B

Ignite Your Adventurous Spirit

**Inspiring travel stories by individulas whose
lives have been deeply transformed**

INTRO BY

JB Owen

Founder of Ignite and JBO Global Inc.

PRESENTED BY

Albert Urena, Aleanu Imbert Matthee, Alexandra Blake, Andonia Reynolds, Angela Legh,
Charlene Ray, Charlie Ropsy, Damian Culhane, Deborah Choong, Elena Rodríguez Blanco,
Eva Kettles, Faraaz Âlì, Hanit Benbassat, Hanna Meirelles, Janie Jurkovich, JB Owen,
Joanna M. Walton, John D. Russell, Kamelia Britton, Katarina Amadora, Kate Withey,
Kersti Niglas, Linda Elie, Mariflor Arcoiris, Micah Nelson, Michael Brighteyes,
Mystère Poème, Nadia La Russa, Ravi Muti, Scott Owen Harrell, Tanya Lopez,
Tara Heinzen, Yaana Hauvroesh, Yendre Shen, Yoram Baltinester

Published by Ignite and printed by JBO Global Inc.

DEDICATION

We all grow up somewhere. We are surrounded by a tribe, grounded in a place, immersed in a culture. We are shaped by local events, beliefs and the environment. All of these things band together to mold us into who we become. But some of us, the lucky ones, get a glimpse of other places. We travel. Sometimes, we may be taken along with parents, friends or clients. Other times, we are awakened by an urge from deep inside of us that speaks for the soul of the adventurer within. As we travel, we get to meet people who are different and experience things from another perspective. These impressions often precede the birth of new ideas and change how we see the world, ourselves, and others. This book is dedicated to your inner adventurer. It is a homage to the voice that begs you, "Let's go; let's explore the world." It is a call to your spirit to grow and for your soul to live life to its fullest. From our authors' hearts to yours—Go travel! Travel can, and indeed will, change who you are forever!

~ Yoram Baltinester

Author Testimonials

Writing my story for the first time was a profound healing experience, helping me overcome the voices of my own self-doubt, allowing me to get in touch with my authenticity and giving me the courage to share it with the world. It truly Ignited my life.

~ Albert Urena

Participating in Ignite your Adventurous Spirit allowed me an outlet for my story. It gave me the opportunity to share my biggest adventure and what I learned from it. The coaches and editors were invaluable in giving impact to my story, validation to my experience, so that now it can be shared with the world. Thank you so much, Ignite team! I can't wait for my next chapter.

~ Nadia La Russa

The Ignite series has proven to be one of the best ways to get yourself out there. I also enjoyed reliving a moment in my own life that I get to look back at. It is an opportunity to help others who might be struggling and, at the very least, fill someone's heart and bring a smile across their face as they live through each story.

~ Andonia Reynolds

Every moment is an opportunity for something to ignite within our heart and soul. Whether we notice, recall and record it is up to us. Taking the time to write the detailed and vulnerable stories of two profound moments in my life transformed the way I saw those moments. It stirred a new appreciation for the value of capturing the magic and the details of your experience in words. That process can transform tragedy into triumph and experience into insight. Truly profound and powerful.

~ Mystère Tasra Poème-Dawson

This is my second time contributing to the Ignite compilation book series. I keep coming back because I find the writing process so rewarding and therapeutic. It gives me a glimpse into myself; a chance to get very intimate with my own thoughts and experiences of past events that have come to shape me into the person I am. Telling my Adventurous Spirit story allowed me to see the thread that runs through my urge to explore and travel. It was a search for belonging and the desire to find home — something deep down we're all looking for. I encourage anyone who wishes to know themselves better to consider this undertaking. There is such love and support from the Ignite family to help you along and you'll be proud you did it.

~ Yendre Shen

Published by Ignite and printed by JBO Global Inc.
5569-47th Street Red Deer, AB
Canada, T4N1S1 1-877-377-6115

Cover design by JB Owen
Book design by Dania Zafar

Designed in Canada, Printed in China

ISBN# 978-1-7923-0670-9

First edition: December 2019

Ordering Information: Quantity sales. Special discounts are available on quantity purchases by corporations, associations, and others. For details, contact the publisher at the address above. Programs, products or services provided by the authors are found by contacting them directly. Resources named in the book are found in the resources pages at the back of the book.

Ignite Your Adventurous Spirit

INTRODUCTION BY
JB OWEN

ad·ven·tur·ous

adjective

   1. Willing to take risks or to try out new methods, ideas, or experiences.

spir·it

Noun

   1. The nonphysical part of a person which is the center of emotions and character; the soul.

Since the beginning of time, adventurers have been thought of as people who were in search of something. Columbus traveled to find new lands. Marco Polo did so to open new trade routes. Most early explorers had a purpose or cause and sought out travel as a means to a desirable result. Without knowing the minds of these early explorers, can we say for sure if that was their only reason? We can never truly know, but it is hard to imagine risking one's life on treacherous, unbridled oceans and through hostile enemy territory if passion, yearning or inner conviction wasn't part of the equation.

Going against rational thought and venturing forth for months at sea, or traversing snow-capped mountains (with nothing more than animal skins on their feet), may have had a deeper intention than simply expanding commerce. The swell of excitement at seeing land mystically appearing on the horizon or the tenacious desire to discover what would unfold over the next rocky ridge had to come from a powerful internal motivation as much as, if not more than, from a ruler's command.

Today, travel has become easy, and adventure more accessible. Boarding a plane or taking a short train ride can bring you to an exotic new place or magical unknown town. A quick Google search or call on your phone can have you booked on a ticket around the world. Gone are the days where traveling to the coast took weeks or boarding a transatlantic ship meant you were bobbing at sea for months on end.

It is estimated by the World Tourism Organization (UNWTO) that 1.4 billion people travel every year, spending hundreds of billions of dollars. According to statistics, Finland has the most well-traveled population in the world with the average Finn making 7.5 trips a year (including staycations and abroad). The United States, Sweden, Denmark, Norway, and Canada balance out the list of whose residents are jetting off somewhere new. Spain has topped the World Economic Forum (WEF)'s ranking for the country best equipped to welcome tourists, followed by France and Germany. Japan and the United States round out the top five.

It seems that millennials (born 1981 - 1996) travel the most, averaging 35 days each year. They were followed closely by Generation Z travelers (born 1995 - 2015) who travel 29 days annually. Generation X (born 1965 - 1980) travels the least; the result of work and family commitments. According to a recent travel trend study, the percentage of baby boomers (born 1946-1964) traveling to relax and rejuvenate is close to 49 percent. This age group tends to, on average, take four or five leisure trips each year. Boomers are the lucky ones who, as empty-nesters, have the desire, time and resources to travel continuously throughout the year.

Of all these statistics, none are more impressive than the fact that 20.05 million people visited Bangkok last year, followed by London at 19.83 million, Paris at 17.44 million, Dubai at 15.79 million, Singapore at 13.91 million, New York at 13.13 million, Kuala Lumpur at 12.58 million and Tokyo at 11.93 million. Cities are filled to the brim with wide-eyed photo-taking fanatics eager to indulge in the historic sites, eclectic sounds and delicious foodie delights.

The top reason people travel are as follows:

- To visit and re/connect with family.
- To spend quality time with friends.
- To take a gap year, a year off or a world trip to signify a momentous time in life.

- To enjoy nicer weather, of course!
- To explore new cultures and better understand different societies.
- To find oneself by taking an inner, transformational quest.
- To find love or romance; to serendipitously meet 'the one'.

The top benefits derived from traveling include:

- Traveling develops skills and perseverance you didn't know you had.
- Travel opens your eyes and exposes you to new ideas.
- Travel helps you learn new languages and ways to communicate.
- Travel creates meaningful relationships with both yourself and others.
- Traveling helps you learn who you are and better understand yourself.
- Travel prompts adventure and the thrill of the dangerous or unknown.
- Traveling gives you a new perspective on how you see yourself and others.

In the pages of this book, you will meet 35 individuals who became one of those statistics and fit into one of those categories. Their desire to travel might have been to see friends or have exposure to a new culture. They may have jumped on a plane and found themselves in one of those 'busy' cities. Or they left their homes in search of personal growth and transformation. What you will also find is 35 unique adventures that went far deeper than just the token tourist traps and destination highlights on a map. These are the *Adventurous Spirits* that took venturing to a whole new level.

Their quests come in all shapes and sizes. Some of them climbed to the top of a mountain while others swam with the sharks, yet all of them took a detour from the charted path to discover and uncover something more. They wanted a deeper meaning, more clarity and answers to a part of themselves that felt lost. Journeying outward became a portal inward to a magical, personal land. Just like Aladdin discovering the Cave of Wonders, home to the most extraordinary treasures, they unearthed the priceless gifts of peace, realizations and the greatest of all — finding one's Self.

Often when we get caught up in the minutiae of life, we forget who we are. We tend to conform to what others want and lose our sense of purpose. We find ourselves chasing goals that don't seem to matter. Habits, routines and following other people's expectations can lead us down the same street over and over again with disappointing results. Repeating old patterns creates a well-worn path to a life we don't really want. As Robyn Young said, "We travel not to escape life, but for life not to escape us."

One of the greatest gifts of exploring is discovering who you are. Travel allows the mind to expand beyond your everyday thoughts. It turns your view-finder away from the obvious and focuses it on new possibilities. A last-minute theater reservation might result in meeting a brand new friend. A lost train ticket could unknowingly have you eating at the best restaurant of your life. Late flights, wrong turns or unexpected detours could divinely orchestrate an experience, gifting you with something that will change the trajectory of your future forever. These are the beautiful by-products of travel and just the tip of the iceberg of what can happen.

True inner happiness comes from exploring every aspect of who you are. It is about experiencing the bliss of being alive by challenging and expanding your norm. It is about the boundaries you push and the uncharted trail you blaze. It is about the people you meet, the cultures you embrace, and the deep and meaningful connections you build. If you live within your limits, all you will ever find are more limitations. Adventure breaks apart that idea and catapults your thinking to an entirely new level, awakening your spirit, tantalizing your senses and feeding your soul.

This book and the stories in it show how stepping out of your comfort zone can yield a plethora of wondrous results. Simply exploring a new place can burst open your ideals and activate an unconventional approach to life. Travel, trekking and touring the many facets of the globe allows clarity of purpose to be found and true happiness to be experienced. Be it from the vista of a rock formation or when wiggling your toes in the sand, nirvana and utopia can be felt from within. *No one place is the right place.* The only right place is the one that is right for you.

Our wish is that when you read through these chapters, you are deeply transformed by the many examples of other explorers following their deepest desires—both externally and internally. May the discoverer in you be Ignited by the brazen and beautiful stories of others blazing a brilliant new trail. I hope that your mind opens and your self-awareness awakens to how adventurous your life can be. I hope that you feel the possibilities and potential that each author shares, and the supportive intentions behind it. All the writers wrote their stories so that you may relate to their passion for travel. Every word was crafted with the idea of instilling a personal desire in you to discover more of *you*. By encouraging you to go somewhere different, you may uncover and enjoy a magnificent life with you at the center of it.

As you turn the upcoming pages, you will find each story begins with a *Power Quote*. It is like a mantra or a self-activating statement. Every individual has one and here the writers declare theirs. It is a phrase that pushes you to do more, take risks and journey a little deeper. It is what the sticker on your luggage would say, or what you'd write at the end of a postcard. Power Quotes are words that you can repeat when you need some extra confidence or when the tears are flowing from both life's hardships and its rewards. Each Power Quote reminds you of what you have inside, what you prefer to feel, and how you can unleash an exciting and more adventurous side of you.

Next, you will read each author's *Intention*. These are the insights and ideas they wish to inspire in you. They are personal messages filled with meaning and purpose. The authors want to IGNITE YOU to begin living your most extraordinary life and they share what they hope their explorations will do for you. Each intention sets the tone for their story and is intended to both awaken and elevate your vision of what's possible.

Then, their adventurous spirit *Story* follows. It is an epic account of a trip they took and the transformation they experienced from it. Their explorations explain how they found the answers to some inner and personal questions. These are their genuine recollections of consciously awakening to the *Ignite* moment that instigated a journey inwards toward finding their true selves. We all have *Ignite* moments in our lives that change us, define us and set us on a new path or trajectory. These stories are those moments, told in the most vulnerable and heart-felt way. They show that we all have *life-changing* moments that not only impact us but ultimately define us.

Once you have finished each story, you will find a list of fun and enjoyable *Ignite Action Steps*. These are the tangible things they did to overcome their worries and move through any doubts; including disregarding the naysayers. Each author shares easy-to-do, practical tips for you to try out and implement immediately. These are the processes and practices that worked in their lives. Each step is different and unique, just like you are, and has proven to yield wondrous results when done consistently.

We all know actions speak louder than words; never is that more important than when it comes to travel. You must take action for any of it to happen. Action IS the key. To move closer to your next adventure, we encourage you to try one action step each day and do it consecutively for 30 days. We have outlined many different action steps to undertake, so find the one that will get the most results for you. Each one is potentially the step that could change your life forever. Start with what resonates the most, and follow through to see significant and wonderful improvements.

The most important outcome is for something you read to *inspire* you, for one of our stories to have a profound impact and push you in a new direction, for something to hit you so strongly that you *have* to take action. This is the most important thing — that one of our suggestions pushes you into a new conscious realization and you feel ready to transform, ready to soar, READY TO ADVENTURE!

You get to decide how to live, where to go and what to see; no one else is in charge of that. You can excitedly move forward and find your bliss. Your life can be absolutely extraordinary on every level; you just have to decide first and then move consciously in that direction. Let these stories remind you that you can do anything, be anything and accomplish anything you choose... and make the most of that power.

The Gift of Community

We know that many people read compilation books to be inspired. If you feel that your story is still unfolding or you are still trying to figure it out, we are with you. We have all been through difficulties and go through them numerous times in our lives. Our stories show our transformation *in spite of* all that. We still have issues, like everyone else; we have just pushed ourselves to go forward. Everyone needs encouragement to rise and flourish. We all need to support each other in as many ways as we can. The enthusiasm behind our transformations are now behind you. We support you unconditionally and are cheering you on as you uncover your own adventurous lifestyle. We extend our hands should you need a bit of support, some advice or a friend to confide in. We offer our services should you ever want to reach out because something we said resonated with you or what we shared was exactly what you needed to hear. We are all accessible and eager to connect, so please feel free to find us wherever we are in the world. We are happy to support you as you undergo your own amazing self-exploration.

We are ignited by the idea of you turning the next page and reading the many stories of adventurous travel. We want you to be excited to find out how another person stepped into the very essence of their tremendous life. Some may be filled with pain and suffering. Others might be riddled with disappointment or even tragedy. All show a determination and perseverance in the steps they needed to take to get where they needed to be. Their stories are a guide to the unlimited possibilities that are before you in your life. Be motivated by what they have shared and then decide to go out and do more. Feel revitalized to venture forth in your life with a smile beaming on your face. Move and groove with excitement! Reclaim your freedom! That's the true magic in life! That's what makes life worth living!

The stories you are about to embark on are all our stories. They supersede race, culture, age and even gender. They are the human story, the experience of being a Being on this earth. They touch at the very heart of belonging, connecting and sharing. They are raw, real and unrestricted... that's what makes them so amazingly engaging. They cut through all the 'stuff' we want people to see and shine a light directly on the heart of who we were born to be.

Ignite was created to ignite others and impact humanity. Our mandate is to do more, share more and spread conscious positive messages to as many people as possible. We believe in the human connection. We believe that power comes from being heard, being seen and belonging to something greater. We invite you to Ignite others. To let your story be heard, share your experiences and find your voice. We pride ourselves in bringing people together, offering a solution, giving back and doing something good for the planet. That is the mission and purpose behind IGNITE. There is power when one person touches the heart of another and a spark begins. Be it inspiration, love, support, encouragement, compassion or belief — we choose to Ignite it all. Each of us deserves to be Ignited and we hope these stories Ignite you.

May you have many Ignite moments that transform your life into the amazing person you were meant to be. — JB Owen

Please know that every word written in this book, every letter in these pages, has been meticulously crafted with fondness, encouragement and a clarity not just to inspire you but to transform you. Many people in this book stepped up to share their stories for the very first time. They courageously revealed the many layers of themselves and exposed their weaknesses as few do. Additionally, they spoke authentically from the heart and wrote what was true for them. We could have taken their stories and aimed for perfection, following every editing rule; but instead, we chose to leave their unique and honest voices intact. We overlooked exactness to foster individual expressions. These are their words and sentiments. We let their personalities shine through so you would get a deeper sense of who they are. That is what makes IGNITE. Authors serving others, stories igniting humanity. No filters. No desire for perfection. Just realness between us and you.

Where will your Adventurous Spirit take you?

We want to assist you in planning your next trip. Answer the following questions with the absolute belief that what you think about you create, that magic happens when you write it down and declare it. Fill out the questions below and get yourself thinking and manifesting your next adventure.

List the top three places you would like to visit.

_____

_____

_____

What are the top five things that are most important to you when traveling?

_____

_____

_____

_____

_____

What is your Dream Trip?

_____

_____

_____

Think of this map like a vision board for your Adventurous Spirit. Start with your roots; grab a pen and make a mark everywhere you have lived. Find your tribe; indicate where the people who are important to you can be found. Document your adventures and highlight everywhere you have already been. Make extra big circles in those places that have engraved themselves on your soul.

Then start to dream. Place your hand on the map, close your eyes and let visions of all the places you could possibly go dance their way into every corner of your mind. Make a wish; draw a star on every place you long to see and jot down notes about what you hope to experience there. Make it happen; draw a giant arrow to the one you want to go to first and start packing your bags!

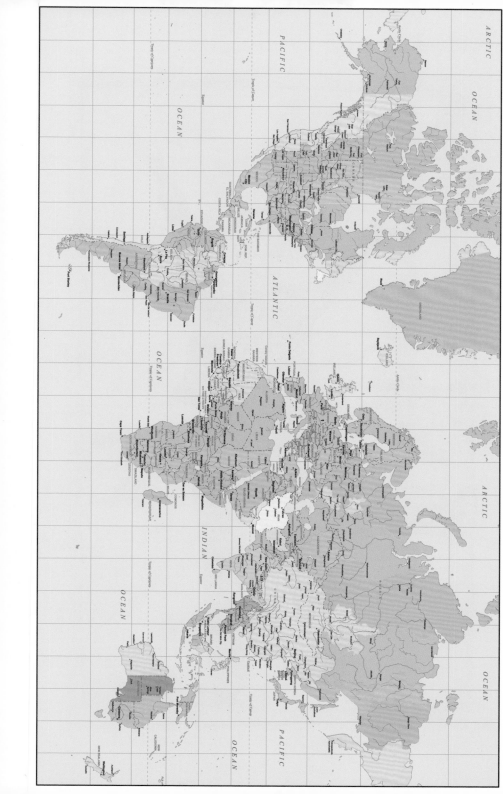

JB OWEN

"The path is never straight for a reason."

My story is designed to open the door to your heart and awaken your emotions. We often go looking for something outside ourselves when all that we need can be found within. By reading about my journey, you will see that the adventure outward became an exploration inward; there, I found the most wondrous things.

THE ROAD HOME

One of my very first memories at the age of five was a trip our family took to Hawaii. Escaping the bitter cold of a Canadian winter, my parents, sister and I spent a month-long holiday on the big Island of O'ahu. I remember EVERY-THING about it, as it was filled with things I had never seen before. The moment I stepped off the plane into the open-air airport, my nose was intoxicated by the sweetest, most exotic smells and my eyes drank in the sight of people wearing flip flops and shirts drenched in flowery patterns and jolts of color.

The crystal blue shimmer of the ocean and the blazing yellow sun were in stark contrast to the barren, brown farmland of the prairies where I grew up. The heat was delicious, tickling my skin and making jumping in the pool the most glorious thing. For a whole month, our family escaped the freezing snow-covered Christmas of Canada and basked in everything island life had to offer. I ran endlessly across the beach, dipping myself in the ocean waves and bodysurfing the shoreline. I was like an otter pup, baby duck and blue-nosed dolphin all in one. It was the first time I had ever experienced the magic of the sea and I loved it!

Hawaii held a multitude of firsts for me. First time I snorkeled and got salt-water up my nostrils. First time I ate a buttery macadamia nut. First time I was buried in the sand up to my ears. The first time I saw a pig roasting on a spit, its snout turned up by the stick that ran the length of its body while it rotated over hot coals. I was fascinated by everything Polynesian. The way the women hula danced at the luau and the men ate fire to impress the crowd. Their richly colored costumes of rattling shells and vibrantly adorned with feathers captivated my childish love for excitement and splendor. I delighted over the new foods I tried: purple poi, lomi salmon and crackling pigskin. I ate so much tantalizing sweet pineapple that my lips hurt. Hawaii awakened my mind and breathed adventure into my heart. I was hooked! Right there and then, I decided I wanted to see everything the world had to offer and all the wondrous sites in it.

By the time I reached high school, I was a seasoned traveler. My parents had whisked us away to numerous sunny destinations to temporarily escape the frigidly cold winters. In my junior year, I traveled to Hong Kong and Bangkok with the school's travel club. There, I gleefully ate yummy steaming noodles from vendors cooking on the street corners, maneuvered my way through the bustling market on Temple Street, and paddled on the Chao Phraya River, buying fruit and stopping to watch a wild reptile show.

The following year, I was off to England, taking pictures while standing rigidly next to the Queen's Guard at Buckingham Palace. Placing my hand on the wet misty rocks at Stonehenge and climbing the worn steps of Edinburgh Castle. For my senior year, it was the Greek Isles and historic sites of the Parthenon and the Temple of Zeus. I ate gyros, souvlaki and baklava as if it were the only food on earth.

All of this cultivated an insatiable desire to explore. I felt unbridled freedom to go anywhere and experience everything the world had to offer. I had learned that escaping life, the cold weather, a boring job or overworked schedule was best remedied by a travel fix. By the time I reached college, jumping on a plane was a commonplace event. If life became too hard, I was off somewhere, avoiding my responsibilities, ducking out of my real life to chill in the sunshine or party on the beach. A week after I graduated, I was on a plane heading to a sunny vacation spot in the Dominican Republic.

What I didn't tell you about all the travel was, it was my parents' way of trying to be happy. Their marriage was a cold one and spontaneous trips were an effort to address their emotional desires to try and warm things up. That first luau I went to was with my mom and sister because my father didn't want to attend. Exploring Disneyland were just us girls as my dad stayed at the hotel. Dipping in the pool, all you can eat buffets and sandcastle competitions had only my mom watching from the sidelines. Their strained marriage put a lot of strain on me and by my twenty-first birthday, the relationship with each of them was almost non existent.

By the time they finally divorced, my cocky teenage attitude had further chipped away at our relationships. Once I got to college, I made little effort to talk to them. I had all but written off my father and connections to my mom were strained and tenuous. As much as she tried, I blamed her and let my selfish, young-adult opinions forge a wedge between us. Going to the Dominican was partly an escape but mostly payback for all the crap I felt they had put me through. Running away to a third-world country far away from them seemed like the perfect way to make them worry, piss them off, and show them just how mad I was for all the misery I had endured.

Truth be told, I had grown up with a bit of a 'silver spoon in my mouth.' My parents had spoiled me, provided for me overindulgently and given me pretty much everything I wanted. Their lackluster marriage created just enough guilt for them to overcompensate by providing me with nice things and a privileged life. That left me with both a self-deserving attitude and a somewhat bruised heart — the perfect recipe for a rebellious and ungrateful child desperate to prove she didn't need them. At the time, I felt as if being away from them was the best medicine for all, so instead of just spending a week in the DR, I purposely missed my return flight and stayed.

Growing up, I would have forgone a few of the material things I had and traded them in for more of a real connection with my parents. By the time I dipped my toes into the Dominican waters, relations between us were at an all-time low. In the early nineties, before cell phones and email, the only way I could talk to my mom was on a once-a-week collect call from a payphone on the side of the street. The constant roaring of motorbikes and noisy mufflerless cars made it impossible to have a decent conversation, not to mention the static on the line and long delays. Within minutes we'd both be frustrated and annoyed. As a result, I'd go weeks without successfully talking to her and, over time I eventually gave up.

Fax machines had just hit the airwaves and so I took to sending a quick fax to her office, letting her know I was alive and well. It was the least I could do (and it cost much less than a long-distance call). The grating edginess of our phone calls had kept my rift going, but the freedom of a fax liberated me to share whatever I wanted *sans* feedback or without commentary from her.

Like with all my trips, immersing myself in the culture and customs of the Dominican Republic changed me on a cellular level. I had given up my nice apartment back home and was living in a cinder block box on a dirt road, surrounded by clucking chickens. I had quickly learned to love the food, especially the 'concon,' a scorched crunchy rice browned at the bottom of a cast-iron pot, cooked over an open fire. I learned the essential words I needed in Spanish, got a job and soon danced merengue like I was a local. The Dominican was the opposite of everything I knew growing up. The people were fun and gregarious, happy to laugh, excited to dance and willing to share whatever they had, eating together without needing to be invited.

Despite the third world conditions and obvious poverty, they were a loving and welcoming people. I felt less of an outsider there than I did in my own house growing up. They didn't have a lot, but to me, they had everything. They talked to each other, sat on the porch hanging out, shared food, told stories and worked as a family unit to ensure each had enough. I watched my neighbor, a 40-year-old man walking to the market hand-in-hand with his 80-year-old mother and my eyes wept at their loving connection. I watched kids run from house to house to house in the village and be parented by each adult they passed. My heart longed to be noticed like that. It didn't matter how little they had or how tight money was, every night someone in the village would bring me a small bowl of food welcoming me to the community, embracing me despite being a foreigner.

Their sharing a tiny portion of what they had from an already limited amount cracked my heart open and awakened a feeling of compassion and camaraderie I had never experienced before. I had always thought I had everything, but compared to what I was feeling there, I had nothing. None of the kinship or community that was so prevalent in the Dominican was present in my life in Canada. I had never seen the harsh struggles of third world conditions interwoven with such appreciation for the simplest of basic needs and peppered with gratitude for the most minuscule of indulgences. My heart swelled with a mix of admiration and longing. I appreciated their genuine demeanor and had hope that one day my family and I could have a similar connection.

As the months passed and my heart slowly melted, I started sharing a bit more in each of my weekly faxes. A part of me wanted to talk to my mom as I had with the other mothers in the village. As they happily showed me how to make my own concón, plantains and sweet dulce, I pined for my mom; wishing to be learning from her, at her side. As I softened my broken-home shell, I succumbed to the jovial life of Dominican cooking, dancing, laughing and warm days in the sun. I started to thaw from my frigid past, and my emotions bloomed like the widespread red petals of the caoba flowers that grew in ditches surrounding the village.

Soon enough my faxes turned into letters. I poured out my feelings, describing my newfound emotions and filling up page after page with excitement and epiphanies. My entire Being had been transformed from the love of the people there and I wanted to share just how amazing it felt. Letter after letter, I apologized to my mom for all the terrible things I had said in anger. I lamented my sorrows and I forgave her for divorcing my dad; asking her to look passed all the small-minded judgments I had made. I was deeply fascinated by her childhood, her mother and all the things she had learned as a child. I wanted to know if she had ever stood next to my grandmother learning to cook and embroider as I was doing in the DR? I wanted her to relate to the new me that was bursting forth with empathy and conviction. I was loving the Dominican and personally connecting to the injustices of low salaries, poor medical services and lack of food. The state of the DR's economy outraged me and I vowed to do whatever possible to help my new Dominican families whom I now felt so connected to.

I wrote over 200 letters to my mom, pouring out my heart, revealing my deepest emotions and divulging my most personal thoughts. It was through letter writing that I discovered a profound love and admiration for her and wished to return home to rebuild our relationship.

Without warning, a terrible earthquake hit Los Angeles, California. Hovering over the one small TV in the village, I watched news footage of people trapped, buildings collapsed and thousands homeless in panic and disarray. As a kid, I had seen natural disasters on TV, but it had always been in a far off, third world country like Bangladesh or eastern China. There I was, in a far off third world place myself, and the world was crumbling practically right next door to my mother. The luxuries of a first world nation had not spared them from the wrath of nature and that felt jarring to me.

Watching the footage of the devastation and seeing the rising death toll from the earthquake, I suddenly wondered why was I still living so far from her. Was my anger still justified? How would I feel if something happened to her and I was still holding this grudge? Enough time had passed and enough healing had occurred that I knew I was ready to go home. Boarding the plane and leaving behind many people I had grown to love, I pushed aside the loss and focused on the enthusiasm I felt in seeing my mom. I had shared every depth of myself with her in my letters and all I wanted was to have the most amazing mother-daughter connection possible. The time away had given me perspective. The art of letter writing had allowed me to share in a way that was both honest and endearing.

The interesting addition to the journey is that, for all the letters I wrote — over 200 of them, some up to 20 pages long — my mother never once wrote me back. She never reciprocated my sharing or answered the many questions I asked. She didn't pour her heart out in return or ever mention she forgave me. The letters were sent and simply not answered. It was devastating at first. Resentment grew and I parked her indifference in the same painful place of rejection I had put her in for years. Yet over time, something started to happen; my need for her response slowly and eventually didn't matter. The words on the page had become healing for me. Each confession, resolution and learning I discovered put my mind and heart in a happier place. Every envelope I sent traveled to her with the intention of making things between us better, while making it all better in my own heart. I stopped needing her to reciprocate or validate. While living away, I had rebirthed myself. I had changed. My attitude had shifted. Those old opinions dissolved. Everything I had held against her diminished. All that was left was the love and bond that only a mother and daughter can share… and I wanted all of it.

When I arrived home, I had the most beautiful connection with my mother. She was the same person she had always been, but I saw her through renewed eyes and a loving attitude. I looked beyond the actions and saw her at the core of her being. She did an amazing job raising me and gave me much more than I ever asked for. That entire experience prompted me to write my first book in her honor: *Letters For My Mother — Healing from the Heart*. I diligently wrote the important message of how it only takes one person to heal a relationship. That one person can make a difference and when they shift, everything shifts for the better. I found that in loving others in the harshest conditions, opening myself up and loving my life, I was truly able to love her.

When my mom and I traveled to Toronto to be on National TV and talk about my book, she was there with all 200 letters in hand. She had them in safekeeping and gave them to me to show on camera. She may not have acknowledged my letters when I was sending them, but on that day, I knew more than ever that each one had touched her deeply and meant more than words can express.

The path is never straight for a reason. Where you are headed and what unfolds when you get there has a purpose and a reason. We don't know why it all happens until we look back and recognize how far we've come. Only then can you see the progress you have made and how you got there. You can heal any relationship in your life, make any friends you want, positively influence as many people as you choose. How you show up is the ultimate adventure. How you see more than just what is in front of you and go deeper within will be the *most rewarding journey* you will ever take. See more than you ever saw before, in yourself and others; that is the truest path to the heart and the gift of a real Adventurous Spirit.

IGNITE ACTION STEPS

- **Write Letters.** We have texting and emails, but there is something divine and sublime about receiving a handwritten letter. Take the time to write a letter to someone you love, regardless if they are far away or right in the bed beside you. Express, share, open up, be real, be honest, be authentic and revealing in a letter. Tell someone exactly how you feel, heart to heart, and see how powerful a personal piece of mail can be.

- **Start a Relationship Journal.** Have a blank journal or notebook that you use to write back and forth to someone you care about. Be it your spouse, partner or even your kids—sometimes the written word allows us to convey your feelings more deeply and encourages the reader to hear what we have to say more directly. With no distractions or judgment, this kind of communication speaks directly to the heart.

- **Write a Letter to Yourself for the Future.** Craft a letter to yourself one year from now, on your next birthday or New Year's Eve. Trust yourself to intuitively share exactly what you will need to hear. Those words will be magical when you open and read your own heartfelt advice.

JB Owen - Canada
Founder of Ignite, World-Class Speaker,
International Best-Selling Author
and Owner of JBO Global Inc.
jb@igniteyou.life
www.igniteyou.life
jbowenlovesyou
thepinkbillionaire

YORAM BALTINESTER

"Being absolutely right is a big red flag."

My intention is for you to realize how the more certain you are that you are right and 'they' are wrong in an argument, the higher the chances are that you deprive yourself of the opportunity to resolve the conflict. Every conflict calls on you to examine the other side's position, even when it questions your deep rooted beliefs.

I AM THE CHINESE.

Something must be wrong for a whole class of teens to have to go to the cemetery. On this March morning, nothing seemed right. The funeral was attended by hundreds. A few relatives, a few friends and hundreds of people came to show support to the family of the deceased. So many, in fact, that my friends and I were nowhere near the fresh grave where our murdered friend and classmate, daughter of our beloved art teacher, was about to be laid to rest. The air was infused with pain. Our teacher's youngest daughter was crying at having lost her sister so abruptly. We cried with her.

I sensed the grief in our teacher's voice as he prayed. Our teacher, who always started his lessons with Psalm 51:10: "A pure heart create in me God, and a willing soul renew in me," was now reciting the Kadish, the mourner's prayer, for his daughter. He struggled through the words which we all knew so well both in text and as a song.

He who makes peace in his high places
He will bring peace onto us
And upon all of Israel
And say ye, amen…

He stopped briefly as he recited the lines. His voice cracked. "Please God," his voice broke as he exclaimed, "bring that peace already!" His pain was ours also.

By the time I was in middle school, I had already experienced two major wars, countless skirmishes, terror attacks and hostilities. On the surface, my home country of Israel seemed to be winning, except that day, nothing felt like winning. We all felt terror.

It was the same terror that I sensed as a four-year-old when everyone feared that we would all die in the upcoming war of 1967. It was the same quiet desperation that we felt on that October day in 1973 when, in the aftermath of a surprise attack, all our fathers and brothers vanished in a matter of hours as they rushed to their army reserve units, many of them to never be seen alive again. The same horror that we felt during the Munich Olympics massacre in 1972. The same horror that we felt in 1976 when a plane was hijacked and flown to Uganda, whereupon landing, Jews were separated from the rest of the passengers and segregated to become a bargaining chip in an impossible negotiation. All of these experiences revived the memory of the Holocaust that our people had suffered during World War II.

That day, we were laying to rest a high school student who went on a field trip to a popular tourist attraction, a field trip that was short-lived as their bus was hijacked and most of the passengers murdered in yet another terror attack. The country stood still as the extent of the loss dawned on it: 37 dead, 74 wounded. The Palestinian Liberation Organization (PLO) announced its responsibility for the attack and cited the Peace Treaty between Egypt and Israel as the reason. Peace became a reason for terror.

Cabinet ministers and members of parliament attended and spoke at the funerals of the victims. We heard strong speeches. "This is a lowly, cowardly crime against women and children," said the Deputy Prime Minister. "We will only talk to the PLO in the language it understands. This organization, its members and supporters shall be tried and treated as the scum murderers that they are." In the wake of the Holocaust, Israel had a clear policy: no one who attacks Jews for being Jews shall remain unharmed.

"Murderers, criminals, barbaric animals, kill all of them once and for all" was the public sentiment. I listened... and I learned. It was quite simple: they all want us all dead; therefore we must heed the saying, "Those who come to kill you, get up earlier and kill them first." I never thought twice about it. I never considered the effect of that one little word: 'all.' ALL of them?! Suddenly, every Palestinian was a suspected criminal and a murderer, wanting to ruin any chance for peace. A couple of million people who identify themselves as Palestinians live in Israel. Many live elsewhere. Do they *all* want me dead? I never asked any of them.

As time went by and the attacks persisted, my truth was reinforced. Every bus bombing and murder increased the fear and suspicion I felt towards Palestinians, and worse, in my mind, it rendered any conversation or reconciliation attempt pointless. It felt as though we must live by the sword forever.

Many Israelis had different experiences and views about the situation. A lot of people have developed excellent relationships with Arabs living in Israel, including my own father. A full third of his company's business came from the West Bank and he visited there every once in a while. Many other Israelis were under the spell of 'all' just like me, believing that 'all' of 'them' want 'all' of 'us' dead.

By 1992, waves of terror attacks and wars swept over Israel and the Middle East every few years. Being 29 years old, I had been through military service, experiencing the continued confrontation, going from bad to worse.

That was when my girlfriend Shifra and I decided to go on a long trip abroad. Our relationship was young and we decided that the time for an adventure was ripe. We were in love! We loved traveling and, best of all, we couldn't wait to get away from the stress and the tension that we experience daily in Israel. We felt adventurous and wanted to go big. We got backpacks and booked a full-year trip around the world.

With an open flight ticket and a vague plan, we left home and started to head west. We toured the big canyons of North America, island-hopped in Hawaii and Fiji, hitchhiked through New Zealand, and finally arrived in Australia, our last stop before Asia.

Our Asia trip needed planning. Israeli citizens were limited by the fact that many Asian countries would not admit us. China was one of these fascinating but out-of-reach countries. Hong Kong was still a part of the British Commonwealth and we could visit there, but it wasn't the same! We planned for what we could: Singapore, Thailand, Nepal, Japan. But right as we were finalizing the itinerary for our seven months in Asia, the best news found us. China and Israel announced diplomatic relationships!

Just how we learned about the news has been lost in the sands of time. It was before the era of the Internet and cellular phones. In Israel, we listened to news updates every 30 minutes but once traveling, we could not get away from news fast enough. We hardly bothered with newspapers and even less with TV. Yet, somehow this development that would allow us to enter China reached us and fired up our imagination.

Change of plans! We rushed to the bookstore to buy a China tour book: *Lonely Planet* guide, of course, the best travel guide ever! I couldn't wait to lay my hands on it and read everything about China. Breathless, I scanned the bookshelf for the China book, but the book I saw right next to it would change my life: *Lonely Planet: Tibet.*

It stopped me in my tracks. I only had a vague idea of a separation between China and Tibet. I was born after China-annexed Tibet and looking at political maps, there was no separation between them. "Why two books?" I wondered. "And moreover, why was a rush of energy running through my entire body as I looked at the book?" I did not know much about Tibet. I had not even read *Lost Horizon* and had never heard of Shangri-La. As soon as I laid my eyes on this book, my itinerary was decided, sealed, and there was nothing that would make me change my mind. We were going to Lhasa, capital of Tibet.

Tibet was hardly accessible in 1992. There were only three ways to get in. One took 14 days of bus travel over treacherous roads that climbed from the Sichuan province to Lhasa along 2,200 kilometers (1,350 miles) of unpaved roads. Another was to fly from Nepal to Tibet and be driven back to Nepal a week later, not what you'd do when you are inside China. The last option was a 72-hour train ride into the Gobi desert, followed by a 48-hour bus ride crossing the desert into Lhasa. That sounded like a plan. Let's go!

There was one last yet significant issue. Tibet was off limits to foreigners. It often was, and always for the same reason, I learned. The Tibetans were unhappy about the ongoing occupation of their country. China had overrun Tibet about 40 years earlier. Every time the Tibetans protested, China would close the borders as they harshly dealt with the situation. In 1992, Chinese police were the almighty. All tourists needed "Alien Travel Permits" to go anywhere and, at that time, getting one for Tibet was impossible.

Not entering Tibet meant the end of my dream. Or did it? My tour book listed a few options. We could hike and sneak around police checkpoints. We could ask Tibetan truck drivers to hide us in their trucks. My excitement was off the charts. We will show these Chinese that no one stops us! With the perspective of time, I must say that messing with the Chinese police sounds crazy, but back then... it was "Game on!"

We planned our adventure in detail. We bought train and bus tickets to the town of Xiahe, a staging place for us to depart from, and a place where many Tibetans lived. We reached Xiahe at sunset and having completed a long trip, we planned to stay a few days and explore the town and local monastery. The next morning was pleasant and the weather was beautiful. The monastery had dozens of beautiful prayer wheels around it. The monks were all busy inside and we were the only ones in that huge courtyard. It was us, the wind and the prayer wheels. We wandered around the yard, turning the wheels as we went. I was quietly asking God for safe passage to Lhasa. What happened next was not only unexpected; it was virtually impossible.

"Did you hear they opened Tibet yesterday?" At first, I did not even consider that someone had *actually* spoken those words aloud. We were alone so it must have been in my head. Furthermore, it had been said in *Hebrew.* I *must* be dreaming, I thought, yet something caught my attention. It was Shifra, who stopped her contemplative walk so abruptly that I almost walked right into her. We turned around to the sight of two young travelers who, as it turned out, were also Israelis.

"What did you just say?" My amazement was evident. They laughed out loud. "Tibet is open. We are going there before they change their minds and close it again." Shifra and I looked at each other, thinking the same: let's go right now! My miracle happened. Our path was open. Less than 72 hours later, we settled at the Yak Hotel in Lhasa.

Even today, three decades later, it still feels like an invisible hand guided us, putting me in front of the Tibet tour book, creating a timely diplomatic relationship with China to allow us into the country, and opening the internal border for us.

If there was a divine intention for me to visit Tibet, then my true adventure was about to start. And start it did. For the following weeks, visiting Lhasa and taking the Friendship Highway over the Himalayas into Nepal, we saw the same everywhere: devastation.

When China overran Tibet decades earlier, they immediately went to work to 'integrate' it into China. They relocated thousands of Chinese, offering them incentives to settle in Tibet to change its demography. They suppressed any attempt by the Tibetans to regain independence. The harsh behavior of the Chinese towards the Tibetans was evident everywhere and accounts of what happened away from the public eye were abundant.

China's position on Tibet, I learned, was that it is a non-issue. "Tibet is an inalienable part of China," said the Chinese, "and has always been that way."

With that position, they enforce their laws and assert their sovereignty. In theory, all Chinese citizens are equal. In practicality, Tibetans will always be suspected and oppressed.

I felt for the people of Tibet. I did not like one bit what the Chinese had done there. I felt that once I was away from the threat of the Chinese police, I would love to raise awareness and find support to help Tibetans regain their lives and independence. I did not realize at the time that the same guiding hand that put me in that country was softly changing me from the inside.

I never saw it coming. At first, I just felt the injustice of it. Then, I felt uneasy, as if I had already seen this somewhere. Was it on the news? I could not remember any coverage of Tibet that I had ever seen. Something was brewing inside me. The anger that I felt toward the injustices I witnessed was growing. Finally, I realized a truth I never in a million years expected: *I am* the Chinese!

I was shocked. "No, no, our situation in Israel is different." In my mind, I counted the differences. It isn't the same; if anything, it is the total opposite. We are the ones being chased and threatened by a bunch of hostile neighboring countries. I looked for something that would reassure me that the situation in Tibet was different than in Israel, but there was little to make one of these conflicts different than the other.

A fierce internal conflict ensued. My upbringing, the first 20 years of my life, had a single conclusion: *We're right and they are wrong; we are good and they are bad. Israel is OUR land — and has been for 3,000 years.* In Tibet, I could see things from both sides, a new vantage point I never had. I learned that conflicts are solved together, and most of all, that ignoring another's side and what drives them does not solve conflicts.

With this new perspective, Shifra and I returned home to a country where both Israelis and Palestinians have the same stance: *We are right, they are wrong and only a fight will fix it.* Since then, I have witnessed both sides declining any inclination to change. Entrenched in their righteousness, each side further indoctrinates their children with their version of the truth. It is a practice that is both dangerous and unsustainable.

I believe that humanity is one. A single species, a single human race. Yet, we hold on to conflicts, making things worse by the generation, and soon enough, we might hit a deadly end. We must change course and heal. I also believe that if humanity is to heal itself, it must start with the deepest wound it has, which lies in the Middle East. Am I just thinking this way because I grew up there? Perhaps. Maybe the Middle East isn't the deepest wound of humanity, but it touches everyone, so how about we start there?

To heal this wound, we must learn perspective taking. This isn't news. Any conflict resolution expert (I am not one, nor do I have the solution for the Middle East) would tell you that perspective taking is one of their fundamentals, if not the most important tool.

The question is: Can we do it? Can we learn to respect each other? Can we heal and unite? I believe we can…

IGNITE ACTION STEPS

- **Follow your heart.** Never disregard your heart when it calls you to travel. It's very likely that you are being attracted to a growth experience and to your true Life's path.

- **The places you visit will teach you about home.** It is easier to recognize a different perspective than the one you have by witnessing a similar situation elsewhere, a situation where you are not emotionally identified with one perspective and scared of the other. Traveling has demonstrated this principle time and again. Travel a lot!

- **Being absolutely right is a big red flag.** In any argument, the more we think we are right, the less we are willing to look at it from another perspective and the less chance we have of ever resolving the matter. The more we are convinced of our side of the argument, the more alert we must be, lest we turn deaf in the conversation.

- **Beware of 'all.'** Generalizations are unhelpful, especially when groups of people and their intentions or characteristics are the subjects of it. Have individual conversations, and understand that different people have different intentions, opinions and characters.

- **Healing Humanity starts with us.** Healing truly starts within each one of us, individually. As you travel, learn from other people in other places, and import your experiences so you can create more peace at home.

Yoram Baltinester - United States
Founder, The LifeDesign Method
www.HeyYoram.com
🛐 yoram.baltinester

FARAAZ ÃLÌ

*"It is better to experience life by doing, rather
than observing and overthinking."*

**I invite you to unlock the traveler within you. To explore places you had
never imagined going to and do things that scare you. Don't just read about
other countries and cultures; experience them from different perspectives.
I have been fortunate to have traveled to over 70 countries with every
journey teaching me a lesson that opened my mind to new awareness. I
hope that the defining moments in my story are the inspiration you need
to take your next journey.**

THREE KEY MOMENTS IN MY ADVENTUROUS EVOLUTION

My travels have barely scratched the surface as they add up to only 29
percent of the world's countries. This story touches on three specific moments
that helped me rise to the next level in my life's evolution through travel which
also included the expansion of my 'exploration team.' Each of these moments
played a transformational role in my mind, heart, body, soul and relationships.

Stairway to the Dead Woman's Pass

"This is not where I die," I kept thinking with every slow step I took into
the pitch blackness of the night. Everytime I had my headlamp on, bugs were
attracted to the light and swarmed my face, but my discomfort with insects

was a minor issue compared to venomous snakes and spiders that could have been a lethal threat. Improvising, I used the headlamp as a torch in my hand, shooting out short flashes of light to capture knowledge of the terrain for my next steps. This was my maiden camping trip and my inexperience left me in a very uncomfortable situation. My paranoia was running wild as to what was out there in the dark with me.

It was the first night of our four-day Inca Trail hike in Peru and I was not a hiker. I had arrived last to the campsite at sunset, thus forgoing my chance to scope out the area. I had an early dinner with my Norwegian hiking group, followed swiftly by bedtime. Several hours later, I woke up in the middle of the night needing to venture out of the tent to do 'something important.' After checking my boots for scorpions and spiders, I stepped into the darkness. To be honest, I had no clue what I would have done if I had found something dangerous in my boots. Perhaps I would have screamed, waking up the whole campsite! The city slicker in me was strong and the outdoor mountaineer was a work in progress, but the brave evening explorer was simply non-existent.

Leading up to this, my deepest concern was about getting bitten by a venomous creature and my friends finding me in the morning with my 'joystick' in hand. Not the way I was planning to go out. Five minutes outside the tent standing in darkness, hearing my heart racing made me anxious. That is when I made the decision to man up and just get on with it. I was not going to find a specific area that would say in Spanish *los servicios*. Right here, right now was fine. No more pitch black analysis paralysis. I finally started to pee.

In the morning, our eager group gathered for breakfast, knowing the day ahead was going to be tough, as we were about to ascend to 4,200 meters to a point called Dead Woman's Pass. As our excitement increased, Lucio, our guide, came to check on us. He asked me, "How was your night?" I was not going to tell him about my hunt for *los servicios* so I replied with "Good" instead. This also gave me the chance to ask about what venomous creatures I could expect here. He replied with a big smile, "NONE, nothing in winter." All that fear I had created in my head, mixed with high altitude brain fog, was my introduction to the lack of oxygen and the challenges ahead. We had a good laugh over my evening adventure. He said, "Take your time and remember the altitude will make things difficult, as we will ascend 1,200 meters today. Good luck."

We had arrived in Cusco four days earlier to get acclimatized at 3,400 meters. I did fall sick for a day but luckily nothing serious, and the comforts of being in a hotel room made recovery a lot easier. I felt confident as I was in good shape having put in serious training for the past six months. One and a half days into the mountainous trail, I had learned very fast that gym workouts meant shit-all when it came to hiking in higher altitudes with rough terrains. Passing the highest point, which was the highest I had ever been hiking, I knew that I had inadequately prepared myself.

With uneven steps that varied in narrowness and height, the ascent was much tougher than I had imagined. With the grueling sun behind our backs, everyone in our group fought their own personal battles to get to the top. The guides did their best to motivate us. There was no turning back; the top was the only savior. It became a mental and physical test that was going to take me to an uncomfortable place. My plan to concentrate on one step at a time helped me progress well. My mind was focused but my body struggled. My attention was narrowed to the very present moment; everything else became a blur. Some of my friends had reached the top. I could see them waving to me. It was perhaps 100 meters away, but for me in that fatigued state, it might as well have been 100 miles away. Energy deteriorated with every step in the midday sun. My mind was in a state of disorientation and my body in fatigue. I was like a *Walking Dead* zombie. I focused on one step at a time, enabling my autopilot so I could rest and move, rest and move, while ignoring the pain. There is this saying, "Fail to prepare, then prepare to fail." I was experiencing this life lesson at its fullest.

There was no background music like a Hollywood finish; it was a real struggle. Putting my head down, I finally made it to the top! It was powerful. I had turned the impossible into the possible. As I sat on a rock at the peak marveling at the views and feeling the accomplishment sink in, I knew this was something special for me. I had just pushed myself past exhaustion, through ALL the challenges, to make it to the checkpoint. We were far from finished, but I was pumped and ready for what was ahead. I had just ignited my fighting spirit. I pushed my mind above and beyond. I was ignited! This was the moment of discovering inner resilience.

The Rambo(ish) Experience

The desert was a beautiful brown and red color against a backdrop of rocky mountains. Here I was in this beautiful scene, on my quad bike, flying off the ground and about to crash land. Airborne, my intuition said, "Let go of the bike — don't crash with it." Within a few seconds, it was all over. I landed on the rocks. I lifted myself up immediately to convince myself I was okay, even before the dust around me had settled. My friend Glen started running towards me to see if I was still alive as from behind, the crash looked a lot more horrific. I felt fine, but this was the adrenaline. As my thumping heart settled along with the dust, I started a self-assessment only to realize I was in a very bad situation in the middle of the Moroccan desert three hours away from any city. Tiny rock fragments had penetrated my arms, shoulders and back. My shin had a huge cut. I needed medical aid fast. Survival became the new objective.

An hour earlier, 13 of us departed a roadside town about two hours outside of Marrakesh. It was a bachelor party and adventure was on our agenda. After some ziplining action, we set off to enjoy an adventurous quad bike drive. The road was dusty and I was worried about my GoPro™ footage being unusable. Partying and a lack of sleep led to my idiotic decision to turn my GoPro camera off while in motion. This resulted in a miscalculated turn that saw me flying off the edge of a rocky sandbank.

Glen's first words when he got to me were, "Oh F@ck!" After self-assessing for fractures, I gave myself the all clear, ready to find help. Our guide's biggest concern, I found out later, was "Make sure the tourist doesn't die, bad for business!" He recommended we go to a nearby Bedouin village. Miraculously, my bike had tumbled several times and lay on its side on the road, but was still working, so I got back on.

Arriving at the village, we met up with the rest of the group; their looks of horror and happiness were priceless. Horror from the fact I was rocked out, literally. Happiness that I was alive. Half the group did not speak English and my French was just as nonexistent. I knew I looked in bad shape; however, I was annoyed by their teasing me in English, French and Arabic. The French even dropped the English word "amputation" with a cheeky laugh.

The villagers saw I was hurt. We were greeted with hot tea and dessert items by the local families. One of the older ladies gestured for me to follow her outside. She made me sit on a bench as she got some warm water and a cloth. We communicated through hand gestures and my limited Arabic vocabulary. The pain was immense as she pulled the rocks out of my skin. I held my brave face knowing that the big rocks were the easy part. Removing the smaller pebbles with a tweezer would come later. After the partial clean up, the bleeding stopped and it was time for me to get going. I thanked the lady for her assistance. We did not speak the same language, but we understood each other. Human compassion transcends language, culture and societies.

After a long hike back to our starting point, sitting in our private bus headed back to Marrakesh, I was in pain but also glad to be alive. I was grateful for the help of strangers who showed compassion despite the language gap. The chance to interact with a local village was an igniting revelation that we are all *One*. This was my moment of deeper understanding of human connectivity and compassion.

The Deep Blue

"We are going to swim with the whale sharks," my wife Maria announced. We were vacationing in Mexico, staying at Isla Mujeres, a small island tucked to the east of the Yucatan Peninsula. This was a couple getaway with the intent of enjoying the Mexican culinary scene and relaxing. Or, so I thought. Maria had different ideas. I had a childhood fear of ocean-going experiences from when I lived in Fiji. Maria was instrumental in helping me overcome it by encouraging me to do more activities in the ocean to make the uncomfortable… comfortable. Snorkeling was the easy part. As the saying goes, "The easiest day was yesterday." That summed up my reaction to the idea of a whale shark swim. I could not say 'no' as I have this thing to always say 'yes' to things that scare the hell out of me — a mechanism to prevent me from procrastinating. On our way there, I sat stiffly. My stomach felt hollow. My heart was racing and my mind was unsettled. I was both scared and excited, the cocktail of emotions before any wild unknown activity. Sitting on the edge of the boat, ready to jump into the ocean, a whale shark around eight meters long approached us. I was frozen.

"Three, Two, One, Go!" that was the call from the guide as we jumped off the moving boat. Now in the water, I looked left and right to see where that whale shark was. The guide tapped my shoulder, indicating I should turn around. Wow! There it was, swimming right towards me! I was mesmerized by its beauty. Suddenly, it opened its mouth to swallow plankton. As it got closer, I realized I had better start swimming. That was the fastest I have ever moved in the water!

I had a magical experience. I swam forward and saw this magnificent whale swimming towards me. It had beautiful grey skin with white spots gleaming with the sun's rays. I looked into its eyes as it approached me. I felt like it acknowledged me as it slowly swam past. Never in my life had I thought I would be that close to such a magnificent creature. The aura of the shark captured me and I admired every second of the experience — until I realized I was too close and its tail slapped me on the chest like a massive high five, thrusting me aside like a submerged bath toy.

Climbing back into the boat, I felt euphoric from witnessing the sheer beauty, size and majesticness of the shark. My relationship with the ocean had just evolved. Gone was my fear of the unknown, replaced by love for the deep blue and its inhabitants. This was my ignite moment, discovering and connecting to the aura of this ocean's guardian. Seeing its embodied spirit made me feel a stronger connection to the unknown.

Creating Utopia

My next adventure was parenting. Parenting, according to what everyone told me, meant the end of the adventurous life, the so-called prescribed societal conditioning and cultural norms that influence people's constructs in their travel evolution. But this limiting belief was not going to become mine. I choose to live my life to the fullest, even as a parent. Experience has taught me lessons that lead to better decision making. Every trip and every moment to that point was teaching me to master a new skill as an adventurer. Knowledge is great, but wisdom is greater. Applied knowledge creates experiences that cannot be taught in traditional education systems. Experience elevates you to your next level. At the end of the day, you are better for it because you have grown in your mindset, skillset and heartset. I am grateful for all my journeys, experiences and survival stories coming from those intense and igniting moments. I was not born an adventurer, but every trip took me closer to what it meant to *BE* one.

My travel evolution from being a participant in family travel as a child to becoming the leader in my family's adventures was coming full circle. I had the chance to travel a lot as a kid with my family to many locations, which was fantastic, despite warnings that traveling with infants and toddlers was high risk. Today, technology and medicine have minimized those risks. However, the old information has a way of not getting updated in society and cultural setups and there will always be resistance and naysayers to change. My decision to travel with my daughter Nicola from three months onwards was met with raised eyebrows, skepticism, condemnation and rare positive feedback. However, my objective was to keep my inner adventurous spirit in full flame, not a shadow of what it was. Finding the perfect balance of exploration and de-risking was always going to be a challenge, but as I always say, "It is better to experience life by doing, rather than observing and overthinking."

Traveling home to Fiji was the very start. Island hopping with a five-month-old baby was awesome. Then the humidity of Singapore was an invitation for more pool time. Driving through the former Yugoslavia was beautiful and Nicola found her culinary desires for exotic food. This continued as we made our way to Belarus and Latvia for weddings. She was constantly surrounded by love, people and educational activities to engage her. We were never alone as our friends were with us in part of the journey. Having had fantastic trips over five months in ten countries, we relocated to Bali for a 'staycation' for over two months. As always, our friends were present there which was a blessing for us as it made the trip so much more fun, integrating social and family life.

One of my treasured memories from our Balinese trip was when Maria, Nicola and I were at the non-touristy jungles of West Bali National park. Off the mainland were the amazing reefs neighboring Menjangan island. While snorkeling I remember coming back to the surface to see Nicola sitting in the boat, smiling and laughing. For her, seeing her daddy pop in and out of the water was hilarious. Our previous trips snorkeling meant she was with a babysitter on land, but not this time. Two trips later, this was the perfect equation of a family vacation with all members present in love and joy. This was my moment of discovering that family adventures should be interpreted as adding a new member to the team to explore, not hanging up the adventurous jacket thinking it is not safe out there.

We are often looking for Utopia, but the truth is, you create Utopia with people. It is not about the location you visit; it's about the energy and chemistry of the people with you… and the people you find there. The journey makes the unfamiliar… familiar. Enjoy the world through your eyes, and the world will see you as you are… and welcome you.

IGNITE ACTION STEPS

- **Live your life** to enjoy and create moments to help honor the authentic you.
- **Love your life**. Get to know yourself better and grow from experiences. Every chance to share that love with others is growing together.
- **Leverage your relationships** with family and friends to create your Utopian moments. Time spent exploring together creates better memories.
- **Learn by traveling** to new locations. *Exploration* and *interaction* are amazing teachers.
- **Laugh and enjoy** the process, and always remember to smile.

Faraaz Ãlì - New Zealand
Chief Empowerment Officer, International Best Selling Author,
Speaker, and Explorer
www.faraazali.com
faraaz4real
faraaz4real
faraaz4real

ALEXANDRA BLAKE

"Independence makes you strong; vulnerability makes you stronger."

We sometimes strive to be as independent as possible, show no vulnerability and are reluctant to rely on others lest we are let down. I want you to know that allowing yourself to be supported by those who love you is a tremendous gift you give to them. By sharing your adventures, experiences and challenges with loved ones, you can discover new parts of yourself. Being open to receiving love is a powerful way to live and does not diminish you or your independence; it strengthens you.

WITH VULNERABILITY COMES STRENGTH

"Just one more step," I told myself, the words swirling in my mind. "You're almost there. You can do this." For four hours, these words had been the only thing keeping me upright as I inched towards the peak of Mount Kilimanjaro. The neck of my jacket chafed against my skin, the gap between letting cold air slowly find its way underneath and making my body shiver with the chill. It was 4AM, six hours since we'd departed the camp. "Let's rest here," I heard the guide call out. A wave of relief swept over me as I took in these rare but delicious words. I paused but didn't give myself permission to sit, frightened I would not have the strength to stand again. Standing close to my side was Troy, my partner and fellow adventurer. Our breaths were shorter now and we knew it was best to save them for breathing, not talking. "You're doing great, Al," his bright blue eyes said to me when I glanced at him. "You too," I silently smiled back at him.

I recall the first time I had 'itchy feet' and felt a desire to be out in the world. I was 11, swinging on a homemade timber swing, its weathered seat worn smooth. Swinging upwards, my toes almost reached the tops of the tall elephant-ear shaped plants bordering the tiny creek that trickled along one side of my backyard. As I swung and looked skyward, I remember wondering, "What is out there for ME to see and discover?"

I can remember as a kid being crowded in our family's tent, squashed between my five siblings as we slept with the smell of freshly cooked popcorn from the camp stove and the sound of waves surfing their way onto the shore. Travel, for my family of eight, consisted of camping at a beach during school vacation and my favorite childhood memories are from these trips. I was comfortable at home; it was a safe harbor to be anchored in. However, I knew it wasn't where I could stay. I was seeking awe, wonder, mystery, adventure and most of all, diversity. People who were different than me and places that immersed me in sights and sounds unlike those I had experienced growing up in Australia.

I knew something of the world, with my limited knowledge being gained through three things: an enormous tabletop world atlas that needed two children to turn a page, National Geographic magazines my parents brought home, and pictures in travel brochures. Every week, on my way home from school, I would dig through the "Take One" box outside the local travel agency, looking for brochures displaying colorful images of exotic locations. I discovered Hawaii, Egypt, Peru, Canada, China and Vietnam. Each week I would add my new 'treasures' to my own cardboard box in the bottom of the wardrobe and feel my excitement grow when given a homework task involving anything geographical. It meant I had a valid excuse to look through them again. When a sibling asked to borrow a travel brochure for their homework project, I would carefully curate the pile and offer them only the ones I was willing to sacrifice. One of my proudest moments in Grade 8 was cutting out images of South East Asia for a school project and researching the region so thoroughly that the teacher told me I had handed in three times as many pages as required. I interpreted this as high praise. My longing to travel and explore, my desire to see these places for myself was Ignited.

Starting university felt like a ticket to launch my life. I can remember walking into my first class and feeling the excitement of not quite knowing where this would lead me, but knowing that it was a step in the right direction... a step towards Adventure! I studied mining engineering and this presented opportunities to work in remote outback towns, something vastly different to an office in my hometown of Sydney. After graduating, I embarked on a four-year cross continent career path during which I called the tiny, mining towns 'home.' The more isolated the town, the braver I felt and after work the possibilities for outback adventures were limitless.

At work, I was surrounded by men. I was usually the only woman working in the underground mine: operating the drilling rigs, driving the trucks and loaders, or loading explosives into pre-drilled holes. Earning your stripes 'working on the tools' was a rite of passage for engineers prior to being considered for a supervisory role. It was exciting knowing I was a rarity and forging a new path for other women. At the same time, it was a burden. As with anything rare, anonymity doesn't exist. My expectation and hope was that I be treated like every other engineer, but that wasn't always the case. The unofficial spotlight placed on female engineers in this era made us a target for skepticism, rumor-mongering and sometimes bullying. It made me feel uneasy and propelled me further into wanting to appear professional and fiercely independent at all times.

Maintaining my professionalism was important to me, even in social settings. There was a fine balance to be held between being a leader at work and socializing with the crew on the weekends. I had an internal struggle around this. The times when I let my guard down and shared something personal, I would hear versions of it on the rumor mill next week at work. This feeling of having trusted someone with something personal only to learn they'd shared it with others was so disappointing and drove me further towards always keeping up my guard. Having no role models in this arena, I was never sure if I was doing it right. Holding this balance was lonely at times and I sorely missed the sense of belonging and warmth I felt with my family.

My time in each town was limited and I was reluctant to put down any roots and develop deeper connections. I knew I'd be leaving at the end of my 12-month posting in pursuit of promotions and a successful career. This didn't bother me. I was independent and needed noone. Convinced that standing alone was the best way to be but still wanting to have fun, I joined in on all the social activities I could find. By ignoring the aloneness and deflecting the discomfort of feeling unfulfilled, I didn't have to show vulnerability.

A job opportunity eventually took me back to Sydney, but within six months I grew restless. I was seeking a connection with nature and adventure outdoors. I wanted out of the city and felt the pull towards something bigger than me and decided to plan a challenging wilderness trek in Nepal.

With my backpack on three months later, I breathed in the freedom of wandering along skinny mountain paths and absorbing the vistas laid out before me in the Annapurna region. I would stare, trance-like, at the intense solitude of the valleys and mountain peaks until they were photographed on my mind. I recall having hiked so high that one day, when looking down, I could see mountain peaks poking up through a white ribbon of cloud. "How am I so fortunate to be having this experience?" I thought. I was mesmerized. I felt dwarfed yet embraced by something so extraordinarily grand, an undeniably incredible creation.

My love of hiking and exploring landscapes deepened on this journey, as did my compassion and love for the people who I connected with in the villages. Partaking in meals and ceremonies with those people gave me an awareness of the beauty of connections and the deep sense of belonging and love in their families. I felt pure joy and a sense of peace there. I vowed I would come back.

A year later, I met Troy. When I first saw him, it was at work. I was drawn to his smiling eyes and felt his warmth, but I didn't want to feel it. The second time I saw him, in a social setting, I felt gravitationally pulled towards him, but I tried to ignore it. The third time, I succumbed to his playful nature and we wrapped our arms around each other and it felt like home. We very quickly discovered we shared a love of physical challenges and adventures in nature. It was exciting to be venturing out with someone who wanted to share fun experiences and be spontaneous. Troy and I were an unshakeable team, spending weekends hiking and discovering new trails, and mountain biking in the nearby hills. During those adventures, we dreamed about and planned our trek to Mount Kilimanjaro, in Tanzania.

That climb was the highest we had done together and we held our breath with excited anticipation while planning it, but the reality of it was something else altogether.

Clambering over boulders to wrestle my way up a rocky slope, I felt exhilarated. My energy was so high I was springing over large rocks while others walked around them. Three days into the climb, my muscles should have been tired and meager, but they were full of bounce. I wondered where this energy came from. Perhaps it was adrenaline or the mountain air, or maybe the fitness training I did leading up to the trek; most likely a combination of all three. Either way, my body was strong and keeping me on target to reach the 5,895-meter summit. It was as though something that I didn't recognize was inside me; I was powered by something that I had not felt before. It was almost spiritual. The best part was, altitude sickness hadn't affected me to that point, and I saw this as further reinforcement that my goal was a reality. I was determined to reach the summit. I was convinced I'd be there, witnessing the sunrise and capturing it on camera. It was galvanized in my mind.

As the afternoon sunlight bathed the surrounding peaks in gold, we paused at our final camp before our push to the summit. Here, we would sleep for a few hours until it was time to complete the last part of the climb. This final push would happen in the darkest and coldest reaches of the night, designed to ensure we reached the top in time for the sunrise.

Waking after a four-hour nap, we fitted our headlamps, pulled on our boots and checked our water supplies. I had slept in all my clothes, too cold to leave any item unused and didn't regret it for a moment. Although I wasn't completely rested after those few hours, I felt energized and eager to start walking. In that frame of mind, we departed camp.

The next two hours were spent steadily ascending the tundra, its grainy yet firm surface providing plenty of traction underfoot. It was challenging but somehow comfortable as I kept up my rapid pace from the day before. My headlamp provided me a two-meter radius and because the landscape underfoot was so barren and unchanging, I frequently looked up at the sky, seeking another perspective. The cloudless night allowed me to feel cocooned in the infinite expanse of stars. Gratefully, I rested whenever our guide advised, but only for a minute at a time. This was adequate to take in small sips of water as well as avoid having the warm sweat on my body cool in the below zero temperatures.

In the next few minutes, I heard a distinct English accent talking loudly yet with a hint of disappointment. Lifting my head up, I could make out a large shadow of a man only meters ahead of me. "I did my best," the voice said. "I'm not going on. I'm heading back down to camp. I'll be home in a few days; give my love to the kids." He was talking into a satellite phone and although I didn't know his reasons for turning back, I looked across at Troy and panted, "Wow, imagine climbing for four days only to turn back hours before the top." I was filled with compassion for this man who had gotten himself so far but could not find it within himself to finish. I couldn't fathom this as a possibility for me.

Gradually the coarse-grained pebbles disappeared, making way for a much finer, slippery material and my pace slowed. Each step onto this fine grey volcanic ash was like walking on clouds as my foot would not stay where it landed. Instead, it would slip backwards down the slope which meant I was advancing only four or five inches each time. My breathing was heavy. The positive self-talk had stopped; how long ago, I couldn't say. I could no longer remember the words. Exhaustion weighed heavily on both my body and mind. I attempted another step, but my foot didn't move. Looking down, I willed my boot to lift up. Nothing. I couldn't reconcile why my mind saw it moving but it stayed where it was. Both feet were locked in place.

"I can't do it," I gasped, my voice barely audible. "I can't move my feet." Despair and panic rushed in as the thought of not being able to reach the summit engulfed me. Before that moment, it hadn't occurred to me that I wouldn't.

Suddenly, I felt a gentle pressure in the middle of my back. "Yes, you can," I heard Troy say. "I'm right here. I've got you." He held his hand on my back and slowly pushed me forward into the next step. The tears came then and continued for many steps thereafter as I felt his hand on my back. The knowing that I could be vulnerable enough to depend on someone for support and still be loved and adored by them was a moment of clarity. Being cracked open to receiving that unconditional support was a first for me. I dropped my guard and with surrender, came relief. I cried because I had surrendered and allowed myself to be vulnerable, and I knew I was going to be ok. I didn't feel weaker in that moment. I felt stronger.

I always felt something was missing, but I buried or swept aside any desire to look for it. I wasn't comfortable being vulnerable and this eventually caused me to play small. It was safer to be tough and remain independent. I was good at it. And I convinced myself it was more exciting. The concept of interdependence was foreign to me; I just wasn't aware that I could have it all: to maintain my independence as a woman, a pioneer in my field and at the same time be in a loving relationship and lean on someone when I needed to. It wasn't a balance I knew how to do well. Instead, I thought I needed to choose one. How wrong I was and how grateful I am to have experienced all that I have.

I did reach the summit that morning and many others since.

Troy and I have traveled together many times since our trip to Mount Kilimanjaro, from weekend getaways to years living in other countries and everything in between. We've been up close to elephants in South Africa, watching from the front seat of a Mini while the herd crossed the road as though it were a family of pedestrians. We have watched bears playing while hiking in Yoho National Park in Canada. I've lain on the ground north of the Arctic circle and watched the Northern Lights dancing above me countless times. These experiences have far surpassed those childhood dreams I formed when looking through that box of travel brochures.

The gratitude I have for my early childhood is immense. It helped me become a curious, thoughtful and independent person and as a result, I've made the conscious decision to share that curiosity and joy of Adventure with my children as together we build a greater awareness of the world around us.

Over the years I have become more at ease with vulnerability, and accepting support by loved ones has become easier too. That place of interdependence is now a place I relish being in. It gives me constant strength.

Independence is a wonderful trait and something you can be proud of. However, being too independent can close you off to discovering deep relationships and powerful connections. Allow yourself to be vulnerable sometimes. It can energize everyone in the relationship and lead to a profound and uplifting sense of togetherness. Your adventure begins when you allow yourself to be vulnerable and truly connect with others.

IGNITE ACTION STEPS

- Travel in as many ways as you can. Traveling solo has its strengths, but when traveling with a partner or friend, or in a group, you can lean on each other to deepen the experience.

- Join a walking or hiking group or start one yourself. You'll meet like-minded people and maybe find someone you can lean on in all areas of life, not just on a hike.

- Take your 'meetups with friends' into nature. Meet at the trailhead and bring the people you lean on most into your adventures big and small, sharing in the places that bring you joy.

Alexandra Blake - Australia
Mining Engineer, Technical Writer, Editor, Author
www.mintediting.com.au

ANDONIA REYNOLDS

"Embrace the adventure of life; there is always a lesson to learn."

It takes courage to step out of your comfort zone and expand your mind. Live free of self doubt and see the world as you are intended to. Making yourself smaller takes away from your experiences. Live and play BIG.

GALLOPING HORSES BROUGHT ME BACK

I was eleven years old. It was going to be my first trip into Willmore Wilderness Park in the Canadian Rocky Mountains. I was going to be spending the summer working for my Godfather. I didn't know any of the people that worked for him, but I was excited and ready for the adventure. I remember as a little girl never being afraid to live big and to have my energy take up space. I loved the feeling of being spontaneous and with that, also blunt, sharing my opinion of right or wrong for all to hear. As we headed out in the backcountry by horse, I found my love for the mountains and knew even then that this was my purpose.

Even though I was more than happy to share my opinions with others, I rarely let anyone see past the surface. My true feelings were always kept for me alone. Horses became my voice and my ability to express what I could never tell another soul. I was exposed to a whole new world that embraced me with open arms and accepted my weirdness and singing-out-loud ways. The mountains became home and the horse wranglers became my family. I spent every summer break for the next eight seasons living in the bush for two straight months, away from the noise and judgment of my home town, living the lifestyle that I loved.

As I got older, my free spirit started to dim. I started to lose my way.

I abruptly quit halfway through my last season at Willmore. New people had taken the place of my original mountain family and I was disappointed with the change. I didn't understand why they were there and I didn't want to be their friends. They didn't belong. At the same time, my Godfather was dying and I felt empty and broken. I kept asking myself what was happening to my home? Everything I knew or thought I knew had changed and I didn't like it one bit, so I packed up my car, my dog and moved to the city.

The city didn't make any sense. It was too much chaos. I never felt satisfied with what I was doing while living in that space, eventually just another hole that brought pain. I continued to fall further away from my true self, quitting everything I started. I had finally hit an all time low and I needed to find my way back again.

One year after my Godfather had passed, I sat in my dark basement suite thinking about the person I am and the person I was supposed to be. I flipped through my photo albums and allowed my memories to come flooding back in. I hadn't touched a horse in at least two years and I missed their smell. The way they would nuzzle me with their head, pulling me into them. My legs pulled in tight to my body with my face in my knees, I rocked back and forth sobbing, feeling everything I had pushed down. I knew change needed to happen. I decided to shake off the past year and regain my focus.

It started with working for a race barn. It was wonderful to be around the horses again, but they lived in a stall 80 percent of the time. Other than their daily feed and hour-long ride with the jockey, there was no opportunity to connect with the horses. It felt like a typical nine-to-five job, operating on cruise control shoveling 200 pounds of manure a day. I was looking for more and soon found myself exploring other options.

An intriguing possibility popped up rather unexpectedly. I saw a posting online looking for horse wranglers in the United States, not too far from home. As a young adult making minimum wage, while the idea of traveling to the States seemed interesting, I knew I would have to be creative to make this happen. I traded my experience with horses for opportunity. Two weeks later, I had a round trip bus ticket purchased by my father. I was thrilled to be leaving for Lander, Wyoming for a few months. With my guitar, a duffle bag and a little bit of cash for food, I felt nothing but excitement as my bus rolled out of town driving towards my new adventure.

The Greyhound drove through the Rocky Mountains to the coastal city of Vancouver. I made a bus transfer and started south to Seattle. This was my first time being in the States. Though my experience was as an observer passing through, I felt like an explorer. I soaked in the changing landscapes. I watched mountains change into hills, hills transform into seascapes. I watched the silver ribbon of rivers wind their way through dramatic canyons. Passing through cities watching the sun reflecting off the mirrored windows of office buildings, I admired their architecture, the art and science of the designs. My heart felt full and that I was heading in the right direction.

By day three, having spent the last two nights sleeping in a seat on the bus, I was bagged. The idea of doing this again to get home filled me with dread.

I met many 'interesting' people on the bus. I chatted with a lovely elderly couple who were amazed and seemingly proud of the adventure I was under-taking. There was this really nice woman with her kids and I helped her out by watching her children while she ran to the bathroom. One man who I remember vividly invited me to join him in his basement for some sado-masochistic sex. I politely declined. At 19 and alone, I felt violated and a little scared. I was sick to my stomach with discomfort until he got off the bus and we were another town away. I wasn't so open to new conversations for the rest of the trip.

My last transfer was in Cody, Wyoming. Red and sage and desert colors dominated my view, the mountains a distant bump on the horizon. I headed off to Lander in a shuttle van, crowded in with five other people as we journeyed on for another two hours. I remember how the sun was starting to rise. The orange and yellow bouncing off the mountain range gave me a sense of comfort.

The van pulled up to a gas station to drop me off. I grabbed my luggage and it drove away, leaving me standing at the curb waiting for the strangers I was going to spend the summer with. It was five in the morning in the middle of nowhere. The only sound was the wind and a lonely tumbleweed blowing across the road. I chuckled to myself as I pictured a scene from *Fievel Goes West.*

Shortly after 6AM, a dually (a large pickup truck with doubled tires on the back axle) pulled up. A man about six feet tall stepped out wearing a black cowboy hat and a light blue collared shirt. He looked to be in his fifties with a soft complexion and kind eyes. He shook my hand and introduced himself, and I felt at ease.

The main ranch was ten minutes from town and on the border of a Native Amercian reservation. I spent one night there before going up to my position to wrangle at 9,200 feet in the heart of the Wind River Mountains. It was off the grid, offering a rustic comfort with custom-made cabins, daily horseback rides, pack trips, trout fishing, natural history hikes and wildlife viewing. The wrangler's job was to help plan the rides for the guests. I was the new gal and the season had started a month earlier. I looked out the truck window as we drove up the rough mountain road and a feeling of sadness came over me, remembering my last trip into the Willmore. I missed my mountain home and my family and wondered if this trip was a mistake. Shrunken down, I felt very small as we pulled into the dude ranch.

I brought my gear into the wrangler cabin. It couldn't have been more than four hundred square feet. The door opened to the inside and to the right was a two-person table, a cabinet with nothing in it and to the left a counter with a small mirror above it. Straight ahead one step down was a separate room with six handmade bunk beds nailed together with a plywood base. One old dusty mattress for me. I had never experienced the pleasure of being in a cabin or having a bed when wrangling; from sleeping on the ground in a tent to a bed. I felt privileged.

After dinner and meeting everyone, I went to bed and lay awake for a while thinking about the days to come and already trying to find reasons to leave. I started having self-doubt. I began questioning my abilities and judging myself as if they were judging me. I didn't put myself out there and kept my head down.

The morning came quickly and I was awake before everyone else. The night before I had helped with the evening chores and it would be more of the same that morning. I grabbed the square bales, cut them open and spread the hay flakes out in the mangers for the eighty horses that were wanting their breakfast. It was a crisp dawn in the high country. A couple of wranglers had saddled their horses and headed out on the range to bring the rest of the herd in. Soon I heard the hooves beating off the ground as the horses moved in sync into the holding pen. In that moment I felt bliss. I hadn't officially met the horses until then. Seeing their hot breaths in the crisp air made me feel safe. My heart fluttered and a deep sense of warmth filled me. I felt the full impact that I was exactly in the right place at the right time.

My first week went quickly; there wasn't time to waste as clients were in and out every few days. From day rides to overnight pack trips, food drops for hikers and clearing trail, we were moving every minute. Things had been going pretty smoothly. With my previous years of experience, I caught on quickly. I embraced the company of the horses, taking moments out of my day to appreciate their majestic ways. I felt deeply connected to the spirit of the animals and the beauty of nature.

The first few weeks, I had mostly been riding with the lead wrangler, helping with the bigger jobs over the mountain passes. Any days spent back at the ranch, we were working on the property, fixing fences and taking day rides out. I'd joke around with the other wranglers, but most of the time I was alone. I still hadn't fully decided if this was where I wanted to be.

In the evenings when we were all together, the wranglers had a habit of arguing over who got to take the herd out. I never participated in the evening bickering. While I considered myself to have the most experience, I didn't mind if I stayed back. I kept to myself, sitting alone in the cabin playing my guitar, reminiscing about Willmore. Secretly, I had been fighting within myself, part of me wanting to jump in and the other side holding me back, afraid I would look like a fool.

Quietly amongst themselves, the crew had been talking about me not participating in the evening wrangling, vying for their own spot to ride. One night when it was time to take the horses out, the lead wrangler spoke up and said, "I'm taking Andonia out." He had decided for us and picked me. I felt a sudden rush of fear. I could feel the blood going to my face. I felt hot and I was nervous. Up until l then I was holding back, but now my skills were going to be put to the test.

A horse was saddled, one I had never ridden. We made eye contact and I ran my hand down the left side of his neck, put my foot in the stirrup and leapt into the saddle. The gates opened and I heard the sound of thunder as the herd started galloping off. As soon as the 80 horses took off, I heard someone yelling, "The babies got out; stop the herd!!!" It was clear the debate about my ability to wrangle had distracted us from remembering to separate out the young horses that could get badly hurt galloping across unfamiliar terrain. I had a choice to make. I could jump off and give my horse to someone else... or I could ride.

In that moment, I remembered who I was.

All my fears and self judgment fell away as I raced after the young horses. I rode the edge of the herd, pushing fast and hard, feeling the power beneath me. For a moment, time slowed down and I spotted a gap through the trees up ahead. If I could cut through there I knew I would be able to break in front of the herd and cut the lead horses off. When riding a horse at full speed your job is to be at least five steps ahead, which is even harder in uneven terrain, trees and on a horse you've never ridden. I galloped through the bush, my heart racing, dodging branches and leaping over gullies. Working with my horse, nothing could throw me from the saddle.

I burst out of the trees just in front of the herd, facing the lead horse, yelling, "WHOA! STAND! EASY!" My horse was vibrating underneath me with the adrenaline rush and excitement of the ride, ready to work, pushing back any horses trying to get by while waiting for direction from me. My horse and I had successfully stopped the entire herd. I was proud, sitting tall in my saddle feeling a powerful energy pulsing and radiating around me. The cadence of the entire herd was with me and it felt magical. I was so in tune and in sync with both the horses and the horse I was riding. It was a powerful moment. I was unstoppable.

The lead wrangler caught up and we turned the horses around, headed back to the ranch and brought the babies home.

In that moment, the horses had brought me back to myself. Their sense of understanding and acceptance allowed me to learn what was to come. They forgave me for stepping away from my purpose and reminded me of everything I had to give. I found my Ignite moment through the eye of the horse.

As we were riding back, the lead hand looked at me and cleared his throat, "You know, I have to apologize."

Confused and curious I responded, "Okay...?"

"I really didn't think you knew how to ride," he said. "You never wanted a turn wrangling the horses and, you see, *everyone* wants a turn. We all assumed you were scared and couldn't ride."

I sat even a little taller in the saddle, feeling a little embarrassed as the blood rushed to my face again. He then said, "You're one hell of a rider. I'm extremely impressed!"

In that moment, I felt very uncomfortable in my body — as if it didn't belong to me — a sense of disbelief that this is who I had become. I realized that by making myself smaller, it took away from my own experience. My self-doubt and lack of confidence put a dark light on my abilities and led people to believe I was not who I said I was. I never felt I needed to prove myself, but I had gotten in my own way. It wasn't until I unleashed my true self that I realized part of my dissatisfaction here was that I had stopped myself from experiencing the full journey and the transformation I was there to have. I was reminded of the courageous, spontaneous 11-year-old I used to be... and the woman I wanted to become.

Sometimes looking back doesn't mean you'll keep going backwards. Often it can be a place of comfort that allows us to see how much we have already accomplished. Instead, move forward with an open mind, knowing who you are and allowing the Universe to take you there. We have all experienced opportunities in our lives when we need to step out of our comfort zone to regain the Truth in who we are. Saddle up and enjoy the adventure!

IGNITE ACTION STEPS

Here are some steps that I follow that could help you get out of your own way.

- When you feel lost, take yourself back to when you felt like *you*. Photos, journals or even calling up a friend to reminisce can remind you of who you really are.

- Write what you want down, make it real. Then be bold and take action to get it.

- Ask yourself, "Who am I? Where do I want to be? What am I doing now to live my best life?"

Andonia Reynolds - Canada
CEO/Founder of Western Horse Academy
www.westernhorseacademy.com

Charlene Ray

"Say yes to the journey; the journey awakens the Soul!"

It is my intention that this story will help you listen deeply to the call of adventure. My hope is that you feel inspired, ready and open to step onto your true path; even if it means leaping into the unknown. Even if it means believing in something you have never believed in before, or forgotten that you knew.

Answering Ireland's Call

*"I would love to live like a river flows,
carried by the surprise of its own unfolding."
John O'Donohue*

Long before I ever saw the green rolling hills of Ireland from the window of the plane as it descended into Dublin, Ireland had called to me.

I grew up in Chicago, a place where an abundance of Irish immigrants settled and influenced the culture of many areas of the city. As a child, one of my best friends lived across the street. She was Irish. I loved going to her house. The smell of soda bread baking and Irish stew bubbling on the stove were delicious and enticing. I loved watching her practice Irish dance. Hearing the beat of the music and the rhythm of her shoes hitting the floor filled me with excitement and made my heart beat faster. I would often look at photographs of Ireland with her and always wanted to go there someday.

At age 30, I moved from Chicago with my husband to the Pacific Northwest and I forgot about Ireland. Looking back, I just focused on other things: my work, exploring my spiritual path, becoming a mother and reconnecting with nature in the beautiful place I was living. Ireland was not forgotten; she was just waiting for me.

In my early 40's I began feeling unhappy with myself and my life, and I started searching for more meaning. Through my spiritual explorations, something stirred within me. Initially I did not recognize what it was. Not until a friend of mine suggested that I join him on a spiritual power journey to Ireland. Without hesitation, I said, "Yes." I knew it was going to change my life. It was followed by six months of planning, excitement and anticipation. I had this feeling that I was stepping into something life changing, but I could not even fathom what that meant at the time.

When it was finally time for the journey I was feeling ready for what was to come. Out the plane window, I caught my first glimpse of the beautiful landscape, many shades of green separated by stone walls and dotted with white sheep. The warm tears welled up in my eyes and I literally felt something in my heart that I never had before. After we landed we were met by our American guides and an Irish woodland bard who later became a dear friend. The bard drove the bus and introduced us to the myth and story of his country. We were whisked away to our lodgings in a castle in the west of Ireland. My room in an upper alcove made me feel like a princess in a magical fairy tale. It all seemed so surreal.

The 10-day journey was filled with unbelievable experiences in places that I had only dreamed of. We did rituals atop mountains, walking amongst megalithic tombs. We did rituals while standing at the source of the Shannon River. We sat among dolmens and stone circles and felt the ancient wisdom of the land. In my room each night, I would write in my journal in an attempt to capture the magnitude of the experience. I would cry knowing that my life was about to change and feeling that my soul was home. I was so moved and inspired by every moment. I could not adequately describe the feeling, but it was like I had taken the first deep breath of my life. My heart and soul were expanded and open.

My friend and I stayed in Ireland for another two weeks after the organized spiritual journey ended. That's when the magic really began. My new woodland bard friend helped us map out an itinerary that took us from one end of the country to the other. When I walked into the pasture where the Beltany Circle was in County Donegal, I felt like I was walking back into ceremonial space that I knew from many lifetimes ago. I walked across the field to the circle of 64 large and ancient stones, grabbed onto the closest one and wept. I heard a voice that said, "Welcome home." My body trembled as I kneeled down, leaning into it. I felt something begin to awaken in me.

We made our way to the west to County Clare and I fell in love with the rocky Burren landscape. It had an otherworldly appearance. We walked for miles amidst sweet wildflowers that popped up between the stones. They were breathtakingly beautiful. I drove along the narrow roads of the coastline to Doolin where I loved listening to traditional music in the local pub. The pub was packed with both locals and tourists, standing room only. The musicians were *so* good and welcomed audience members spontaneously joining them on stage for a song or two. And I was stunned by the amount of Guinness that people could drink. In Doolin, I watched the sun set over the Atlantic Ocean before we made our way to the Dingle Peninsula. We traveled from coast to coast and places in between, falling deeper in love with Ireland every day.

When visiting the Cavan Burren, I took a walk by myself in a forest so magical it was sure to be a fairy paradise. It was lush and green and the light through the trees illuminated the stones with a brilliant glow. I wandered along an ancient stone wall that appeared to be part of a very old settlement, running my hands along the crevices between the stones and examining the vegetation. It was damp and the moss was luscious and soft. I felt pulled into a captivating dream world of past and present.

I became a bit tired and wanting to rest and reflect, I found an inviting indentation in the earth to lie down in. My eyes grew heavy and suddenly I found myself in another time, another life perhaps. I saw people around a fire. My eyes focused in on a young woman with red hair and a white cloak. She appeared frightened. As quickly as I realized she was about to be put into the fire, a man on a horse appeared and, in true mythic fashion, swept her up and away. I opened my eyes and thought I heard the sound of horse hooves moving fast and felt them vibrating on the ground. I put my hands on the earth and looked down. When I turned my face up again, out of the corner of my eye I saw a white blur and felt a rush of wind across my back.

For a few moments, I sat bewildered and confused. Then came the *knowing*. This was *me*; this was another lifetime. I had been here before. I knew my meaning and purpose then. Tears streamed down my face as I felt the awareness of why I had been called to this country. No wonder my soul felt so at home!

I knew I would not be able to speak of this Ignite moment. Who would believe me? I felt I would be called crazy. I didn't know who would understand.

My mind flashed to a memory of myself around age seven, talking to my grandmother. I had told her that I could talk with trees and that I could see the energy around them, and around people. She very firmly put her hands on my shoulders and said to me, "Don't ever let anyone know this; you will be locked up like my sister." She was so frightened and uncharacteristically upset that I took her very seriously and never spoke of it again.

Yet here I was, nearly 40 years later, sitting on the forest floor in Ireland, *knowing* that I just had a vision that forever changed me. I once again felt that it was not okay to speak what I knew to be true. I tried to tell myself it didn't mean anything. I stood up from that experience and searched out my friend who was happily exploring another area. As we got into the car, I turned, looking back at the forest and I told myself that I had a vivid imagination and that my experience wasn't real.

Before I embarked on that journey, my life was not feeling like my true path. Even though I tried not to think about it, this vision lived in me now. I knew that Ireland might awaken parts of me and that change would be inevitable, but when I returned home from Ireland, my whole life was turned upside down. A couple months after this first trip, I left my husband. We had been married twenty years, many of them happy, but we had grown apart in so many ways. I moved into my own place. Our son was eight and would now travel between two homes. This was both freeing and deeply sad.

As I settled into my new rhythms, I could no longer deny my intuitive gifts and healing abilities. The way I worked with clients and the students I counseled at the alternative school changed. Once again I began to see the energy around them. My walks through the local forests were different as I opened up to the energy of the trees and could hear their messages.

And I longed for Ireland.

After the power of the trip to Ireland, I really thought I would return the next year, but it took nine years before my feet touched Irish soil again. After my son started college on the East Coast, I kept going east, by myself this time, back to my soul's home. I landed in Dublin and headed west to see my woodland bard friend. Stepping out of my rented car, I saw a storybook cottage surrounded by three labyrinths he had created. One was made of herbs. One was of stone. I took off my shoes and entered the last, a tree labyrinth. I walked barefoot, crying and breathing in the moist, sweet air as deeply as I could. I spent two weeks in Ireland, walking for miles through the countryside amidst the trees, stones and the waters, listening to my inner wisdom and for messages from the land. Every day I watched the light shift and change on the landscape.

Every moment changed me. Every step connected me deeper to myself. I was uncovering more of the meaning of my life.

I have now been to Ireland eight times in the past four years. The customs agent recently asked me why I come to Ireland so frequently. How do you explain the concept of a soul's home to a government official who is possibly looking for evidence of potential trouble? They always ask when I will return to America and seem to be fine with this being a special place for me as long as I have a plan to leave. It is hard to explain to anyone why I visit so often, as few people understand. I breathe more easily in Ireland. My heart feels at peace.

I often find myself in Glendalough, a national park and ancient pilgrimage site in County Wicklow. I too am a pilgrim there, walking amongst the ruins, the trees and along the lake, listening for the next instructions on how to best live my life. I can now stand in my truth and say that I am a person who walks between worlds and experiences the energy of the land. I can be grounded and present in the world, and open to the way nature longs to connect with us. In Ireland, I slow down and listen more deeply, creating more time and space to be open to this connection.

In Glendalough, I met my Irish 'sister' who is a wise woman of the ancient wells. Together, we collect water from the wells for the workshops we teach and sit there listening to the wisdom. I see the old and sacred wells as portals into the feminine soul of Ireland.

Teaching workshops in Ireland is a blessing. Once a year, I lead a pilgrimage with my friend in Wicklow and the woodland bard in Sligo who I met many years ago. I invite participants to leave behind their daily lives, their identity back home, and slow down. They are encouraged to experience Ireland in the way I feel she most wants to be known: slowly, intentionally, through the senses, in nature and ancient places. We connect with the spirits of the land through the trees, the plants, the waters and the stones. Participants are invited to bring forward what wants to be healed and transformed. Many people have awakenings similar to what I experienced when I first came to the country and now I am not afraid to share my story of what happened in the Cavan Burren.

As the participants open their hearts and minds, they are often changed in deep and powerful ways. It is frequently the healing wells that create the shift but it is often the over 5,000 year-old megalithic stone tombs that change them. Sitting inside one of the tombs, you feel as if the world has stopped. If it is windy or raining outside, when you crawl inside you are in silence. It is a special place to be still and reflect. I am grateful to witness others as they experience their own awakening while finding meaning through this transformation.

There have been many powerful Ignite moments in Ireland, including that very first one in the Cavan Burren. These moments are sparks of inspiration and transformation in my life that have long lasting effects. They have given me the courage to make life-changing decisions and to be true to my intuitive way of being. Ireland has opened my connection to divine feminine wisdom and allowed me to access many of my feelings that, in the past, I kept bottled up inside. Every time I return to Ireland, the smell of the turf fires, brilliant rainbows and ever changing light captivate me once more.

Ireland may or may not be the place that calls to you, but it is likely that somewhere does, if you are willing to listen. Places like this will often grab hold of you and shake up your life as they help you remember who you are. You may notice that living authentically is the strongest desire you have. Don't be afraid. Living your true path is not always easy but your life will be so much richer and more beautiful because of it. There can be no more making yourself uncomfortable for others to be comfortable. You feel compelled to say "Yes!" to your own life. There can be no going back.

Listen. Where does your heart tell you to go? Which places make your ears perk up when you hear of them in conversation? What books or photos grab your attention when you see them? Why not say "Yes" to the call? You just might discover your soul's home. You could remember who you are and why you are living this life adventure this time around. Say "Yes!" to the journey!

Find the meaning in you.

Ignite Action Steps

- Take a journal out into nature and walk until you find a lovely spot to sit and write. Write for 10 minutes without stopping, asking yourself, "Where do I most want to travel? Why? Is there a place that seems to be calling to me?"

- Reflect on your life so far. Have you ever said "Yes" to a journey, knowing it might change everything? How did this adventure change you? Share your story with a trusted friend over a cup of tea or a pint.

- Take a mindful walk in nature until you feel you can leave your daily tasks behind and listen to yourself. Ask yourself these questions: Are there things about you that you feel no one will understand? Do you have intuitive gifts or abilities that you keep hidden away out of fear of what others might say or do? Can you think of one person who might be able to listen without judgment? Can you risk sharing with them? If sharing with another person feels like too much of a stretch, can you share your thoughts in your journal or with a tree?

• Use a vision board to make your adventure dreams a reality. Collect images of the places that call to you from magazines and/or the internet. Create a collage on a poster board that you can hang in a place where it will be seen often. Look at your vision board daily and watch this manifestation tool work its magic. Get ready to buy your plane tickets; it won't be long until your adventure begins!

Charlene Ray - United States
Heart-centered mentor, spiritual counselor and workshop facilitator
www.charleneray.com
⊙ revcharleneray

MIGUEL BRIGHTEYES

"The smallest of moments can reveal the greatest of opportunities."

I am writing this with a sparkle in my eyes because my perspective is about to be shared with you, absorbed and interpreted by you. How glorious! All life is a series of moments where we step into a greater and greater truth of who we are. I hope this story helps you find more of that truth.

THREE MEN IN THE WESTERN KINGDOM

The first thing I noticed about the airplane I was about to board was its size. I had never been inside such a small flying machine and the thought of being that high in the sky in what looked like a crude toy plane filled my fingertips with the bad kind of tingles. The second thing I realized as I boarded were the people on the plane, a group who had lived through many more years than me without any loss of the spring in their step. Thirdly, I noticed the strip of aquamarine blue light glowing along the aisle of the plane. It was a pleasant color, though not my favorite, nonetheless a reminder of my great-aunt who once religiously sported the color while touting that it 'brought out her wisdom.' Seeing it there on the floor, I wondered if it would help bring out mine.

I was on my first solo trip, the start of a whirlwind weekend in Marrakesh, Morocco, one that would be a deep and lasting Ignite moment and would help lead me to walk the life path that I do now.

Once on the ground in Marrakesh, I was immediately hit with overwhelming sensations. An intoxicating smell of dust, spices and passion. The sun was hot and a rough French tongue could be heard in the wind. What a great opportunity to practice my French! I made my way along the corridors and alleyways of the city for much longer than necessary until I found the little hostel I would call home for the next three days.

A man with a voracious smile that was missing three teeth greeted me at the door. He was short in stature but was a giant in the art of storytelling. It was a few hours of tea, crumpets, laughs and more tea before I was able to settle in on an ottoman cushion and take hold of my thoughts. I felt a calmness in that moment, but my calm was soon interrupted by that familiar gnawing anxiety that had troubled me for years on end. Anxious thoughts pulled at my attention until they percolated up to the apex of my awareness. My breath grew short and my feet grew cold as I asked myself, "What am I looking for here?", and then the thought came, "Why do I exist in this world?", which led to, "What does it all matter anyway?" A further wave of disconnection washed over me. I felt as if there was a physical itch in my chest, constricting my thoughts, pulling me into that memorably dark place. I felt a mix of guilt at my pampered and privileged upbringing combined with a lack of passion for pursuing the traditional career paths the world had to offer. It often left me utterly directionless, incapacitated and in pain. Deep breath… deep breath. The morning would bring the sun.

The sun did rise that first morning and it brought with it the sights and sounds of the bustling Marrakesh bazaar. What a wonderful place it was, filled with the smells of leather and sugar and smoke. Just after sputtering out some broken French and cursing myself for not learning any words in Arabic, a local man ran towards me. Overweight but with a noticeable agility in his step and a vibrant energy in his face, he had the biggest natural smile I had ever witnessed and an almost entirely shaved head with a small curly mop of hair on his crown. The man was a sight to behold.

"Hey, you are the Canadian man from the hostel, Michael right?" he said. Bewildered, I thought, "Who was this man and why was he talking to me?" He explained how he had been eavesdropping on the gathering last night from a quiet corner in the hostel, which I would soon find out was quite unlike him. "I am David, pleased to meet you," he said. He stated his desire to walk the bazaar with me, claiming to need someone to talk to as he shopped. In the moments I took to decide, I noticed a few subtle nods of respect from shopkeepers and I could see his Arabic skills, so I said, "Yes."

That day turned into the perfect blueprint of how to give to a stranger in need. David found me the best barber in town and I experienced my first incredibly nerve-racking knife-blade shave. He bargained all my gifts down far beyond any of my capabilities, bought me lunch and showed me secret passageways that held wonders like a house of jewels. Priests, known locally as imams, taught me the basics of Arabic through their holy scripture and a tea and smoke circle. It was a whirlwind and I felt so like a local that I hardly noticed when David slipped out mid-afternoon, promising to meet again.

Walking back among the shops in the bazaar alone, I noticed a seemingly jovial young man soliciting passersby. What stood out though were his eyes. Inquisitive and deep, yet penetratingly sad. They beckoned me over. At first, the man made his pitch… I was in need of moccasins to impress the ladies back home with my foreign style. When I said I had a woman back home, he touted the durability of the slippers for walking outside. When he learned I was from Canada, he cited their extraordinary warmth. I appreciated his salesmanship, but I was not there for a sale. I asked him why he had such sad eyes.

This struck him like thunder. He paused for just a moment, shaken, before regaining his composure and ignoring me to move on to another customer. So I sat on a little stool amidst his clutter of shoeboxes and I waited. For over an hour I sat there, only receiving furtive glances from the shopkeeper. It was so pleasant, watching the thousands of colorful passersby, like ants hustling before they walk home to their nests. Eventually, the shopkeeper came near me and pulled up a second hidden stool. We sat in silence together for an extended period of time.

When the moment felt right, I asked him, "What is your name?"

"Abdallah Haim," he said.

I tried again, "Why do you have such sad eyes?" Abdallah Haim took a deep breath, before letting out a diatribe on the pains of his life. How he talked back to his parents and got beat for it. How fearful he was of his boss reporting him to the authorities for questioning religious doctrine. How mad he was at tourists who live life with knowledge in their brains and darkness in their hearts. We talked about philosophy and religion, travel and space, food and motorbikes. This man had all the natural intelligence that I did with none of the education, which led to him holding some views that seemed so 'backward' to me at the time. He was uncommonly willing to learn and grow, but without having had the opportunities that I had to satiate my desire for growth. Immense gratitude filled my throat and I almost choked on the feeling. It humbled me greatly.

We became friends.

At dinner time, before I left Abdallah Haim, he brought me to the back of the shop. I saw him shuffling the walls to bring out a very pretty hidden shoe. Inside it, he pulled out a spiral pendant, not expensively adorned with jewels or anything, but simply carved, humble, and full of the power of his ancestors. The artistic beauty and simplicity of it made my eyes well up as he offered me the pendant. Shocked, I respectfully declined, but Abdallah Haim would not take no for an answer and I walked away with a spiral in my pocket and new light in my heart.

The next day, I woke up early to go on a guided adventure to the world famous Ouzoud Falls in the Atlas mountains. The ride and hike there was pleasant, with many a smile and good local food shared. Near the end of the hike and with the faintest sound of the powerful drumming of water, I saw a squirrel run across the path and down a slightly overgrown side path. At the entrance to this side path, a little sign said 'Turismo,' and a small plume of smoke could be seen exiting a shack at the end of the path. I wanted to go but the others all insisted we had to follow the tour guide. Reluctantly, I walked on, but it was not long at all before I thought I saw the squirrel again, running in the forest in the direction of the hut. Whether I was hallucinating or not, the little guy reminded me of David, running around the market the day before. I knew I had to go to the shack. No one else would join so I approached the hut alone.

Apprehensive, I kept my guard up as I emerged into the clearing in front of the shack. What I found was a typical tourist hut, with all kinds of local paraphernalia. What was atypical was the man behind the operation, a man I would soon know by the name of Nishim. He was an old Berber indigenous man who must have been 6' 6" tall, and must have weighed 140 pounds. I had never seen such a wondrous toothpick of a man in all my life. His mind, teased by the twinkle in his eye, was even more atypical. Worried about losing my group, I told him how I needed to leave and catch up with my tour. He replied in perfect English, "Son, your group is not going anywhere; you simply have to walk down the path towards the drumming. Besides, you are already lost."

It was my turn to be thunderstruck. At the time, I thought of myself as an outgoing, confident and assured individual, especially in my interactions with other people. I wondered why these words had cut so deeply and how he had known to say them. All I knew was that I wanted to learn from this man in whatever time I had with him.

He turned out to be incredibly accomplished, having fought for indigenous Berber rights at the UN, having been trained as a lawyer and being fluent in seven languages. Each of these facts rightly floored me, and I couldn't believe the incongruence with what my eyes were seeing in front of me: a frail old disheveled man. He taught me lessons that I still remember and draw upon for wisdom today. Namely that life gives you many paths and choices, with each one opening up a Universe of delight if you let it. He impressed upon me not to bring children into this world until I reach 'the conclusion,' a phrase that can be described simply as having figured out your true grand vision and are in pursuit of it. When discussing the corruption so deeply inherent in the power structures of the world, he told me to plant trees all around you even if those higher in society do not. We talked about oneness, drummed together, and sat in extended silence. Funnily enough, I recall this drumming and silence as being one of my first experiences of that oneness. I asked him about the squirrel and he explained that the squirrel is a creator, doing what he wants in life without regard for external systems of control. He said humans are like squirrels but have forgotten much of a squirrel's knowledge. His simple way of speaking emboldened me to live a life of greater vitality and awareness to this day.

The rest of my days in Morocco consisted of time spent wandering the streets, smelling herbs and spices, motorbiking and camel riding in the desert, and feeling the sun's power and warmth on my skin. When it was time to board the little plane back home, I paused at the top of the rickety metal steps that connected to the threshold of the plane's door and looked behind me. As far as I could see, thick, sandy fog swirled in the air, hiding the larger world around me, but in my heart, I felt free.

Asking the right questions at the right time can unlock the answers to mysteries that you never consciously knew you needed the answers to. Sitting here writing this now, I realize how much this one trip helped to Ignite so much of what I am doing in life professionally, and how I carry myself personally. I did not know it at the time of sitting on that ottoman cushion that the questions I was asking myself, "What am I looking for here? Why do I exist in this world? What does it all matter anyway?" would become a catalyst for so much growth and learning.

The strangers around me, David, Abdallah Haim, and Nishim, provided so much learning in each and every moment I spent with them. David helped me adjust to a new environment and made me feel comfortable simply because I said, "Yes." It turns out that we would meet again later in Denmark to share in interests I was pursuing at the time and he remains an important part of my life, helping me work toward my dream of opening a retreat centre in Portugal. Abdallah Haim needed my perspective at that time of his life, someone to vent to, someone to see himself in. If I had not insisted on seeing him for his true nature with a simple question, who knows where he would have directed his sadness and fear. One of the few regrets I hold in my heart to this day is losing track of that pendant he gave me, but I wear the spiral inked on my skin in his honor. Nishim is a sort of alchemical figure to me and the moments we shared were full of beauty.

These men, these three kings, were brought into my life for a reason: furthering goals and dreams, being there for someone in a moment of great need, and experiencing an unexpected moment of beauty. Three reasons to pick your head up and engage with the world around you. Most especially, to engage with the people in it. The simplest of moments can change your life or someone else's, and in turn, brighten the world. In fact, they are the only things that can.

Traveling is brilliant in that it speeds up the process of growth due to the sheer number of differences like smells, architecture, style, and perspectives that bombard your senses. But, and this is the most important thing, the possibilities that exist traveling are just the same in your regular life. They may be harder to see. But they are certainly there. Today, I have used the lessons from Morocco and thousands of similar interactions to spend my days developing the three pillars of my life: Connection to others, Intuition with the heavens at large, and Power within myself. I coach people in these areas. I put on gatherings where people can breathe and dance and express their creativity and divinity. I write. And I wander the streets elevating and learning from myself and others through simple interactions and energy exchanges. I cannot say that the three original questions that haunted me back in Marrakesh have been fully answered. I do not know if that is possible for anyone. But I do come at them with more grace. I am not looking anymore, but doing my best to be. I am not stressing over existence, but doing my best to follow the pulse and rhythm of the great unknown. I am not worrying about what matters, but doing my best to make things matter.

You too can be, and follow the rhythm, and make more things matter. We all can. Next time someone gives you the impression they may need help, say yes. Next time you feel pulled to chat with someone on the subway, say yes. Next time you think you recognize a crazy squirrel leading you down a path that is not part of your routine, take a deep breath, smile, and say yes. There is a diversity of beauty and opportunity around us that will lead you to that place of grace.

IGNITE ACTION STEPS

People who live out their dreams, adventures and authenticity often manifest their greatest self through a system they use and reflect upon. Try these four simple steps:

Craft a heroic vision. Goals are not strong enough to pull you out of bed as the ultimate and most ferocious version of yourself. You have to think bigger. You have to go through a deep review of your present and past self, your strengths, weaknesses, good and bad memories. Afterwards, metaphorically or literally burn it all, let it go. Then brainstorm and heartstorm the most amazing version of yourself in all areas of your life. Think in terms of emotions and feelings, and always ask why to get deeper and grander.

Develop time-specific goals. Find the best time period that works for your life. Short enough that it stays relevant and you do not lose focus, but long enough to give time for the Universe to work its magic. I suggest between three and six months. Base your goals on developing the different areas of your vision that you crafted. Ask yourself what value you are going to bring to other people by accomplishing a goal. Tell yourself why you are worthy of it. Consider what daily action would bring you closer to the goal.

Generate your daily intention. Every morning, meditate and feel into the emotions and images of your heroic vision with your five senses. Only with this persistent reminder and orientation can you begin to awaken your sixth sense enough to make your visions real. Do activities like a HIIT workout, tai chi or breathwork to enhance your power. Walk in nature, sit in silence, or dance in a state of wonder to prime your intuition. Then sit and plan your day, including when you will complete your daily goal actions.

Engage with the world. View the world as if it is always conspiring in your favor. Look for meaningful signs in the people and places around you. If you recognize a stranger or feel pulled to approach someone with lingering eye contact or find resonance in a pattern or color, take a deep breath and approach. Micro-prime yourself with thoughts of light or a warm memory. Get out there and watch the momentum and magic grow.

Miguel Brighteyes - Canada
Content Creator / Healer / Connection,
Intuition and Breathwork Facilitator & Coach
www.Bebrighteyes.com
⊙ brighteyesmiguel

JOANNA M. WALTON

"Embrace your fears and set sail; life is beyond the harbor."

We are all on our life's journey. A journey with many uncertainties along the way and a definite end point. All too often on this journey we are stuck in fear, blind to the beauty unfolding around us. We are hiding in our boats, sometimes too scared to even leave the harbor. We tend to forget how rich and full of awe life can be if we dare to set sail. With my story I would like to remind you of the radiating colors of life we can rediscover if we befriend our fears, embrace the uncertain and start to trust ourselves.

LEAVING MY LIFE TO LIVE MY LIFE

Eyes wide open, my heart jumping up and down in pure excitement, I'm staring at the majestic beings slowly moving towards me. Holding my breath to not disturb their peace. I'm in Africa, witnessing one of the oldest and most beautiful forms of life that still exists on our planet. And then it happens. An elephant stops right next to me and gently looks into my eyes. Time suddenly stands still. As we're holding each other's gaze, a whole universe starts unfolding. He's telling me the story of his ancestors, his past and how we are all connected: the essence of life.

Only a few months earlier back in Germany, every day felt the same. Get up, work, eat, sleep. Repeat. I felt like a robot, doing the same things all over again. Rushing from meeting to meeting, sending endless emails without seeing any visible impact from my work. On the outside, everything seemed fine. I had a good corporate job, nice colleagues and earned good money. On the inside, I felt stuck. I was not growing anymore, feeling tense, both mentally and physically tired. Instead of learning new things, I had the feeling I was losing connections between my brain cells by the hour. Driving to the office on Monday morning I was already longing for the next weekend.

I was functioning and playing my part in the paying-the-bills game. Pretending my deepest feelings to be a little hiccup that passes and not allowing them to surface, distracting myself by staying busy. Over the years, I had negated my feelings so much that I had forgotten who I really was and what I was here for. I didn't remember what it was like to feel completely free and joyous from the core of my being anymore.

I had accepted this reality as my new normal. As I wasn't paying attention to my emotions, my body started looking for other valves to show me that something was not right. Keeping me stuck in a latent feeling of dissatisfaction and anxiety showing up as tension in my body. Slowly but steadily I realized that I had to break free. I was longing for time to get back in touch with myself again.

As soon as I started realizing the consequences of this inner desire, my mind began to agonize. Did I really want to quit my safe job and *waste* all of my years of hard work? The cost felt unbearable. In my heart I knew that something had to change. But my mind was not ready for the final jump yet. It would have felt like failing. What would be left of me if I gave up my job? Who would I be?

As I wasn't able to continue like this, I convinced my mind to do an experiment.

Instead of working five days, I would reduce my working hours to only three days a week. That way I would still be safe, earn money and have more time for myself. In theory, this sounded like a nice idea. In practice, the three days I was working, everything got even more stressful as I had to complete more in less time. I was living for the extended weekend which was not the paradigm shift I had hoped for.

However, during those months, something happened. In the newly gained time I started remembering what inner freedom really felt like.

I finally understood on the level of my being and my emotions what I had been craving so much all those years without being able to put it into words.

A tiny flame started flickering inside of me. After more than five years on the job and five months working part time I was ready to fully release the safety leash and embark on a journey to make that feeling of inner freedom my new normal. Handing in my resignation was now merely a formal act. I was giving up my job to not give up myself.

After quitting my job, I still couldn't believe I had finally done it and was a free human being. Free to go wherever my heart wanted to without any obligations. I wanted rawness, to connect with nature's forces and no longer hide inside but dance with the wind. A radical change of perspective on the outside was necessary in order to be able to shift and heal from the inside. I needed to find a valve to let go of all the things I had been piling up inside. I was longing for something that would make my heart sing again like when I was a kid. Being awestruck by the simple beauty of a butterfly.

My heart called me to Africa. A continent I hadn't been to before, with incomparable beauty but harsh living conditions at the same time. As my days had been so structured and overly planned in the years before, I was longing for the opposite. Being completely free, not having a plan on when to go where and deciding on what my next destination should be. I booked a ticket to Cape Town and said goodbye to my old life.

Of course my inner being hadn't changed overnight. As soon as I was on the plane, fear started creeping up. Was it safe to go to Africa all by myself without knowing where exactly I wanted to go? Would I even get to the city safely at 10 PM at night as cars regularly got robbed or hijacked on the way from the airport? The cab driver who picked me up that night must have had the same thought.

"Aren't you scared coming here all by yourself?" he asked me.

Silently I screamed to myself, "Yes, of course I am!!!" I told him, "Yes, I'm scared. But I also don't want to spend my life hiding."

While I was saying those words to him, a sudden sense of peace came over me. What I realized in that moment was that I was just talking to another human being like myself. A human being who had asked me about my fears and thus showed me he knew the feeling of fear himself. I knew that I would be fine. I was no longer paying attention to the movie that had been playing in my head because of all the unknown around me. I felt present and connected with the man next to me due to our common similarities.

To the cab driver it seemed quite insane that I would leave my prosperous, safe country to travel alone to the one with the third highest crime rate in the world. A country that still has a big open wound from the past years of segregation, exploitation and hatred— with assaults being the order of the day. What would unfold in front of me were two months with some of the saddest stories I've heard in my life but also the most beautiful moments I had ever experienced. Experiences I would never have had if I'd stayed in my safe harbor.

In the beginning of my trip my old companion of fear still kept visiting quite frequently as it was so used to getting nourished at my table. However, in contrast to the fear of unanswered emails and too long to-do lists back home, I now understood why it was here. I didn't know the city, the customs, what areas were safe to walk around or to visit as a woman traveling solo. It made sense to be mindful and not wander around naively. I realized how important it was to accept that the fear was there. It served a purpose and wanted to protect me. However, I had definitely not come all this way to hide in a hostel. We had to find a way to become friends.

Making a first step towards my fear, I started looking for ways to distinguish whether my rush of adrenaline was a signal to really be alert or just a gentle reminder that I was out of my comfort zone. I started asking local people around me where they went, what they did, what they avoided. I teamed up with other travelers and volunteers along the way to share parts of the journey and great moments. Strangers becoming friends, going on hikes, exploring nature, wine, food markets and local music together. And after some time, as I got more used to the way things worked and understood the ground rules, I was able to notice faster when my mind was trapped in a movie.

Finally, after more than a decade, I started appreciating my fear as my safeguard and friend again instead of fighting it as my enemy. A shift from fear-based control to feeling safe through trusting my intuition had started.

When it came to the fear of death, I also learned to take on a new perspective. Due to the high crime rate as well as the rough living conditions, death was omnipresent in the conversations I had with local people. In our culture we often negate death as a part of life. We occupy huge industries to avoid every possible risk and pay huge amounts of money to feel safe. We're trying to avoid confrontation wherever possible; we don't speak about it. In the end, however, it's one of the most natural things on earth; every being that is born dies one day. Impossible to circumvent.

For the local people, death was something natural, nothing to be hidden. A ranger in Zimbabwe showed us a video on his cell phone where people were dissecting a crocodile that had killed a local boy. There had been a lot of grief and sadness in the community about this loss. At first I felt aghast—why would he show that video to us? Slowly I understood that for him there was nothing unusual about it; he didn't keep the incident under wraps nor was there any sensation-seeking around it. It was a story about life. Only if we appreciate death can we value life to its fullest.

Africa made me see the fading of the colors when somebody dies in a new light. On the other hand, it also reminded me how bright and radiant life can shine when we live it fully.

I was finally feeling completely free, far away from cities—our modern human habitats. Thriving in the middle of the rawest nature where some of the first humans had lived and hunted tens of thousands of years ago. Where they had left paintings in caves to show their tribe where to find water or the best hunting grounds.

I was feeling incredibly grateful, immersing myself in the most beautiful energies and landscapes I had ever seen. Deep red sunrises and sunsets, endless sand dunes and deserts, peaceful river deltas, clear night skies filled with trillions of bright stars. Wild animals co-living in their habitat, passing on their knowledge from generation to generation. Elephants, rhinos, springboks, giraffes and zebras all standing together at watering holes drinking. Having the same basic physical needs as we do. Making me realize how we are all made out of the same basic elements. Leaving me with a dazzling feeling of presence and connection with everything around me. Reminding me of why I am here. Not only in Africa, but on my journey of life. The tiny flame was finally turning into a fire again.

With this new fire burning inside, I noticed how the local people I met were shining their lights brightly. Despite all the threats they were facing in their everyday lives, people of all ages and genders were working relentlessly to improve their communities' lives. Bright, warm-hearted, creative and innovative changemakers. People setting up community art projects to bring hope and perspective to young adults who had grown up without a future. Businessmen experimenting with energy extraction from natural wastes to solve the challenge of regular power outages in the cities. Volunteers spending their time teaching young kids hockey or surfing to not let them drift into the vicious circle of crime and despair. Courageous people without safety nets.

In our lives in the so-called developed world we often forget how simple, raw and beautiful life can be. Tough at times but full of bright colors and vibrance.

We forget what it means to live connected with ourselves and what is around us, to live fully in the moment.

Way too often we get caught up in fear, in movies in our mind, hiding in our roles, our cubicles, our comfort zones. Our need for safety and the fear of the unknown hinders us in experimenting with new things, being innovative, creative or taking risks as we don't want to lose what we have. We are scared; will the next thing be *equal* or *better*? We don't leverage our safety to actually empower us. We're tied down by it.

That's how we end up in inertia, hiding in the boat in our harbor. We're unhappy always seeing the same inside walls of the vessel and are not experiencing the life that is going on outside. We are feeling the waves as the boat is moving up and down. But we are just being shaken around as we have not decided to set our sails and use the wind to take us in the direction we want to steer our life to. We are not taking responsibility and are complaining about the ups and downs of the waves we are exposed to. What we are not aware of in that moment is that our boats are not built to last forever.

We all have our own unique talents and gifts to be shared with the world. Sometimes we have to leap into the unknown, let go of identities and false safeties to rediscover the raw, real beauty underlying everything and ourselves. For me, my journey to Africa was the starting point to a new way of life. Learning to follow my own compass, befriending my fears and remembering the beauty of life. From (over)thinking to feeling. From control to trust.

I'm on my boat on the sea, feeling the warm rays of the sun on my skin, the caress of the wind in my hair. I know it's not safe. Nothing is. Each storm that passes is making me stronger. I'm getting better and better at reading my compass and using the wind. I left my life—to finally live my life.

While traveling, we experience different ways of living and gain a new perspective on ourselves and our lives. Possibilities to step outside our comfort zones and befriend our fears. However, we don't always have to travel far or do radical things to find what our heart and soul is longing for. If we just take a moment to stop, connect with nature and ourselves, we can observe the most beautiful lessons right inside and around us.

Ignite Action Steps

Change is possible exactly where we are right now. I would like you to ask yourself where you are currently standing in your life and where you want to stop playing safe to finally live the life you desire. Find a quiet spot where you can deeply connect with yourself to answer the following questions on a piece of paper:

- Is there anything you're refraining from doing because it is *safer* not to?

- If yes, is it *really* not safe? What would happen if you did it?

- What are you missing out on because of your perceived safety?

- What is your heart really longing for? What is your deepest desire?

- What action can you take today to free your heart a bit more?

Revisit them after a week and notice the change in you and how you are feeling and what you may have done differently. Use these questions as a compass in your own life, repeat them regularly—every three months to check your position on your journey.

Joanna M. Walton - Germany
Lover of life, Project Manager & Coach
www.joannamariawalton.com

KATARINA AMADORA

"Traditional Medicines can be powerful allies to illuminate the Shadow and to Heal the Spirit."

To show the reader that sometimes life's greatest adventures happen when we go inside and explore our own inner landscapes. For this, we must leave our comfort zone and perhaps travel to places that may push us to our edge.

EXPLORING YOUR INNER LANDSCAPE

Nervous and excited, I finally arrived at the hotel in Iquitos, Peru. After two days of travel from my home in California, I was excited to begin this new adventure. I put my heavy backpack down and scanned the lobby for someone that I knew. I felt instant relief when I saw my friend who had invited me here to the gateway of the Amazon for my long awaited meeting with Grandmother Ayahuasca. I gave him a big hug; it was good to see a familiar face!

More people began to arrive: fellow explorers who would be sharing this deep dive into the soul using ancient plant medicine. For about a year, I had been hearing Grandmother's call but every time someone recommended an opportunity to meet her, my guides said, "No." This changed when I met two new friends at a talk on Ayahuasca Shamanism in Berkeley last spring. We went to dinner after the lecture and one of them shared about his experience with a specially curated retreat at the Temple Of the Way of the Light in the Peruvian Amazon. I had learned about the Temple at the Psychedelic Science Symposium in 2017. I remember thinking then that this was where I would want to go if I ever decided to try Ayahuasca. When my new friend encouraged me to apply, I knew immediately that this was the invitation I had been waiting for. I took out my pendulum and my guides responded with a resounding, "Hell yes!"

My arrival in Iquitos followed months of transformation. I had announced a new name, been published in the first Ignite book in May, and attended my second Mindvalley University event in Pula, Croatia. After that, I attended my first Burning Man where I led four workshops and a speaker series, and burned up my old identity in the Temple of Direction.

From the hotel, we took a bus to the river where we boarded two boats. They dropped us downriver at the start of a long footpath leading to the Temple. It was an hour by foot through the jungle. As we walked, I had a fascinating conversation with another spiritual warrior who heads an organization in Spain which conducts research and raises awareness regarding the benefits of plant medicine. It was fascinating to be in the same retreat with persons doing such important work. His breadth of knowledge and understanding of these medicines assured me that I was in the right place. It also gave me a slight twinge of impostor syndrome… Did I really belong in this group? Is the work I am doing important enough?

My intention in coming to the jungle was the question, "What gets in the way of connection?" Since my separation five years earlier, I had taken a deep dive into spiritual and personal growth. But no matter how much I learned about myself or how much I honed the modalities I practiced, I didn't feel I was making the impact I knew I was capable of. At the same time, my love life was going nowhere. I had a few long-distance lovers, but none of them had the potential to really be a part of my life. I wanted to know why. I had always felt like an outsider my entire life. Always feeling like I was looking in from the outside, trying to fit in. This caused a lot of pain and suffering. I was ready to be done with it once and for all!

As we crossed the rough hewn wooden bridge over the creek bordering the temple grounds, I saw the Maloka, a large round structure built with rough wooden beams and a conical thatched roof. I felt a soul recognition that I had come to the right place. I just didn't know yet what Grandmother would show me about myself. My experiences with other plant medicines had rewired my thinking profoundly and I trusted that Ayahuasca would further rewrite my nervous system to release whatever belief was keeping me from manifesting a more promising future.

In the first ceremony, I asked to be shown "my barriers to love," inspired by my favorite Rumi quote. As the medicine took hold, I could feel the power of each Maestro and Maestra as their song pierced deep into my being, probing the blocks that I had brought into the jungle with me. I could feel lines of energy moving through me. They seemed to have colors and textures that were new and interesting, unlike any of the other medicines I had worked with. There were no deep revelations in my first ceremony, yet I could feel the medicine working its magic.

The first three ceremonies took place every other night. I went into the second ceremony with the intention "Show me Love," yet this time I was disappointed. I got no messages whatsoever. I felt abandoned by the medicine. I could feel her in my system; the now familiar nausea rising, yet there were no visions, no answers to my questions. Others around me were having profound experiences yet I felt utterly bereft. Why was she not giving me the answers that I sought?

At meals, I would try to sit with different people each day so that I could get to know everyone. At first, everyone seemed open, but as the days passed, I noticed there were certain people who seemed closed to me. I also noticed that when I arrived early and was sitting alone at a table, the other tables would fill first, before anyone came to sit with me. Why? The old stories began to spin in my head... 'I don't belong...' even here, I did not feel accepted. My usual pattern of feeling like an outsider was playing itself out yet again. The Third ceremony felt depressingly similar. Why was I not getting the answers I wanted? Were they beyond me?

In between ceremonies, I continued to do journaling and introspection... examining my responses and the stories that I told myself. As I worked on this chapter, I recognized how I wanted to be in control, even though I had known for years that control was only an illusion. I had seen how my relationship with control had impacted my marriage and the way that I parented my girls. Although I had done much to shift this pattern, I saw ways in which it still showed up in my responses. Parenting is a balancing act. Kids need a sense of structure and predictability. But there is a difference between providing struc-ture and being controlling. I find that when I try to exert control over others, I am only met with resistance. I recognize that this relationship with control is really about fear. It comes from a lack of trust in the Universe. Although I believe that the Universe is a friendly place, there were still ways in which my old pattern was asserting itself.

When is the last time you decided to trust the Universe and allow an adventure to just unfold? To trust your intuition in the moment rather than getting caught up in weeks of planning? The most beautiful synchronicities in my life have often happened when I let go of control and allowed my intuition to guide me.

An example of this came when I was at Burning Man earlier in the summer. I was supposed to meet someone who I had encountered previously that day. Instead of finding him at our meeting point, I ran into a man who had been in my workshop earlier that morning. At first, I thought I would just pass a few moments talking to him while I waited for my friend. As we spoke, I became aware that part of me was hoping that my friend would not show up. I wanted to get to know this new man and spend the evening with him instead. I was grateful for the synchronicity that brought us together and kept my friend away, because this turned out to be the most delicious connection that I made during the entire event.

There is a principle at Burning Man called Immediacy… it is about being fully present in the moment and trusting that whatever is happening is absolutely perfect and to go with it. This principle encourages you to let go of expectations and release the need to control your experience. I am so glad that I trusted my intuition and flowed with what was presented to me. This one chance meeting led to some of my sweetest moments at the Burn and ignited in me a realization that I wanted to live more of my life following the principles of Burning Man. It is so much more than just a party in the desert. It's about community. It's a way of life. It's about stewardship of your environment. It is about giving without expecting a return and living in the moment.

There are so many lessons all around us if we just open up our eyes to see them. Sometimes the need to plan and control doesn't serve us. If I trust the Universe, it will lead me exactly where I need to be and send people into my life to aid in my growth and evolution. Sometimes this growth may be challenging. It may not always feel good. But by surrendering to what is, and by opening myself to the lessons in each moment, I gain the equanimity to handle whatever arises. I grow confidence in my ability to read my intuition and to navigate each new situation I am faced with.

Working with Ayahuasca involves reflecting deeply about life and awakening to the true nature of your being. It is not a substance to be taken lightly. People develop a relationship with her because they want to reconnect to themselves. She allows a person to rediscover their innate wisdom, often cut off by trauma and cultural conditioning. This allows people to understand themselves at a deeper level, which often takes them to the depths of their subconscious mind. Ayahuasca will teach you about yourself in ways that years of psychotherapy cannot.

Her healing power comes from so much more than just drinking the medicine. In fact, the primary technology is the *Ikaros,* or songs, which are channeled by the traditional medicine carriers and healing can be done even without drinking the medicine. This indigenous knowledge is passed from generation to generation. The journey to expertise is a long and arduous one. It is simply not available to westerners, unless we grow up in their culture and share the depth of this journey from a young age. Children don't 'decide' to become a shaman. They are seen and chosen by elders, or called by their own healing crisis. Shamen are taught in native languages, and this knowledge is acquired with deep study in difficult dietas starting from an early age. Ayahuasca is a medicine of the land, of the Amazon rainforest. Those who work with her have spiritual technologies which cannot be reproduced by outsiders. It takes a lifetime of dedication to reach this degree of mastery.

Traditionally, only the Maestro would drink the medicine to allow them to tune in and see where healing was needed. As westerners, we drink because it helps us to surrender and to connect to something far more powerful than ourselves. As the Maestro sings, they are actually channeling a healing technology which can see and unwind the blockages that the patient carries in their energetic body. There is something magical about being with her in nature, in the jungle that is her home. This is lost when you take the medicine out of the rainforest and separate her from the native wisdom tradition.

Although there are many who work with this medicine in the United States and other countries around the world, they are frequently working at a disadvantage. Issues of illegality have forced most plant medicines underground in spite of the tremendous impact that they have on healing. There is a growing recognition that plant-based medicines are *not* party drugs. They are powerful tools for self healing and personal growth. Psychedelics have shown immense promise in treating things such as PTSD, anxiety disorders, addictions and many other mental health conditions. These medicines can also be beneficial in hospice situations as they help people face end of life with grace and peace.

Ayahuasca itself is a marriage of two different plants… the masculine Ayahuasca vine and the feminine Chacruna leaf. The vine contains a monoamine oxidase inhibitor (MAO) which is a substance that stops you from digesting and deactivating the dimethyltryptamine (DMT) which is found in the Chacruna leaf. The Chacruna leaf is the feminine spirit of the medicine that gives the spiritual adventurer visions and insights. The feminine is the center of our intuition, our inner knowing. The masculine Ayahuasca vine allows the feminine to be expressed. The synergy of the two is transformative.

I am still integrating the experiences that I had with Grandmother Ayahuasca. The fourth ceremony broke the 'every other night' pattern, which meant having ceremony two nights in a row. I knew that this was it, my last opportunity to really deeply explore my shadow. I chose the intention of "Show me Trust." It was my most profound journey with her on this trip, taking me very very deep. The medicine first showed me people whom I had trusted, only to be used and discarded. They cost me tens of thousands of dollars and caused me to question the path that I had chosen because they had been mentors. From there, the medicine showed me how I had been susceptible to being used and manipulated; I was constantly looking outside of myself for approval and affirmation. I never felt that I was enough. I needed to feel that I was important… that I could make a difference, so I would say yes to things that were against my own best interests.

She then took me back through all the years that I had been bullied, treated as an outcast and a pariah because I was different. She showed me my desperate need for love and approval and she showed me the devastation of always feeling like an outsider. I recognized how frequently I reacted from my childhood wounding… from a deep-seated belief that I was unlovable. I recognized how this had created the conditions for me to be rejected again and again.

She took me all the way back to my infancy, back to the source of the belief that I was unlovable, and showed me how this belief has affected my relationships and actions throughout my life. It caused me to always look outside myself for love and approval. I needed to be liked and required constant affirmations of my worthiness because deep inside I did not feel that I was worthy of love. To see where this belief came from and all of the ways that it had impacted my life was profoundly healing. I am still coming to terms with where this continues to show up in my life. Before this experience, I did not understand how prevalent this belief was for me. Now, this understanding gives me the opportunity to make different decisions in the future.

Inner growth is a journey, not a destination. I know that I will never fully arrive. But with each new layer of the onion I peel away, I come closer and closer to my true self. I am able to love and reparent that part of myself that felt unlovable, and I am able to see new possibilities for my future. I know that my next relationship will be far different from my last one and I welcome the opportunity for growth that it will present. I feel blessed to have had this opportunity and I look forward to continuing the work, wherever it might take me. In order to receive this healing, I had to surrender to the medicine and be willing to see how I have created my present reality. Taking responsibility for how I have created my life gives me the power to change it.

The most important avenue to self realization is understanding how you have created your own life. When you take ownership of this, it gives you the power to change it.

IGNITE ACTION STEPS

- When looking at opportunities for travel, consider an inward journey where you come to a deeper understanding of yourself. This may be the best investment that you can make, the sooner the better. The more you learn about yourself when you are young, the more you can heal patterns that can be destructive to your life and the more empowered you will be to create a brighter future.

- If you wish to embark on an inward journey through the use of visionary medicines such as Ayahuasca, do your research. Choose a center that does this work with high integrity and with a connection to the wisdom traditions that have evolved with the medicine that calls you.

- Get recommendations from friends who have worked with the specific medicine you are interested in exploring. Speak with others who are knowledgeable about the journey; each medicine is different and can teach you different lessons. The transformation that is possible from plant medicine surpasses most other roads to healing and can shave years off your healing journey.

Katarina Amadora - United States
Holistic Health and Intimacy Coach
Certified RTT Hypnotist
Certified WildFit Coach
Tantra Facilitator
www.AmadoraTransformations.com

YAANA HAUVROESH

"Be open to having your beliefs challenged."

I share my story with you in hopes that you may be inspired to awaken to your full self in this lifetime. May you be moved to seek out those teachers and experiences that will revolutionize your existing paradigms. May you be motivated to explore what is possible in terms of the human potential and be reminded that there is so much more available to us. May your Adventurous Spirit take you on both magical inner explorations as well as extraordinary worldly journeys!

THE LIGHT WITHIN THE DARKNESS

When I used to think of the word 'adventurous,' I thought it wasn't a category that I could put myself in. I wasn't somebody who had trekked to the top of Mount Everest or circumnavigated the globe in a sailboat. I did not have stories to share about encountering a black panther, boa constrictor, or wild rhinoceros. I hadn't parachuted out of an airplane, taken up scuba diving, or even braved a bungee cord jump. In terms of worldly explorations and outward adventures, I appeared quite conservative indeed.

However, with regard to inward adventures, I recognized it was quite a different story…

It was a Tuesday morning and my phone was ringing. I picked up the phone and answered, wondering who was calling from this unknown number. It was an invitation to an advanced meditation retreat. I listened intently and my curiosity was aroused.

Having already braved several vision quests in the desert, I was no stranger to sitting in silence and solitude. Thus, when the call came, I welcomed the opportunity to participate in an exploration of even further reaches into the inner world of the body, mind, and spirit.

Although I was quite familiar with extended juice and water fasting, I had never heard about the type of exploration that I was next to embark upon.

I had been contacted by a group who was hosting a unique retreat and had been told about my experience and background in using food to heal the body. They requested my assistance in preparing the juices for the participants of their program. I was very honored and agreed to do so, as liquid nourishment was an integral part of my lifestyle and I was passionate about sharing it with others. Specific to this retreat, however, juices would only be taken on the first and last days, before and after the period spent in what was called 'dry fasting.' This meant that neither food nor liquid, including water, would be allowed for an extended period of time. In conjunction with this extreme protocol, we would be immersed in what is referred to as a 'dark room' retreat. As neither of these practices had been part of my journey, I did some quick research online and the idea of experiencing them for myself was absolutely intriguing.

Having spent the last few years experimenting with various types of cleansing diets and practices for physical healing, as well as spending solo time in nature connecting with Source, I was fascinated to explore what more was possible. According to what I read, a dry fast could significantly accelerate the detoxification and rejuvenation potential of the body. Dark room practice, I learned, was a complete immersion in absolute darkness for an extended length of time. It was considered to be an advanced technique to bring about expanded states of consciousness through activation of the body's own biochemistry, affecting the pineal gland, or as some refer to it, the 'third eye.' This was known to facilitate one's inner awakening.

It seemed perfectly aligned with my journey. Cleansing the body and stilling the mind were practices that I had already come to appreciate and integrate into my life over the previous years. This opportunity to now delve deeper was most compelling and yet at the same time somewhat unnerving.

It was compelling in that pushing to discover the edges of what is possible, was a key thread in the very fabric of my being. Taking things to the furthest limit had been a part of me since I was a child, much to the dismay of my parents. I recall the look of exasperation on my father's face — you know *that* look — brought about by relentless and repeated questions on endless topics of what I considered important.

In my continued quest for answers, I was delighted to say 'yes' to this retreat. Despite this anticipation, imagining myself going through the actual process was still unsettling. Although I was comfortable and experienced at extended periods of taking only water, I was not at all certain how my body would manage on air alone. In addition, although I had overcome my fear of snakes and scorpions while spending time in the desert, I had never fully outgrown my childhood fear of the dark. Not to mention the fact that in the darkness of this retreat, there would be strangers in the space around me yet invisible to me. I wouldn't know who was next to me, how near they actually were, and if I would feel safe or at ease. All of these factors together saw me arriving for the first day of the program with a heightened sense of alertness and apprehension.

Fortunately, settling into my role of assisting with the juicing was a familiar and comfortable place for me. It was grounding and I was able to relax some-what. As I began meeting the others whom I would soon be stumbling around in the dark with, my concerns were further eased. But only for a short time.

When the moment for 'lights out' had almost arrived, we were reminded to begin mapping the number of steps between our mat and the nearest restroom. We were encouraged to make a last note of the placement of our toothbrush and toothpaste along with any other items we thought we might need for the next few days. As I realized I was soon going to be without any light or water, panic started to set in. I wondered and heard myself asking, "How do you get yourself into these types of things?" My father's voice and words repeated and echoed in my being. My mind raced and thought of excuses that I could make up to gracefully depart the premises, leave the program, abandon the project, my post, and go back to the safety of my home.

However, since I had never given much consideration to my father's com-plaints about my inquiring nature, I decided not to at that time either. Instead, I quickly talked myself into rallying up my most courageous face, all in the name of thorough 'research and development.' And, of course, perhaps with an added dash of 'rebel' thrown in for good measure.

As we were invited to take our last drink of water and the lights were dimmed, I settled onto my mat, not expecting to find what awaited me behind the veil of darkness.

The first few hours were spent fidgeting, listening to the breathing of others, delaying my trip to the toilet down the dark hallway, and wondering how my organs were actually going to manage without water for 48 hours. As a safety measure, I had already explained to the retreat facilitators that in the past I had a near death experience, that my body had gone into anaphylactic shock and the reason had never been determined. I shared with them that although I didn't think it would happen in this particular situation given that we were not eating, I still wanted them to be aware of the possibility that my body might go into distress.

Feeling uneasy and vulnerable, I reached under my pillow to reassure myself that the EpiPen was still there. I once again tightened the wool sash that I had placed around my abdominal area to bring warmth and additional support to my kidneys during this process. Wanting to further ensure that, without water, my body would continue functioning and eliminating toxins, I massaged acupressure points on my hands, feet and ears. Already feeling hunger pains and hearing the growling of my tummy, I was shocked when the facilitator told us that only a mere hour had passed. With 47 hours remaining, I decided the best strategy to settle myself might be to sleep for a little while. Even though it was early in the day, and I was aware of each breath and movement taken by those around me, I easily drifted off into a deep state of rest.

When I finally awoke, it took me some time to recollect where I was, what day it was, and why it was so dark that I could not even see my hand in front of me. As the disorientation lifted, I soon reconnected with the fact that I had signed up for this unfamiliar and untold expedition of a dry fast in complete darkness. And yet, despite that awareness and a momentary wave of fear, I began to notice that my body was deeply and markedly relaxed. It was as though this cloak of absolute darkness somehow allowed and supported my cells to slow down so much more than ever before.

I continued to doze in and out of sleeping and waking states, unaware whether it was day or night. Eventually I let go of my need or desire to know.

As I lay there in silence during what seemed like the next day, I was conscious of how much more still and settled my mind was. A state of presence and peace existed that previously I had only experienced after many days of being deeply immersed in nature. I recognized, to my surprise and curiosity, that the very darkness which I had feared, had actually become my place of refuge and sanctuary. Without light and therefore the many visual inputs that I was generally accustomed to taking in, and fascinated by, my mind was now able to drop into a state of deep rest.

I realized that without the aesthetics of the world informing me and filling my eyes with much to see and evaluate, I was able to reach the state of 'empty mind' or 'quiet mind' so much more effortlessly. I became acutely aware of how affected I typically am by the constant colors and lights reflected in clothing and textiles, as well as the shapes and sizes, placement and alignment of objects within my view. Generally the only time I would be free from this kaleidoscope of images would be while sleeping. However, here I was, fully awake and yet having the sensory input of physical sight completely eliminated.

It was such a unique, profound and powerful experience. There was a level of quiet and calm that descended upon my mind, heart and soul that was unlike any I had ever known. How ironic and yet understandable that the very experience I was so attached to and took so much pleasure in, the joy of seeing the world around me, was in fact keeping me from reaching the places I wanted to reach within myself.

An Ignite moment indeed.

It was a revelation, a gift. In that moment, I recognized the power in letting go of sensory pleasures that may be hindering my spiritual progress.

On that same note, I discovered that my body was completely at ease without any food or water. All of the fears that my mind had about not being able to tolerate the dry fast eventually fell away. In fact, when the forty-eight hours had passed and all the participants were celebrating with their first drink of water, my body and my Being called for more time without any input of liquid. I continued through one more night and completed another twelve hours of dry fast, indulging in the grace of it all.

On the last day of the program, as I prepared the transitional meal of fruit and salads for the participants, I noticed that my body had absolutely no interest in ingesting any solid food. I was not surprised, however, given that it had only been 6 days and I was very accustomed to fasting for weeks on liquids alone.

Returning home, my body continued to ask only for juice, water or tea. Again, I expected this and was not concerned in any way. However, the days soon turned into weeks and eventually months. It seemed that my body and soul were calling for and enjoying a 'spontaneous remission from food.' A dramatic shift had occurred. My primary nourishment was no longer physical food but instead the energy and elements that surrounded me, such as sunshine and oxygen. I had read of people in this state, who were both temporarily or permanently '*living on light*' or the life force of '*prana,*' and were referred to as breatharians.

I then embarked upon a quest to research this phenomenon that was present in many cultures through the ages and concluded that indeed this was occurring for me. Although I had lost weight in the first few weeks, I had now been almost three months at the same weight and felt better than ever. My energy was high, I had physical vitality and mental clarity, required very few hours of sleep, and was extremely productive throughout the day. Clearly, my body was being nourished and fed by prana. It was an epiphany; a profound insight into the furthest reaches and potential of the human body, mind and spirit. Another Ignite moment on my journey!

I was amazed and even amused at the irony of my body's desire to explore life without physical food. All things related to eating and nutrition had been such a passion of mine for the last 30 years. I loved food. Food excited me. Being able to fuel my body with the highest vibrational nutrition had been my focus for so many years, and now…

It seemed that optimal eating might be *not* eating at all.

With my all-encompassing and inquisitive nature, I soon decided that I wanted to understand everything I could about this discovery and its implications for human evolution. I continued to learn about those who had walked this path before me, both historical figures and the many current teachers, some living only on water for decades. I was fascinated and intrigued. Within weeks I had chosen the first teacher I wanted to meet and learn from, purchased plane tickets, said my goodbyes and left for what would unknowingly become a three-year journey through uncharted territory. I never expected to go on such a profound walkabout. I explored fourteen countries, studied with the top pranic teachers, visited various sacred sites, attended two world conferences on breatharianism, participated in an 11-day dark room retreat, filled notebooks with research and was invited to assist with a book interviewing others living on prana. What began as only adventurous curiosity with regard to my inner journey had most certainly taken me out into the world and beyond! A fully embodied Adventurous Spirit had been awakened at last.

I feel so blessed to have been guided along this particular quest of exploring the heights and depths of human potential. I appreciate my unbridled and steadfast passion for inquiry, and am grateful for my willingness to push further and reach higher. I know that the discoveries and miraculous moments of the last few years will continue to be integrated and embodied throughout the rest of my lifetime.

I wonder how reading my story might encourage you to push a little further and reach a little higher, to believe a little more in what's possible for you in your lifetime.

IGNITE ACTION STEPS

- **Be curious about your nutrition.** Listen to your body's messages surrounding what you consume. Question what is actually necessary and required. How much of your food choices are made from conditioning and concepts versus responding to your body's real needs? Be willing to investigate and challenge your beliefs.

- **Be open to exploring the dark.** Do some research regarding the healing benefits of spending time without the input of light and the world of sight. Find out if there are dark retreat programs that might interest you, or even experiment with extended meditation and time spent in the darkness and comfort of your own home.

- **Connect to your Adventurous Spirit.** Consider where your interests might take you in your lifetime. Ask yourself what your areas of inquiry are, what particularly fascinates you in this world, who inspires you, and what adventures would light up your heart and soul. Awaken your Adventurous Spirit by reaching further and higher than you thought possible.

Yaana Hauvroesh, MA. - Canada
Body-Centered Psychotherapist, Marriage & Family Counsellor,
High Vibrational Lifestyle Consultant
www.purestessence.com
f *purestessence*

LINDA ELIE

"Always follow your bliss; it's an indicator that you
are under the influence of the Divine."

I want to reassure the reader that living your life is not in the 'doing,' it's in the 'being.' Breathe, relax and embrace the moment. It can be that easy.

HOLDING SPACE

Growing up as an only child, I often felt alone in the world. My parents both worked long hours at their blue collar jobs to give me bigger and better opportunities than they had. With them gone at work, I was cared for after school by my maternal grandmother, a woman who believed children should be seen and not heard. I hated going to her house and I'm sure the feeling was mutual. I was just an interruption to her chain-smoking, soap-opera watching life.

My childhood programming taught me to be of service to others and to always strive for more. For as long as I can remember, I just knew "what I do must be big." Unfortunately, what I did… was never good enough. My mother expected perfection. My grandmother expected invisibility.

Since my grandmother lived in a senior's community, I kept myself busy playing outside all alone. Sometimes I explored nature to see what I could find. The way a box turtle could completely disappear inside his hard shell fascinated me. The grace and ease with which birds floated through the air captured my young imagination. Other times, I lived in my fantasies. I pretended I was a horse galloping across the field. I would spread my arms and believe I could fly. In my imagination, I was never alone. I had many conversations between me, myself and I. I dreamed of far away lands I heard about in school, like the pyramids in Egypt or the temples on the hilltop in Athens.

The year I turned nine, my grandmother died. Old enough to be trusted on my own, I became a latchkey kid. I spent my hours at school striving to meet my parents' need for my perfection, and the hours at home watching TV or reading about horses. I was forbidden to leave the property.

Being alone has always felt safe. I had a vivid imagination and a rich inner life. When those failed me, books and television were quick to fill the gap. I often felt lonely though, because I did not have friends to play with. At my grandmother's, there simply weren't other children around. At home, our neighborhood was mainly young couples with no kids. The only time I was surrounded by peers was at school, and school was a challenge.

Without friends to interact with, my social skills as a child were nearly non-existent. I was teased and bullied mercilessly. Nothing made sense to me. My life felt like something from *Alice in Wonderland*. I was caught between desperately wanting to fit in with others and not wanting to disappoint my parents, who were always pushing me to be "the best." It was a no-win situation. I tried to hide my natural academic gifts, or at least be invisible at school in an attempt to fit in, but the punishment at home for the slightest mistakes was a strong motivator for maintaining perfect grades.

Transferring to a very small private school attached to our church in fifth grade meant I was surrounded by the same people everywhere I went. The physical bullying stopped, but I was introduced to a new world of emotional and psychological bullying that continued well into high school.

Shortly before I became an adult, I had had enough of people and their visions of what I should be, especially as I never seemed to live up to it. When my path started to diverge too far from what my parents wanted, they gave me an ultimatum: conform or leave. I left, and they disowned me for it.

Without my parents' financial support, college was no longer an option so I chose a career in accounting. Numbers don't lie. As a bonus, I also didn't have to deal with people. I spent my days poring over checkbooks and ledgers, but the sameness of it month after month, year after year… was utterly boring.

In my 20s, I began to travel. I acquired a passion for it in the Blue Ridge Mountains of the eastern United States, the most beautiful part of God's earth that I had ever seen. My first husband's parents had a cabin in northeast Georgia. When we visited, we would hike to magnificent waterfalls surrounded by majestic, tree-covered slopes. The feeling of the mist on my face and the sheer power of the thundering water reinforced the innate knowledge that there was a Presence out there that had my back. I don't care what you call it — God, Universe, Higher Self, Yahweh — there is no difference to me. I had walked away from my fundamentalist religious upbringing when I stepped into adulthood; there were too many hypocrites in it for me. But even as a child, I had known that there was *something* out there watching over me.

There in the mountains, I was in pure Heaven. The rest of the world disappeared and I felt peace. But it was also there that I faced my biggest dilemma. I could easily have become a hermit and lived alone in those woods, but there was that constant gnawing of the childhood message: "*You must do something great in the world.*" My parents had repeated that mantra to me many times and its underlying message was clear: "You are very smart. You *must* do something great or you will be a failure. And failure is unacceptable."

When I became a parent, I did not want to repeat the patterns of my childhood and started questing for a better way to raise my daughter. In my late 30s, I was introduced to the world of personal development when my friend Cindi suggested a course. Since my life did not feel as if it were headed in a positive direction, I figured I had nothing to lose. The course wasn't expensive and only lasted a weekend. I've always been curious to try new things to keep my life interesting. I took the plunge.

I stepped out of my car into the humid Florida air and made my way to the conference room. The air indoors was overly air conditioned and I froze the entire weekend. The course itself was amazing. It had a major impact on me. *How* it impacted me is difficult to describe. I soon noticed The Presence, guiding me step by step to take more courses and connect with new people who provided new insights into my life.

Working on myself in this way made me a better parent to my daughter. It helped me learn to be more present for her and willing to look at things from different perspectives. I am proud to say that I raised a magnificent, responsible daughter without resorting to physical punishment as my mother had. For that alone, I am eternally grateful. But there was still a lingering feeling of "What's next? What big thing are you going to do?" Now, long after my parents had passed, what had started as parental judgment had become internal judgment of myself.

The internal message that what I was doing wasn't "big enough" has stopped me **so many times** from listening to the universal Presence. When I have listened to my heart, things have always worked out, often in mysterious ways. However, "old habits die hard" was not merely a saying in my life. It was an operating system.

Even as the battle between my personal growth and the lessons my parents had instilled in me waged on, I felt successful. My accounting practice, while not lucrative, did pay the bills. I was able to purchase a small farm and carry out my childhood dream of training horses. I got into dancing, a personal joy. I even taught a dozen or so students, which was fun and inspiring. Yet none of this was 'big enough' to satisfy my childhood programming, and so I continued questioning and searching for my purpose. When I threw it out to the Universe, the only thing that came back to me was travel. Was that the answer? Was travel big enough?

I kept asking the questions, "What am I supposed to do in this lifetime? What's my purpose?" The same answer kept coming back to me: travel. But that couldn't be right!

I took a leap of faith and began traveling since my daughter was now grown, the farm had been sold, and I could dance anywhere. I would joke with my friends that I was "collecting passport stamps," always feeling a need to justify the fact that I was traveling. It wasn't until a mentor asked me, "Who in your life is making you wrong for traveling?" that I realized the only person I needed to satisfy, was myself.

With this new awareness, trips began to show up everywhere I looked. For me, it was an indication that Universal Guidance was definitely at work. I was led toward connections with certain people, and that led to even more trips. I was growing and expanding my limits, but I was still haunted by the questions "What am I supposed to be doing? What's next for me?" Little by little, I was learning that when I say "yes" to the Presence, to that Universal Guidance, I was saying "yes" to having things work out for the better.

I signed myself up for a trip to Spain and Portugal and reached out to Deborah, a friend I'd made on earlier trips. I asked her, "Hey Deborah, are you going on the trip to Spain and Portugal? Maybe we could room together again?"

"No," she replied, "I was looking at this trip to Egypt and the woman who was going to be my roommate just backed out. Why don't you join me?"

The Presence was speaking to me again. I was already going to be in Europe. I knew and trusted the people putting on the trip. Deborah's roommate had backed out, leaving an opening for me. Coincidences? Perhaps not. I took a moment to consider my finances, but I knew my only possible answer was "Yes!"

The group I was traveling with was fairly esoteric and contained many psychics and mediums. It was exciting to be exposed to new concepts and practices. The likelihood that I would have found this group on my own was slim to none. This was THE perfect group for this trip. They had so many connections in Egypt that we were able to do things the average tourist cannot do. We started with a group meditation inside the Great Pyramid (at 4:00AM!), then proceeded to study the Sphinx close up, a rarity now. The sites and energies in the different pyramids and temples were amazing. In many of the temples, you could *feel* the energy shift as you went into the sacred temple chambers. This was particularly true for me in Edfu.

Sami, our guide, told us that the temple in Edfu was known for its 'aggressive' energy, which spilled out into the surrounding community. I found the culture in Egypt was aggressive already and Edfu took this to a new level. At the temple, I was waiting to feel this aggressive energy. Sami led us around, explaining what we were seeing. The whole time we walked through the temple, I kept waiting, but still didn't feel the energy. At the end of the tour, I went up to Sami and asked about it. He didn't say a word. Instead, he gestured and silently led me and three others to the sacred chamber where the sacrifices once took place. He deliberately leaves this chamber out of the tour, but since asked, felt we needed to experience it. And WOW! Stepping over the threshold into a room about 8 by 15 feet, the whole energy shifted. My skin began to crawl. My hair stood up on end! If I had just wandered into that room, not knowing what it was, I would have turned and run the other way. But stepping back out of the room, the energy immediately dissipated. It was contained, it seemed, by that single doorless room. I was feeling things I had never felt before.

On the next to last night, Hollister Rand, a medium, offered an impromptu group session. Half of us attended the reading, and several received messages from her. I did not. At least, not until later.

At the conclusion of the session, she asked us to thank everyone who had shown up. I thanked Hollister for sharing her gift with us. She replied, "Thank you for holding the space. You did an excellent job." I was stunned! "What did she mean by that?" I wondered. I'd heard the term "holding space" before but didn't have a clear understanding of its meaning. I thought that she must say that to everyone. Later, asking others, I discovered she had not. I decided to question her about it at lunch the next day.

"Do you have a minute to answer a question?" I asked.

"Of course," Hollister replied. "What is it?"

"Last night, when you thanked me for holding space, what did you mean by that?"

"Oh," she began, "when you hold space…." she stopped as she was looking at me. "Oh," she paused, "OH……you don't know, do you?"

"Know what?" I asked, puzzled.

"My dear," she said, "you are a 'space holder.' You have a gift, the gift of presence and that gift is one of ultimate service to the planet. You are an open channel to the Divine. In being that open channel, you create a safe space to allow another to step into their Higher Self." She could see that I wasn't grasping her words, so she continued. "It's almost like you are the water bottle that holds the water. In this case, you are the container that holds the energy. That container protects the energy inside, just like a water bottle protects the water, both from spilling out and from being contaminated. Does that make sense to you?" she asked. I nodded slowly, still not quite certain I understood the full significance of her words.

Hollister went on, "It probably feels like you aren't doing anything, doesn't it?" I nodded again. "That's because it is not something you do, it's something you are. You don't control it. It is a space — the other person gets to choose what to do with it. It truly is one of the most important, unselfish gifts you can bring to the world."

I was dumbfounded. I think I mumbled a "Thank you" as we parted. The way Hollister explained it sounded so simple and yet it was so profound. Could this be the answer to that nagging question of "What's next?"

For the next week my mind went over and over our conversation. Could she be right? I searched the internet for "holding space." I spoke to a trusted friend who had used that term many times. The more I looked at the possibility, the more things I recognized in my past that "fit". As I considered the implications, more and more situations and conversations came to mind. It seemed that all the time I spent alone as a child had honed that gift of holding space. That moment in Egypt unlocked an understanding of myself that totally changed the direction of my life. It gave me **permission to breathe, relax and just "be,"** something I'd never done before.

I had an adventure planned for the summer. Armed with this new information, I relaxed into it and allowed things to show up. And show up they did! I made heartfelt connections with people I met along the way. I wrote blog posts from inspired moments experienced during my hikes in nature. Most importantly, I eased up on myself. I no longer judge what I am doing as selfish or "not big enough."

Most of us have grown up with "operating systems" imposed on us by someone else, yet we never question that within ourselves. The next time you think you can't or shouldn't do something, question the reason: Is the reason yours, or something passed down to you by another? It takes courage to follow the road less traveled. Be true to yourself and your life will take on a whole new meaning.

IGNITE ACTION STEPS

- **Know that you can only be yourself.** When you find yourself passing judgment on your life, take a time out to re-examine whose values you're expressing.

- **Always follow your Bliss.** When something brings you joy, you are Divinely influenced and that expression will resonate and bring light to the planet. Not only will you be happy doing what you love, you'll show others they have permission to do the same.

- **Accept another's journey.** Others are on the path that is right for them. Everything and everyone on the planet is necessary for the expression of the fullness of life.

- **Look for the similarities to others.** We spend more time looking at the differences than seeing the similarities. Look for the similarities and see how the energy shifts.

Linda Elie - United States
Award Winning Speaker, Teacher and Adventurer
◆ lindaelie360

ANGELA LEGH

*"Life is filled with ebbs and flows. Knowing when to flow
with the tide can add a quiet grace to your life."*

My intention is to lead people into a path of non-resistance in life by teaching them to allow... to surrender. What would happen if you relaxed and accepted when the traffic stopped? What if you simply flowed with what was happening and enjoyed riding the tide?

LEARNING TO SURRENDER

The second time I almost drowned, I was in Portugal, swimming in the Atlantic. The day was hot; the sun beat down on the rocks lining the shore and the heat in the air was unbearable. I jumped into the sea to cool off and spend some quality time with friends.

I don't think that I am a magnet for disaster, but I do have to wonder. I have experienced near drowning twice, once when I was four and again when I was 55. I have also experienced losing everything in a wildfire twice, once when I was four and again when I was 53. Clearly, the Universe has been knocking on my door with a message!

The first time I almost drowned, I was a mere toddler on vacation with my family in Santa Cruz, California, where I was happily wading in a 'safe' swimming area at Capitola Beach. Something caught my attention and I wandered away from the group. I was alone. I stepped forward expecting to find sand beneath my toes only to find that there was no ground beneath my feet.

I plunged off the edge, under the water, feeling the coldness as it reached the top of my head. Time stopped for a moment; I had fallen into a deep void. I knew that in order to breathe, my head needed to be above the water. I struggled alone, underwater, trying to find a way out, to save myself. My arms and feet were flailing around; I did not know how to swim.

No one had noticed my distress; I was the only one who would save me.

I continued to struggle as my head became lighter from lack of oxygen. My left foot kicked upward and my toes felt the edge. I had a toehold!

To this day, I don't know how I did it, given that I had barely the tip of my toes on the ledge, but I pulled myself up with great difficulty. I could breathe! I collected myself and ran to my mother, who was on the beach talking with my aunt. She had not noticed the crisis. She did not understand why I was crying and seeking her comfort, but she gave it freely. That was the first time I felt the sensation of drowning.

Later that year, my family experienced a disaster when our flat as well as several nearby apartments and homes burned down. I remember sitting at the kitchen table at about 6 AM scribbling outside the lines in my coloring book when I looked up and saw beautiful dancing lights leaping around the laundry porch. I felt a sense of wonder at the way these colors were moving and flickering so beautifully. I asked my older sister (who had her back to the porch) why there was a merry-go-round in our house. She looked over her shoulder, jumped up, and ran to tell my mother.

I didn't understand what she was doing, but she was old enough to grasp the urgency of the moment. Mom got us out of the house and, like the hero she is, alerted our upstairs and downstairs neighbors and helped them get out as well. I remember standing in that cold, dark San Francisco morning, wrapped in a blanket provided by the firemen, feeling a sense of loss.

These two incidents from my early childhood are clear in my memory. These stories were stored in my consciousness, ready to come out when I was older and wiser, to help decode the message I was being sent by the Universe.

My second experience with wildfire happened when my home was destroyed by the Tubbs Fire that devastated Santa Rosa, California, in October of 2017. The fire was a wind-whipped inferno that stymied the firefighters' attempts to contain it. The conflagration torched over 5,000 homes and killed 24 people; a huge and devastating loss for my community. In mere minutes, my house and everything inside had become a two-foot pile of ash contained by the concrete foundation. A neighbor who had not evacuated sent us photos of our house, first when the roof caught fire and then five minutes later when the whole structure was engulfed in flames. He told of the violence of the fire — windows exploding outward; glass shards reaching 40 feet into the street; metal melting; the structure gone completely in 10 minutes… a lifetime of stuff instantaneously destroyed.

The loss of 'stuff' can be overcome, but the loss of the structure that stored all my memories, the memories of my children and extended family, was devastating.

My husband and I were sent into a tailspin. My children, who are adults, were cast adrift, feeling a sense of loss, of no longer having a childhood home.

The fire was an Ignite moment in my life, though I did not recognize that for a full year afterwards. I struggled to re-establish life for my husband and me, finding housing, replacing necessities and creating a safe space. Over time, I realized that no matter how hard I tried, I was unable to create a peaceful environment because I was playing a victim role in my marriage. I did not ask to be, nor did I expect to be treated well. I allowed things to happen that did not serve me. About one year after the fire, I had reached a point in my life where I asked myself, "Is this the life I wanted to live for the rest of my years?"

The answer was a resounding "No!"

Devastated by the prospect of a failed marriage, I decided to leave. It took some time to work up the courage to do so and for months afterward, I was a wreck — a shell of a person, grieving the loss of the marriage but also the loss of time that I had chosen to spend in a toxic relationship. What could my life have been if I had chosen a man who respected me? Or if I had known enough to establish boundaries and expectations? These were moot questions, for I now know that everything happens for a reason. The story of my marriage was a necessary component to create the person who I am today.

A month or so after I left my husband, I was on a website listening to a course. As I worked through the material, a notification popped up announcing *Mindvalley A-Fest Bali*. I was intrigued. I pulled up a search to find out what A-Fest was. After reading a quote on Forbes.com that A-Fest was a unique combination of TED Talks by day and Burning Man style parties by night, I was hooked! It was a 4-day extravaganza of personal development, complete with an emphasis on celebrating life! I had to attend! I applied, and to my great surprise, I was accepted.

I left for Bali In November to attend this life-changing program. Traveling alone to a foreign land was intimidating. This was the first time I had traveled by myself, but the end goal of transforming my life was bigger than any fear I was experiencing. When I walked into the hotel conference room, I knew I had made the right decision. I felt seen and understood in a way that I had never experienced before. I had found my tribe! A room full of people wanting to make the world a better place. The connections I made will stay in my heart forever because finally I could be myself and fully accepted.

In May that year, I left my job behind and, once again solo, trekked this time to Portugal. I was going to my second transformative event, which I had signed up for even before saying goodbye to everyone at the first one. I decided to travel alone through Europe for 2 months; pretty outstanding for a middle-aged woman. The trip started with the event, but the rest was unplanned. I serendipitously visited any European city that caught my eye.

I felt empowered while shedding old paradigms that confined me from the past.

When I arrived in Portugal, my heart expanded. I was greeted with the beautiful sight of our hotel clinging to a cliff overlooking the Atlantic. I took a deep breath of the warm ocean air, feeling like I was on the verge of a great adventure. It was a lovely location filled with amazing people and I knew I was in for a wonderful ride!

It was on the day leading up to the final festivities that I nearly drowned. After lunch, a young couple I knew suggested that I join them by swimming to a nearby cave. I met Jay and Mo at our agreed meeting spot and we set off down the public path to the cliff's edge. The path ended with a gate to a more precarious pathway, complete with a sign warning us to stay away from the dangerous combination of cliff and sea. We marched through, feeling confident and fearless, a quality instilled by the self-development we had undertaken. The descent was difficult as we made our way to a point about three or four feet above the water and jumped in.

We began swimming toward the cave, which was about 250 feet away. The tide was strong; for every stroke forward, I was also pushed back. I was not the strongest swimmer and I was not used to the strong tides of ocean swimming. I knew that I could swim the length of an Olympic swimming pool, but I was unsure if I could do much more than that. However, I was determined.

I would stretch my boundaries and do this!

The swim to the cave took us around a rocky point before we could see the entrance. I swam confidently to that point before realizing that I was tiring. Once past the turning point, I could see the rocks just beneath the surface inside the cave. I was short of breath; the appearance of a place to stand seemed to be fortuitous. I thought I might be able to rest for a moment before I continued into the cave. Just as I put my feet down on the rock and stood, taking a deep breath, a strong wave came and knocked me off. Whatever air I had found was forced out of me as I was pushed over by the pounding water. It dragged me over the jagged rocks that littered the cave. My arm burned where the sharp, coarse surface tore off my skin. I was washed onto the beach inside the cave, my arm bleeding from my elbow to my wrist.

My friends rushed to my side, concerned for my well being. I assured them that I was okay. I felt shaken and a little fearful. Fortunately, we stayed inside the cave for about an hour, giving me time to recover. Jay and Mo played with their underwater camera, creating beautiful shots of crashing waves and submerged treasures. I explored a little before I sat and rested on the sand, preserving my energy as I felt worried about the swim back.

As the hour wound down, Jay and Mo felt equally concerned about leaving. We had all hoped that the tide would turn and that the waves would diminish. We stood at the edge of the water, watching the unending onslaught hitting the cave's opening, waiting for a moment of calm that did not arrive.

Our window of time was narrowing; we had to make the decision to return. The sun was lowering on the horizon. A monstrous wave crashed on the shore; as it pulled out a relatively calm space was created. We jumped into the water for our return trip, before the next wave descended upon us.

I struggled to swim as each wave crested, the tide pulling me backward toward the cave. I made it to the turning point, swimming close to the edge, hoping that the waves would not pummel me against the rocks. I swam two feet forward to be pulled one foot back. It was exhausting! I was struggling, getting tired. As I tried to get around the turning point, a wave washed over me and I unwillingly swallowed water. I faltered, trying desperately to stay afloat. I thought, "This is how people drown." I was terrified that I would not make it. I knew at that moment that I was in peril.

During this moment of darkness, I heard Mo shouting out to me. Younger and stronger, she and Jay had reached our destination about 100 yards ahead. Mo called out encouraging words as she voiced the instructions that are now a road map to my life. She encouraged me to float when the tide ebbed and swim like hell when the tide rolled in my favor. I took her advice, conserving my energy when being pulled backward, and swimming with all my might when being pushed towards the shore. I realized that I only had to use half the strength I had been exerting. The rest of the swim went quickly. Before I knew it, I was standing in shallow water beside her, utterly relieved to have my feet in the sand at the bottom of the cliff.

We all were a bit shaken by the experience, humbled by the power of the ocean. I felt foolish to have dropped into the water without taking any safety precautions. I had not taken the time to learn how to swim in rough conditions and I had not really thought this through.

I resolved from that moment on to live my life in surrender.

Mo's words have become a life lesson. Resistance is futile! My struggles to move forward while the tide pulled me backward was nothing less than a complete waste of my energy and effort. I reflected on how this applies to every area of my life. This inspired me to choose to allow and surrender as I continue to adventure through my life.

Life will always bring hardship, left hand turns and unexpected delays. Surrender does not mean to give up; it means learning to accept what is, but also knowing when your energy is best used to push forward. Allowing your 'will' to be guided by the flow of life is the ultimate surrender.

Taking actions based on the flow of life is also surrender. What areas of your life can you apply this? Can you ebb and flow as needed? When can you let go and when do you push like hell? Your journey is awaiting your discovery.

Ignite Action Steps

Allowing or Surrendering

- **Know** that everything that is happening to you is something your spirit wanted to experience. Know that divine love goes before you, carving a path that leads you to the ultimate goal, of being one with your divine spirit.

- **Trust** that all obstacles are growth opportunities. Fears, doubts and anxieties are opportunities for you to let go and allow, letting your spirit guide you gently along the path of least resistance.

- **Stay in the flow** – make decisions but allow changes; allow the Universe to happen, be with it like the water. When a river has rocks in it, does it stop, or does it flow around the rocks? In allowing change, you are allowing God, the divine, to lead you through life. Make goals, make plans – keep your eye on the prize!

- **Remember** that you have spiritual guides, angels and divine light assisting you; you do not have to do all the work. Your job is to surrender and let divine love guide you.

Angela Legh - United Kingdom
Intuitive Subconscious Shifter
www.angelalegh.com
☉ angelaavery.revealchange
🖪 Revealchange

MYSTÈRE POÈME

"Walk into the mystery that awaits."

Call upon your adventurous spirit for the courage to face your fear, feel it deeply and release it, remembering who you were before fear entered your life.

WALKING INTO THE MARKET OF MEMORIES

I found my feet again in the winding market maze of Marrakesh. Smells flood my senses. Sights and sounds weave their way into my center. Drum beats and deep voices call forth something within. No more sleepwalking or shadow hunting. No more holding myself together, forcing, fretting and fearful. In this market moment, time stands still and we move through it. Until I find myself deep in the desert. Vast. Barren. Expansive. Day has come, the light is here. It's time to bask in the sun.

It was my last day in Marrakesh, Morocco. I had only a few hours left in this vibrant city and felt the ancient Medina calling me to visit one last time. It was hard not to be enticed by the maze-like twists and turns of the souks selling everything imaginable. There were miles of shops still unexplored and my search for the perfect gifts to take back home was not complete, so one more venture out into the streets was essential.

Walking alone or trying to find a taxi was still intimidating. Hailing a cab seems like a simple task, but in the chaos of the crowds and cars, it felt overwhelming. I was also acutely aware of the 'tourist tax,' the increased cost to foreigners visiting the country, especially anyone who didn't speak the language. I wanted to break through that fear. Fear of being alone, being taken advantage of and getting lost along the way were very real to me, not just in this moment, but in *too many* moments of my life.

Even though I had walked the crowded Moroccan streets by day and by night and had visited the market mayhem before, this would be the first time finding my way there by myself. If I was brave, I would muster the courage to negotiate, in a foreign country, in a foreign language, to bring home gifts of this vibrant city to the ones I love.

I wanted to push away the thought about whether or not I would be safe. I wanted to incinerate it in the desert heat, but it gripped my gut and my shoulders felt stiff as I took a few steps forward. The heaviness was familiar, one I'd lived with my entire life. Afraid of walking alone... in a crowded city where I could get mugged, in an empty parking lot where I could be attacked, in remote nature settings where I could be assaulted. I had been victimized more than once in my life and adopted a victim mindset. One that made me hypervigilant as a means of self-protection. I held tight to disempowering beliefs in a futile attempt to keep myself safe. Year by year, my life and world kept getting smaller.

Two and a half years previously, I had faced that fear and said, "I'm done. I'm doing it anyway." I started making plans to become nomadic. And then, I made it happen. The fear was always there, I just pushed it down and away so I could do more of what I wanted and stop hiding out, afraid of my own shadow. From the outside, no one would have known that I was bone-tired of cowering in fright, or that what appeared to be bold and brave decisive action was accompanied by careful calculations to manage the terror I carried inside.

There I was in Marrakesh, with another choice, but this time I didn't want to push down the fear. I needed to feel it, face it and release it. I desperately wanted to find my feet again. The urgency of my final hours in the city and the final gifts for my loved ones were enough to help me move forward and start taking steps in that direction.

It was midday and the sun was shining bright. The bread sellers stood next to their carts filled with fresh baked bread kept warm by the sun. I'd seen how the traditional Moroccan bread, or *khobz,* was baked early every single morning in a community-size wood-fired oven. The bakers rotated throughout the day, as the heat from the oven fire on a hot desert day can be almost unbearable. Served at almost every meal in Morocco, the round bread accompanies the deliciously cooked vegetable and meat *tagines*. The bread is considered sacred and they don't throw uneaten pieces away, but give them to someone in need or feed them to animals to respect the nourishment it provides. My feet carried me past mothers and children sitting on blankets, arms outstretched and asking for money. More than that, I think they were asking to be seen, to be protected, to be safe. They wanted the same thing I did. We were not that different.

Cars, cabs, carriages, bicycles and scooters shared the busy streets in both directions. Traffic surged and stopped, busier than usual with the visit of an important government official to the city that day. Palm trees lined one side of the street. Natural colored buildings made of clay and earth with bright colored doors lined the other. I took it all in, but kept my stride, glancing at the map on my phone, still headed in the right direction.

I saw two young men, taller than me, stronger than me. Fear crashed over me like a tidal wave. They were slightly hidden behind a set of large palm trees. One saw me, then motioned to the other. He looked my way. I panicked. Air got stuck in my throat. I couldn't breathe. Was I safe? Would my worst fears come true? These questions instantly began pummeling my mind from every direction.

I willed myself to take a breath. The cadence of my steps on the sidewalk and the movement of my entire body toward my destination helped the fear move in and out without getting stuck. I felt the terror rise, witnessed it and pushed back against being dominated by this misperception that the world was unsafe, that my safety was at risk, that I had to be hypervigilant to keep myself from harm. Just because I had the thought that I was in danger *didn't mean it was true*. That insight helped me feel more contained and in charge of myself again. "I'm safe. I'm safe," I repeated. "They simply see a potential customer. They have good intentions."

I was almost to where they were standing. "Smile," I thought, somewhat surprised with the idea. But the surprise of that thought slowed my thinking long enough for me to take a deep breath. And then another. In a moment, I passed where they stood. I smiled. They smiled back. And it was over. Just like that. A primal fear reaction triggered... then faced... and released, all in the span of a few seconds.

My smile didn't fade. Instead, it grew to envelop my chest as I took an even deeper calming breath. That smile engulfed my heart as I thought about the men who meant me no harm and how my heart knew that. Then it began to encircle my entire body and I suddenly felt power and strength return to my steps. In a moment, I went from feeling weak and ungrounded to solid and stable. My legs became tree trunks connecting me to the earth and grounding me with unseen roots.

I knew in that moment that all would be well. I could handle anything. When the courage to face the fear showed up, the opportunity to make a choice appeared. I was not a victim of my thoughts and fears no matter how long-held they might be. Deep within my core, I knew that I am walking this earth for a reason and everything is possible. I am able and capable. I felt the strength rise up in my belly. My walk was strong and confident, each step anchored to the earth through my hips and legs. I'd found an even more valuable treasure in the market that day, my strength, my confidence. And I knew I'd carry it with me in my life every day going forward.

If I can handle the streets of Marrakesh with grace and a smile, what else is possible? I was on the other side of fear, finally. The experiences of the market and the desert, the camels and the nomads, had cracked through the wall of fear to let the light in and reveal the undeniable abundance within and without. With every subsequent step, my insides were weaving themselves together again with rays of hope, delight and curiosity. The rest of the walk to the market passed quickly as I marveled at the vibrant colors of the women's dresses and the cacophony of sound from every direction.

Once inside the market, I was again confronted by the ancient Medina and the magic that it holds for those who enter. Street vendors lined the narrow and cobbled streets of the walled market sections. If you stopped even for a second to admire a jewel-covered genie lamp or a deceptively small dagger or scabbard, the shopkeepers would be beside you. "Best price. I give you best price," they would gush in your ear. Even if you didn't stop to look, they would call out, "Come back, no charge to look." Arms inviting and outstretched, they wanted you to see what they were offering, in many cases the same goods that their ancestors had sold for ages. The brilliant blues, flame-like oranges and passionate purples of the stalls breathed life into the market in a way that made the calling out for attention just part of the experience rather than a threat.

My mind was brought back to the street where women with babies to feed were asking for money. I thought of the nomad mothers living in a camp in the desert where their entire home can literally be blown over in a windstorm. Of their children who have no access to medical care or dentists to keep their teeth from getting stains from the water. Of the 16-year-old girl asking simply for books to read in English so she could learn and make a better life for herself.

The sounds and smells of the market surrounded me as I walked, lost in my thoughts. I am okay. I will be okay. My mind will return to these memories any time I feel stressed or worried. I will carry with me the resilience and beauty of this mystical culture.

Something came alive in me as the market and the memories wove themselves together with every step I took on the cobbled streets. I strolled and listened to the melodic sounds of the snake charmers as they sat perched on their boxes, tempting fate. The smoky smell of roasted nuts filled the air and pulled my attention to the stall with olives of every size, shape and color. Orange, red, brown, and yellow pyramids of spices defied gravity as they graced the circular trays they sat on. This all felt so foreign and so familiar simultaneously. Could it be that this place was a part of me? A part of me that I never knew existed? Is this where the vibrance of my life had gone? To a home I'd never known and was only now discovering? I didn't even know this world of dualities and dichotomies existed. I certainly didn't know that I could ever feel safe, or at home, or dare I say, even belonging.

That was what I was feeling. Self-remembrance from a rooted place in my soul. I had been here and would be back again and to other places as well. Everything was aligning into a place of harmony and coherence with who I am, my real nature and identity. I felt a sense of creative urgency. That this is my work. This is why my heart is so tender. This is why my compassion is so strong. To be a conduit. A vessel. A channel between the worlds of abundance and need, for generosity and healing.

I felt myself pulled back to Mexico at age 16. A mission trip building a home for the orphaned children. Singing with them. Teaching them. Hugging and holding them. That experience changed my life and limited worldview. I didn't have to force or plan, but could be a channel for what life wants to bring forward. I was willing to lean into and surrender to what this time and place was calling out of me; to use all that I am, my art and creativity, my eye for beauty, my desire to transform all around me. To show others the beauty of these people and this place and bring hope and health and generosity to the people most needy. That will be my mission. To have a community that will support that vision. To partner with me in giving and caring. To share the abundance of what we have. I have been given the gift of travel and nomad life, a wanderlust and Adventurous Spirit so I am equipped and able to go where I am most needed.

I've already felt the swelling of connectivity when my son and I traveled to San Francisco and walked through the city handing out meals to the homeless. That act compelled by a memory of visiting the city alone at 18, meeting an older man dressed in a suit and bow tie. He was dancing and entertaining to earn his way. His smile was contagious and it made me smile. But I walked by, afraid to engage. As I walked away, I felt a pounding in my chest and an ache in my belly. "Go back," I heard. I retraced my steps, but he was gone. I've never forgotten that man or that missed moment.

The thoughts are coming fast now, washing over me in beautiful waves of grateful recognition. I felt the calling when my son and I took our groceries and shared them with the woman in Edinburgh. I felt it when we went out on Christmas Day and gave cash to people in need in Seattle. When my daughter and I prepared care packages for people in the military. Shopping to buy gifts to fill boxes for kids in Africa with toys, dolls and treats. Such a small thing for us and so monumental to those in need.

I recall my own need as a little girl growing up and how people gave us food and money. How I got used clothes from the share closet at church. My shame at being needy and my indescribable gratitude for those who gave and did it in a way that preserved our dignity. I relive the night someone dropped off cash at our front door in an envelope so we could buy food. I look back to when I was a single mom in my 20s and my cupboards were bare and my friends brought over boxes of groceries and unloaded them until my cupboards were overflowing.

Immediately, a lump swells in my throat as I connect the lessons of each of those moments in my heart. I remember the young me, the vision of me teaching. Anything to help others live life better and with more ease. *Oh sweet awakening.* I feel this in my bones. Pain pushed me out of my comfortable small world to become a nomad and it kept me always moving, seeking and striving. This felt different, as if the vision was pulling me in to my expansive future through insight rather than effort, ease rather than dis-ease, harmony instead of hustle.

My vision was revealing the path before me. Showing me the way. Opening it up with the deep rhythms of wisdom, magic and miracles. I believe in this divine timing and this mission. I am ready to embody it. The Elder. The Artist. The Healer. The Teacher. The Adventurer. It's time to raise up a fierce tribe. Photo shoots, adventure and service retreats, gifts from and for places around the globe. Spiritual and grounded. Women empowering women. Bringing dignity, hope and healing to those who need it most.

The markets of Marrakesh brought me back to me. The desert sands released me from society and unfounded beliefs. The nomad hospitality reached deep and showed me the future, past and present all in one meeting. My heart will never be the same. This place resuscitated the dying places, quenched the thirsty spaces, emboldened the timid traces. There I stood, and I knew this was a full circle moment. Somehow, a portal had been opened. I left the past on that road in Marrakesh. Taking it all in, every step of the way, knowing from this moment forward, everything had changed.

I can still feel the desert sands running through my hands, reminding me that, in the end, we all wind up in the eternal forever. It's *this* moment that really matters. Trust and surrender. Open your heart. Embrace all that is tender. Each moment is simply magic waiting to happen; everything you ever wanted and never even knew, exists. Watch it all come together. No more grasping or hoping, just reaching out with open hands and delight in what gets delivered. All that you dared to dream. Now it's time to reclaim.

Where are you being called to walk? What adventure is waiting right outside your door? Sometimes all it takes to unravel everything is a short walk to the market. Or perhaps every walk to the market is an opportunity for unraveling, to see and feel, all that needs to be known and released. Will you have the courage to face the fear and feel it deeply? To call upon your Adventurous Spirit to wade into the deep? I believe you do and one day soon, I'll meet you there.

IGNITE ACTION STEPS

Listen to your intuition. Live unapologetically. Leave nothing undone.

Mystère Poème - United States
Director, "Invisible Illness" Film
Certified Ayurvedic Health Advisor
www.mystere.life
mystere.life
mystere.life
mysterelife

NADIA LA RUSSA

"Seeing the world through your child's eyes will forever change you."

Travel experiences are the best gift a parent can give to children. Through my adventures, I have also learned that it is the best gift a child can give a parent. You might think that traveling with children is a recipe for the worst vacation possible. When you travel with your children, you are taking on the risk that the entire experience might not be rainbows and sunshine. There could be tears and hardships. The important thing to remember is to do it anyway; weather the storm. Dare to experience a different climate. Live in your bathing suit for a while. When your children look back on the experience of travel, they will remember the best of it.

LIVING IN BATHING SUITS

The greatest adventure I've ever been on started as an idea in the fall of September 2016. I had been perusing the blog of my friend Samantha, who had earlier that year traveled with her husband and two daughters to Ecuador on what she called a 'family sabbatical.' She took an extended trip with the people who live in her household and experienced life in another part of the world.

I don't actually know what sparked this desire in me; perhaps it was the amazing photos that kept popping up on social media. I knew that my daughters, at the time 14 and 11, and stepsons, twins aged 12 and their younger brother aged 10, would soon be slipping from my parental hold as they made their way through their teen years.

The realization hit me — if there was a time to plan a massive family adventure on a different continent, it was now. Far too soon, the idea of simply skittering off for a month with no regard for anything back home would be impossible. I had to act fast.

The very next day, I approached my husband Brent on the topic. It was the classic and typical manner in which we are so compatible.

"So," I began, "I'd like to go to Bali for a month in the summer. With all the kids. I'd like to give them one big family experience, and create memories that they can take into their adult lives." I had a whole slew of justifications for the idea, which I knew might have sounded completely crazy, and desperately wanted to be ready to ward off any objection.

He sighed.

And then he pulled out his phone, opened the calendar app and responded. "Okay babe. What dates are you thinking?"

The next thing I knew, we had booked ourselves for the wildest adventure I had ever imagined. Less than a week later, I had two separate sets of flights arranged courtesy of three different credit card points. I had found a lovely AirBnB™ villa in Kuta Utara, Bali and we had the kids and the exes (mostly) on board.

And then, I got on with life.

As we approached our departure date, and because it had become a comfortable and easy idea, I had been inserting details of our trip into random conversations with friends. Not because I was looking for shock value, but because it had just now become a part of my plans. I had forgotten that most people weren't quite expecting me to say, "We are taking the kids to Bali for the summer." The biggest question I got during the weeks before our departure was, "Why?" "Why were we doing this? Why Bali? Why now?" By the time we actually left, I had my rationale down to an elevator pitch:

Our kids are at a critical age and stage where they are growing into adults with thoughts, beliefs and opinions of their own, but they still want to hang out with us. We recognize that we have a very short window of time left where they are under our influence in this way and I want to show them a different part of the world. I want to give the kids my travel bug; walk them through busy, crazy, loud international airports and have them experience different languages, currency and food. We want to show them that their North American lives are not the only way people live and we want to teach them the value of living in a culture that is completely different from our own.

It also helped that my research had shown that while Bali was expensive to get to, it was relatively inexpensive to live in. This, of course, was a big factor traveling with five growing teens and pre-teens. As if this whole plan didn't have enough of an adventure component, I gave strict instructions that this was to be 'carry-on only.' We had long since learned that the 'lug' in luggage was something we wanted no part of.

On July 22, 2017, my daughters and I boarded our flight and headed off to the other side of the world. Brent and the boys left 12 hours later, which gave the girls and me time to set up the house, get groceries, get sleep and figure out what the heck to do next. A mere 24 hours later, I was sitting on a beautiful beach only a 10 minute walk from our temporary home listening to my children laugh and squeal as the waves washed over them. I knew at that moment that I had made the right decision. I knew that whatever unfolded over the following six weeks was simply meant to be and would be forever woven within our family's story. Little did I know what lay ahead.

My idyllic dreams of beachfront laziness, perfect weather and endless laughter were squashed the following day. When we woke up, our two daughters, two of our sons and Brent were crippled with what I later learned was a case of 'Bali belly.' An Internet search informed me that this was common, temporary, but terribly unpleasant, all of which was accurate. Thankfully, it whipped through the family rather quickly and by the third day, everyone was back to normal.

'Normal,' however, took on a whole new meaning. When I planned the trip out, I prepared a detailed and meticulous budget. I've worked my entire adult life as an accountant, an expert on preparing budgets. However, I had catastrophically failed at determining a reasonable grocery budget for the family trip. Looking over my calculations on the seventh day of our adventure, I discovered that I had already spent nearly $1,350 of the entire trip food budget of $2,500. Apparently, my calculations did not allow for the increased caloric requirements of five growing children who were now spending their days outdoors running around. One of my vivid memories was after a full supper one evening, I then had to cook a dozen eggs, all of which were devoured.

By the second week, Brent and I realized the other thing that wasn't accounted for was the fact that for the first time in our lives we were together as a family 24 hours a day, seven days a week. Gone was the going to work and school, visiting grandparents, kids hanging out with their friends, going to church, or anything that separated us as a family of seven. It was all us, all kids, all the time. Needless to say, it didn't take long for the grumpiness of dealing with each other on a non-stop basis to reach a head. I actually googled 'flight cost from Bali to Canada leaving today' and thankfully, for everyone involved, the number was too high to fit on any credit card I had. I refer to this part of the trip as that time that 'everyone was a complete jerk.' I recall being in the kitchen of the villa crying, listening to the twins in a heated argument, the girls hollering at each other in the loft and our youngest slamming his door after lipping off to Brent.

It was a learning phase for all of us and I knew that despite my feelings of anger and frustration, it was our job as parents to set the tone. It was important for the kids to experience life and travel with others in ways that they wouldn't have necessarily chosen to. And it was time to let them develop their own ways of resolving conflict.

Rather than wallow in my newfound dislike for everyone in my family, I decided to check my crummy attitude and plan weekly adventures for the crew. We settled into a great routine: trying out local food, going to the beach, and hitting up the fun things to do on the island. Over the six weeks, I was able to treat all of us to an adventure park complete with zip-lines, the world's largest waterpark, white water rafting, snorkeling over a shipwreck and an elephant safari.

After the end of the fifth week, Brent and the boys ventured home and left the girls and I behind. This had been planned in advance as the boys' biological mother had not wanted them to be gone for the full six weeks. Once they left, the girls and I had nine days together to finish off our journey. It occurred to me that since we were there longer than a month, it was time to get our travel visa extended.

I made my way to the visa renewal office alone with my passport and the girls' passports in hand, fully expecting a simple process costing approximately $30. Little did I know what was in store.

Rewind to arrival day — a blurry-eyed, tired Nadia gets instructions from the immigration officer that sounded something like, "Your tourist visa is good for 30 days; make sure you renew it before it expires," which translated in my exhausted brain as "You have a month to figure this out."

Not so.

When they said '30 days' what they meant was '30 days and today is day 1.' And that is NOT the same thing as one month, especially when that month is July, which has 31 days. Having arrived after 37 hours of travel on July 24 at midnight made my arrival at the immigration office on August 24 at noon a full two days late to renew.

Apparently, this was a big deal. I asked the quickly-becoming-less-and-less friendly counter person, "So what do I do now?" and the answer was, "You leave the country. Immediately."

I felt my temperature rise and my heart rate increase. I knew right away that I was not in a position of power in this circumstance. I internally questioned if I was understanding the situation fully or if this was a language barrier.

I had no means to 'leave the country immediately' for several reasons. I didn't have my children with me; in fact, I didn't have anything with me. I started to protest, which was rapidly met with me getting ushered — and by that I mean I was taken by the arm and led — into a small, grey room with a table and two chairs. You know, the same as the rooms you see on television when someone is about to be interrogated.

Then... entered Big Balinese Immigration Dude and Even Bigger Balinese Immigration Dude. Both dudes were not pleased.

For the next 10 minutes or so, I was subjected to a very loud and stern talking to about the importance of respecting authority, following process, and removing myself from their land. It didn't take much to have me do what any self-respecting, confident woman would do — I burst into tears and sobbed uncontrollably.

That was their cue. They left the room without a word. A very small, sweet, kind and helpful lady entered with tissues. Calm Sweet Lady apologized for her mean friends and suggested that there might be another way to get my visa extended. It all became clear at that point what was happening.

"Money?" I said. "You want MONEY? Frick, why didn't you say so. How much do you need?"

And it was done, just like that. I handed over $500 and all of a sudden I became a respected and esteemed visitor. Not only was I allowed to stay, but now my passports were going to be 'fast tracked' through the 'speedy system.' The next day, the girls and I made our way to the central immigration office and were escorted to the front of the line for photos and fingerprints. Amazingly, our files were already waiting for us.

Life without the boys in Bali was different, but good. The girls and I spent our days shopping, eating lunch on the patio at our villa, swimming and going for walks.

Three days before our departure home, I woke up feeling unusually warm.

By mid-day, I was exhausted, so I announced that it was a 'stay in' afternoon. The girls hopped in the pool while I napped. I woke up a short time later, feverish, drenched in sweat, with a blinding headache. I also felt chilled, and scared. I couldn't even imagine what was happening, but I sensed it wasn't great.

The next morning, it was even worse. I found myself unable to get my temperature down one moment and the next I was piling blankets on me trying to stay warm. And the headache — I can't even describe how terrible it was. As a previous migraine sufferer, I was trying to identify if this was, in fact, a migraine — but I couldn't quite put my finger on what was different about it. The following day was a complete blur. I vaguely remember handing money to my daughter so she and her sister could get food.

I woke up some time later that evening feeling worse than before, and still feverish. Groggily, I padded off to the bathroom to splash water on my face and brush my teeth. I removed the toothbrush from my mouth and saw that it was bright red. I lifted my eyes to look in the mirror and saw that my teeth were red with blood. I knew I urgently needed to see a doctor.

Being vulnerable is not my normal mode. However, I was feeling the worst that I have ever felt in my entire life. Seeing the blood on my teeth from my gums made me question my decision to travel alone with my children in a foreign country. Without alarming the girls, I requested an Uber and prayed that the driver would be someone I could trust.

My panic and self-doubt were rampant. After all, here I was in a foreign country, clearly very ill, and effectively a single parent. I had absolutely no working knowledge of the medical system, but I felt a little short on options. I certainly wasn't in any shape to board an airplane the following day as scheduled. In fact, I was beginning to question whether or not I was going to make it at all.

I left the girls at the villa with strict instructions not to leave or let anyone in, and I made my way to what was rated as the 'Best Hospital In Bali' (thank you, Google reviews). I was pleasantly surprised to find myself in a bright, clean, up-to-date hospital, complete with English-speaking nurses and physicians. Within the hour, I had received a diagnosis of dengue fever, a common mosquito-transmitted virus that, although uncomfortable, had very few serious risks associated with it. I was given a thorough examination, kept overnight for observation, heavily medicated, and made it back to the villa the following morning in time to pack up for our journey home. Every fear that had been running through my mind as I left for the hospital was proven to be false.

The great family adventure concluded on September 1, 2017. As we landed home, jetlagged and exhausted, I knew the trip had been the right decision.

It took about a year for the kids to start talking about Bali. It comes up all the time now as they recall the adventure we had together. Everything they have to say about Bali is positive; it's as if they only remember the good parts. Now, they are asking about new adventures and wanting to see new places. I learned that travel and experiences are the best gift a parent can give to children. But I also learned it is the best gift a child can give to a parent. Having seen the other side of the world through their eyes is something that has forever changed me for the better.

The moral of my story is… It is okay to live in your bathing suit. You cannot plan for everything when you are traveling with your children, so plan to have *no* plan. I believe the best way to travel is to take your family and live somewhere else for a while. In doing that, you get a richer experience of the culture, people and all the magic the world has to offer.

IGNITE ACTION STEPS

If you are on the fence about undertaking a major travel adventure with your children, just jump in with both feet. Give them the gift of travel, experience and culture. Let them see how other countries operate. Set aside your expectations for them — and for yourself — and watch how they reflect on the experiences later. You won't regret it.

Travel light; have your children and yourself bring only what you need. You'd be surprised how many days in a row you can live in your bathing suit.

Go far and stay long. A one- or two-week vacation isn't long enough to experience the way another culture operates. Stay away from the resorts and rent a house in a neighborhood. Find a place where you can stay for a month or longer, even if the kids miss a bit of school. They will be just as educated through travel as through the classroom.

Nadia La Russa - Canada
Wife, Mother, Step-mother, Entrepreneur
www.nadialarussa.com
 nadiaannelarussa
 nadialarussa

CHARLIE ROPSY

*"Dare to explore yourself until you become the
unknown and the unknown becomes Home."*

**With my story, I invite you on a journey to meet that forgotten part of you.
I wish for you to maintain deep faith in this resurfacing power, especially
in moments of loneliness, for it will guide you step by step to your most
ambitious dreams.**

A GOLDEN EMBRACE

In order to become a master, we train and practice. We do it again and again
until one day, we've mastered the skill. From my youngest age, I've practiced
separations. My parents divorced when I was 18 months old. I lived with my
mum who started a new family. Due to circumstances, we had to move every
six to twelve months, which often meant changing schools. When I was 8, we
left Belgium for the south of France, leaving friends and family behind. My
dad settled in Thailand after a few travels around Asia, and some years later
also started his own new family. I did my best to connect people and blended
families that didn't want to have anything to do with each other. In the midst of
family disunion and my own identity disorientation, I felt alone and incomplete.

I have always felt like there was something missing in my life. There was
a void inside that I could physically feel like a pain in my core. You know that
grieving ache when you lose someone or after a breakup? I grew up feeling
that 24/7. It was not until later in life that it finally came out: I miss my twin

brother. I have always felt like I was supposed to have a brother and that for whatever reason he had given up his life for me to make it. That's a heavy thought to carry and there is no rational proof of this. Yet, I just knew. This perpetual feeling of grief and these physical discomforts were very confusing to me. I couldn't relate to who I was nor to anything out there. I guess that's what also developed a need for my reclusion. Maybe if I go back into my cocoon, I'll meet my brother again.

To fill that void, I tried to find a boyfriend who would also be my best friend, twin brother and answer to my feeling of inadequacy. I felt like I won the jackpot in my early 20s when I completely fell for Charly. Charly and Charlie. "Perfect!" I thought. When Charly and I broke up, loneliness struck harder.

Five years later, Luke, my next romance, and I were sitting on a bench outside a hotel in Kampot, Cambodia, hugging, crying. My bus was due to arrive any minute. Tears were coming down my cheeks and the pain in my chest made it hard to breathe. We loved each other deeply but we didn't want the same things out of life and we were holding each other back from reaching our dreams. I remember our hands slipping away and losing touch. I climbed on the minibus, looking straight ahead of me, trying to find all the strength I could, to keep myself together. But there was nothing there for me to grab onto and comfort me. No hope, no liveliness, no one to hold me anymore. I knew I would never see him again. I didn't want to face that separation and wished for the grief to be over. We had to let go of each other and however paradoxical it seemed, we did it for Love.

It was almost 11 PM when that heart-wrenching bus ride ended and I arrived at my destination. I opened the apartment door to an asphyxiating stench of mold. I ran in to open the windows and purposely ignored the view. I knew it too well. I didn't want to be reminded of where I was and even less of why I went there. I grabbed a silk sarong from my suitcase and wrapped myself in it, using it as a sleeping bag and my jumper as a pillow. I laid down on the sofa bed, rolled onto my side in the fetal position and cried myself to sleep.

When I woke up, I couldn't ignore the situation anymore. I was in my dad's empty apartment in Pattaya, Thailand and I had just lost my best friend, lover and confidante. I felt disconnected from myself and life. I had left my homeland, Belgium, three years earlier and had not been in touch with family members for several years; including my father. Luke had been the only person who really knew me and who I felt I really knew, and suddenly I was without anyone to love or anyone to love me, no project to undergo, no income and not much taste for life.

My dad's apartment was not my favorite place to be. Summer holidays there were filled with loneliness. I had no friends and wasn't allowed to go out. It was a prison to me. I stayed for five days, not willing to leave this unhealthy place and face anyone for anything, not even food. I remember passing in front of a mirror and my reflection catching my attention. I couldn't believe what I was seeing...

I touched my arms and looked at my thighs. Where was I? I couldn't recognise myself. I had melted 10 kilograms away. My survival instincts kicked in and, starving, I got myself together and found the courage to go to the restaurant and have proper meals. Back on a balanced diet, I found my way to the mall and bought myself some new, better fitting clothing. I started shifting out of my mental and physical rat hole. But I still felt lost within.

One day, I stared at a giant poster on the wall titled 'The World Map.' Every place reminded me of Luke: Australia, where we met; New Zealand, where we traveled; Vietnam, where I had moved to be with him; Cambodia, where we parted. Thailand, where I found myself currently and, further west, Belgium, which I had left in as deep a state of depression as I was in now. What was the point of fighting so hard to survive and make a life for myself if I was to end up in the same position again?

Looking at the map, it was clear that there was nowhere I belonged, no place for me to long for and no place calling for me. I recognized these thoughts; I had already experienced them years earlier and I knew that they were dangerous. I closed my eyes and took a deep breath. I thought to myself, "Charlie, think outside the box. When what you know is painful, start thinking about what you don't know." This new perspective awakened my imagination. In all the shapes and colors painting the countries, I saw opportunities, new stories, adventures and experiences. In reality, there were so many places to go. My visa was about to expire and I had to make a decision I was not ready to consciously make. So I left it to the odds and pointed at the map: Nepal.

I researched the information necessary to get there, watched every video I could find on YouTube and booked a ticket. A week later, I was flying. I was definitely not ready for this cooler country, but the challenge and excitement of a new experience sparked something inside of me that gave me the courage to get on with it. I took a bus to Bangkok, bought my first backpack, left over ten kilos of travel gear and books behind, then got on the plane and flew towards a new life.

Once in Nepal, the Himalayas started calling me. I knew I was up for the challenge. I got a trekking permit and headed west. After seven days of hiking through the mountains, and despite excruciating pain in my legs, I couldn't wait to finally reach the Annapurna Base Camp. It was three in the morning when my alarm woke me up. Despite the early hour, my eyes were wide open: this was the day I was going to accomplish my first ever trek.

In silence, I slipped out of my sleeping bag, plunged into my waterproof trousers and dived into my walking shoes. The cold grabbed me as I exited the guesthouse. I was facing a couple of hours of walking to get to Base Camp and my plan was to be there by sunrise. I was not the only one with that idea; other trekkers along with their guide and sometimes sherpa, were getting ready to tackle the last stretch of their walk through the Himalayas too. Some of them had already departed and their headlamps drew beautiful meandering lines of light in the distance. I closed my jacket up to my chin, put on my woolen hat and drew out my walking sticks. Let's go!

I could barely see in the dark, but step after step... I kept climbing. Looking down at my feet and focusing on my very-soon-to-be thrilling achievement, I pressed on. As a 'westerner,' I was used to the robotic busyness of everyday life. Get up; automatically find your way to school and follow the rules. Let's be honest; we're all programmed that way. There isn't much space for us to reflect, be present and enjoy the moment. This time, there was no noise and expectations for me to fill up but the ones I created for myself... and I did create them. I was in the stillest place I could ever experience, yet I wasn't aware of it. I was too focused on the need to get to Base Camp. I was creating a never-ending loop of chaotic thoughts that were kidnapping me from living in the moment. I had identified with the familiar busyness of my life and had imprisoned myself in it, thinking the same sequence over and over again: "I have to get there, I'm finally going to get there..."

Then..."STOOOOOOP!!"

I jumped. The voice came out of nowhere. My heart was pounding. I was so confused. I looked up in front of me and switched off my headlamp to see how far the other groups were. But there was no light shining in the distance. I immediately turned around, but again, there was no one in sight. It hit me then, the sudden danger I was facing. Was I really alone in the pitch-black Himalayas at 4 AM? How the fuck did that happen?

I had never experienced so much darkness before. I couldn't see anything. I felt like somehow I had ended up in another dimension. The world had been taken away from underneath my feet. I hoped it was only a nightmare and that I would soon wake up. All of my senses were on high alert as there was no more path for me to follow. Full panic hit me. My survival instinct took control of my thoughts and carried me deeper into fear. Draped in darkness and trapped in nothingness, I was trembling. Emptiness had engulfed me. There was nothing there but silence and absolute blindness. Lost in the fearsome Himalayas of my imagination, my mind slipped into the abyss with images of freezing to death and being eaten by a snow leopard. I didn't exist anymore, only the threat did. With quick and shallow breaths, looking left and right, up and down… I waited for Death to strike.

From above, the frozen moon grabbed my attention and yanked me towards herself. I was captivated, hypnotized by her majestic presence and her feminine beauty. Locking eyes with her, all my worries and fears were instantly swept away. I stood in awe as the moon caressed my soul with comforting gentleness. She emitted groundedness and confidence. Mesmerized, I submitted to her embrace as she shone her wisdom onto me. I was hit with energy. '*Hhhaaa*'… I opened my mouth widely and felt the air rushing down my lungs, reviving me. '*Choooo*'… The air left my body through a lasting exhale and I landed back in the blackness. But something had changed: the void was no longer emptiness. The unknown had become alive. I connected with all of the things I could not see, nor touch, nor hear — we were all One.

I had become the unknown and the unknown had become Home.

A tickling arose in my heart center and started moving in circles inside my chest. At first, it was very subtle but as it gained speed, it grew bigger and bigger. I couldn't identify this new feeling but I could see the golden energy slowly embracing my core. Its warmth imbued me with a new sturdy confidence, stability and determination. I received this gift with gratitude. The golden energy expanded to my whole being and in a fraction of time, imploded and locked itself inside of me.

The revelation that came with that energy was profound: I was not alone; I was with Myself. This beautiful truth was a pure epiphany. I had never been alone because I had always had Myself. I had Myself to guide me, to support me, to motivate me and keep me going in the hardest moments. Myself had been there with me since my beginnings, but I was too busy and caught up in the hustle and bustle of the outer-world and had never noticed it. I had believed that I wasn't enough. I thought I was a failure and a burden. I thought I needed to be fixed and needed someone else to complete me. I had drawn on everyone else's judgement for my identity without checking in with Myself to see if any of it was true. I was finally free to be Myself, whole and complete where it wasn't about anyone else... And, I knew that I would never be lonely again.

Black turned into deep indigo blue as the mountains appeared all around me. I was still alone and lost on the mountainside, but the fears had faded away. Calmness and peacefulness occupied me, along with a deep faith that I was going to be okay. I followed the path before me until an assortment of houses emerged in the distance. I paused and looked at them with wonder: the Annapurna Base Camp. I was saved.

I couldn't believe what had just occurred over the past couple of hours. There was no logical explanation for what I had felt, yet I had experienced it all.

It is said that many yogis who reach a higher level of consciousness can choose to leave their body, transforming their immortal life energy to forever prevail. Many ancient yogis have passed on in the Himalayas and an aura of intense life force eternally inhabits the mountains. This would explain why so many of us experience life-changing breakthroughs there and come down these mysterious peaks a new person. We tap into a tiny fraction of their spirit and expand our own consciousness. Becoming aware of this energy I am, helped me reconnect to the whole of my being. I gained an inner compass and an access to my own truth as well as a wiser way to respond to the outside world. Of course, you don't need to get lost in the Himalayas in order to experience Yourself but when you start exploring the unknown and surrendering to the infinite mysteries of life, every possibility can manifest.

I learned, when we dare to tap into our adventurous self and do something out of the ordinary, our spirit awakens with joy. It is 'Ourself' that is the fuel to reaching these advanced states of being. Our inner willpower is undefiable when rooted into confidence. Finding Oneself is the most freeing thing one can do, for judgments no longer find shelter in our insecurities and old depleting patterns like self-sabotage, aren't welcome anymore.

A month after my awakening in the Himalayas, I participated in a month-long event on personal development where I met amazing like-minded people and who became life-changing friends. I also traveled around Europe, flew to North America for the first time and transformed my life for the better. And I did it all alone… with Myself.

Growth is a never-ending self-study and action-taking process. Going on any adventure brings you closer to a spiritual aspect of life and yourself. As well, going on an inner, reflective journey can definitely take you on a roller-coaster ride towards discovering *Yourself*. There is always more to experience and uncover. So, as a hint for when you have your own personal '*I experience Myself*' breakthrough, fall deeply in love with Yourself. And that my friend, will be the start of your next spirited adventure!

IGNITE ACTION STEPS

- **Experience:** There are things about you that you don't know, and the only way to discover Yourself is by experience. Go somewhere you've never been. Book a trip, find a place on the map and go there. Dare to explore Yourself until you become the unknown and the unknown becomes Home.

- **Ask:** When we're alone and need guidance, we start talking to Ourself. And that's the whole point! Yourself knows everything you need. So start a conversation with it and ask it what your next step should be.

- **Listen:** When I told my godmother I decided to go to Nepal, she said she already knew it. I was surprised. She reminded me that when I was in Australia, I had dreamt of myself alone in the Nepalese mountains. The way had already been shown to me but I had not listened. Recognize that voice, acknowledge it and even dare to follow it. Keep track of those messages, journal about it, write it out and read it daily.

- **Nurture:** Pay attention to your own needs and desires. Reconnecting with Yourself means nurturing it. Ask Yourself what it needs and then give that to Yourself. Make it important, map out a plan, make a list and do your best to do it.

Charlie Ropsy - Belgium
Soul Explorer
www.charlieropsy.com

SCOTT OWEN HARRELL

"Get out of your HEAD and into your HEART!"

My intention is to create an entertaining story, a snapshot of my life that reveals insights that were not always clear to me but I now see from a higher perspective. My intention is to show you that, even if your life experiences don't fit what everyone says they should be, they are *yours*. Those feelings are never wrong. The deeper the feeling, the more it shapes you as a person.

AS SEEN FROM THE WINDOW SEAT

I was raised in a fairly typical suburban middle-class American family in the 1950s and '60s — Mom, Dad and three boys. My Dad was an airline pilot. Back then, being a pilot was pretty glamorous. As a kid, I was proud of my father's role, flying a plane and traveling all over. My Dad had a cool job — and a uniform. The prospect of air travel was always very exciting, but also second nature for our family. A vacation would just as likely include hopping on a plane as it would a long drive in the station wagon.

In the early years, my awareness of the world around me increased in tandem with my travels and education, but flying on a plane was the ultimate thrill. I always scrambled for a window seat so that while taxiing on the runway, I could marvel at the aircraft around me — a TWA Constellation, Pan Am 707, United DC-8, Eastern 727 — and even the smaller airlines — Mohawk, Allegheny, Piedmont with their quaint propeller aircraft.

Once in the air, I was transfixed by the New York skyline, the Tappan Zee bridge, the Pennsylvania countryside turning into checkerboard Ohio farms and the vast agricultural landscape of the Midwest. It was utterly fascinating to see the tiny little towns, or try to guess what state we were flying over — and what was that distant city that seemed so interesting? Chicago? The Great Lakes shimmered on the horizon. "What are the people like there?" I would wonder. Look — the Rocky Mountains! And there's the Grand Canyon! Growing up on the East Coast, I had the privilege of nearly annual family trips to California. We had relatives there, and we would typically travel during winter months, which was an exotic escape from the cold New Jersey snow, ice and sleet. Disneyland! Palm trees! Knotts Berry Farm! Tacos! Those trips were among the highlights of my youth. California was more than just a vacation destination — it represented a different, more exciting way of life, filled with great weather, pretty girls and an indescribable energy that captured my imagination. It was the optimistic promise of the good life and I knew at an early age — someday, I will live in California. And of course, that's where I live now.

I always looked forward to each trip, hoping it was a newer, faster, bigger aircraft that flew higher than the last. On one such flight, from my window seat high above the clouds and the earth's surface, I could actually identify the curvature of the earth. I felt attuned to my world and I imagined the sense of awe that the astronauts must have felt in space. That beautiful blue horizon. That triggered a spiritual awakening, a true "Ignite moment." Suddenly, I wasn't just some kid from New Jersey — I was a citizen of the world — on a planet called Earth. I knew right then that I wanted to have a life that would be exciting and bigger than the world I came from.

Even though 'our' airline, United, was only a domestic carrier at the time (United went international years later), I managed to see a lot of different places in the United States. On one such trip, I got to see the entire West Coast and the gorgeous mountain ranges dominating the coast. That same trip culminated in my first international visit — to the beauty of Victoria, British Columbia, Canada. It was an inspiring feeling to experience another country, so terribly exciting, so different, with colored money — and the metric system! I felt like I'd *arrived*. I could only imagine what it would be like to go to other countries — places like Asia, Europe, Australia and South America. I couldn't wait!

When we weren't traveling, life at home was pretty routine, even though Dad would be gone a lot. I always considered myself to be a normal, typical kid my age despite being ignited by subjects like Ethics, Philosophy and creative writing. My studies of religion, science and consciousness were key to my next spiritual awakening at age 17. I was alone in my room, deep in inquiring thought. My head was filled with questions about God, the Universe and the nature of reality. We're supposed to believe, but in science, we need to have proof, I reasoned. I jumped up in a fit of youthful energetic bravado, and demanded an answer. "God, if you're *real*, show me a sign, *prove* to me that you're there!" Suddenly, I was enveloped in a massive burst of energy that started in my feet and worked up my entire body. It wasn't a shock, but rather, a loving bolt of pure energy that was unmistakably the answer I was looking for. "Yes, I AM." In that one magnificent moment, God showed me that He *is* real.

Nothing was exactly the same after that, although I mostly kept the incident to myself and went about my business, living an ordinary, mundane existence. So, God is real, but I'm still in high school.

My travels continued to broaden my horizons and offered new experiences. A winter trip to Hawaii introduced me to the tropical beauty of the islands. Body surfing in Waikiki gave me a thunderous pounding. A ski trip to Winter Park, Colorado was my initial trip to the Rocky Mountains. On our first day, the sight of the steep expert slopes with their seemingly near-vertical drop were a source of sheer terror. That mountain was scary and well beyond my skill level, black diamond flags and all. Each new day brought a rush of adventure, improved skills, and many, many falls. On our final day there, I conquered that mountain. Careening sharply down the long expert slope over moguls and hazardous terrain, a victorious sense of adrenaline-charged satisfaction ignited my system. That trip inspired me to go to college out West rather than my initial choice of Syracuse University in upstate New York.

The summer after my high school graduation, my brother and I drove cross-country in an epic four-day voyage. My family was moving to the sunny beach city of Santa Barbara, California — a big change for all of us. I said goodbye to my friends, New Jersey, and my childhood all at the same time. While our journey mimicked the cross-country flight path I had taken many times before, this was happening at a much slower pace. A decent collection of 8-track tapes provided the soundtrack for the long stretches of pleasant, mundane interstate highways punctuated by ordinary towns and cities like Columbus, Indianapolis and Oklahoma City. My then-new 35 millimeter camera helped to document our progress as we moved westward. Sprawling cities became tree-covered towns. Fields of green yielded to pastures; prairies to mountains. Desert horizons finally gave way to palm trees and the great blue Pacific. Life was moving too slowly and changing too rapidly.

Less than a month later, I took off for the University of Denver in Colorado.

Life at school was interesting and educational, of course. I made some great friends who are still in my life today, but my time there was not always happy. Perhaps living in three different states, thousands of miles apart, in the space of a few short months added to the pain of trying to figure out my identity while transitioning from teenager to adulthood. Photography and music were my salvation.

By the end of my first school year, I was feeling a bit sorry for myself. (What am I doing? Where do I belong?) I was offered a summer job and a place to stay with friends back in New Jersey, so I retreated to the safety of my familiar turf. Even though my future was quite uncertain, the summer yielded some unexpected life lessons. On my own for the first time, away from the comforts of home or the dorms, I had to actually cook, or pay for my own meals, and I worked long hours on the night shift in a plastics extrusion factory. It was there at the factory that I had my next spiritual awakening.

During one 3 AM break on a warm summer night, I was outside, staring up at the stars. It was a particularly fine night for stargazing — perfectly clear skies in the rural New Jersey countryside. I marveled at the heavens and the infinite vastness of the Universe and all its mysteries. I closed my eyes looking for answers, seeking to know what is the purpose, why am I here? Then it hit me — a brilliant vision in my mind's eye appeared — a glowing sphere, a great orb of energy before me. I instantly understood what it meant. It was my 'Oneness' moment; the sphere represented the consciousness of all that is. I knew then that we are all part of the cosmic Universe, yet we are individuals. Each one of us is a microcosm of everything else — but we are also part of God. Every thought, every person, every planet, star or Being - we are all part of *The One*.

That vision has infused and informed my life ever since. Let's just say it was a little weird going back to work that night. And, by summer's end, my direction became clear and I knew my time in New Jersey was over. I quit the job, made my exit, and headed back to Santa Barbara and then off again to Denver.

Even though my parents had moved to California, my father was still flying and commuting cross-country. It was stressful for him and later that year my Dad had a heart attack while commuting from Newark to Los Angeles. He wasn't the pilot, he was merely in transit ('deadheading' in industry jargon), and he nearly died. That event immediately ended his career as a pilot, causing a ripple effect and a major shift in our lives. I was scared and concerned; my future felt uncertain. Things would now be different. Although I enjoyed my studies, school became a bit of a drag that year between the family stress and feeling like I didn't belong. I felt confined in Denver with no car, no money and limited options, so I decided to leave. I would finish out the term, return to Santa Barbara and take a year off to work and travel a bit.

Santa Barbara was another new experience very different from LA and I didn't know anyone other than my family. After working as a delivery truck driver full time, I was able to venture out and explore the area on weekends. A popular destination was to go hiking and camping in the mountains behind Santa Barbara. It was there that I had my next spiritual encounter — a frightening near-death experience while mountain climbing.

I was camping with my younger brother and his friends. Climbing alone, I explored one modest little peak (more like a hill, I thought). It was easy going. I scarcely noticed that the trail was bare and slippery. While making my ascent, I had to stretch and jump to get higher and higher. After reaching the top, I realized that I was in a very precarious position. I was on the crest of the hill with nothing but bare, slippery rocks below me. Getting back down was going to be much more difficult. I knew that if I slipped, I would die. I was overcome with a palpable sense of dread. My heart was pounding; beads of sweat dripped into my eyes from the hot sun. My legs felt wobbly, my feet struggling to keep me stable on the rock face. It felt precarious and dangerous. I knew I had to confront this danger in order to save myself.

Suddenly, I was filled with an eerie calm, no longer nervous. I had to be still. I quieted my mind into complete, empty silence. In that exact moment, without thought or hesitation, I summoned a serene power from within and effortlessly, without fear, made the jump into midair to the precise landing spot below. It was a moment of utter clarity, without time and with not a thought in my head, only presence. After landing on my feet, I had no clue exactly how it happened, but I was able to easily make my way back down to the campsite area. The intensity of the experience, the feeling of presence, being only in the moment — that is something I have carried with me always.

What does one do after experiencing oneness and nothingness? In my case, I traveled and then went back to college. I was a mass of contradictions. On the one hand, I was attuned to spirituality and higher consciousness. On the other hand, I worked and had fun, too, which I did for quite a few years. What had felt special was put aside for a time.

After my father stopped flying, things changed and my parents settled into a different phase of living. My family, who had launched my love of travel, had shifted into being something smaller than what I was becoming. As I sought more and continued to grow, they wanted me to be successful, but not *too* successful, and we had clashes of values. Over time, our relationship became strained and contentious, and we had no contact for several years.

At the same time, my spiritual, adventurous side took a back seat as I focused on my career and my own growing family. My wife and I raised three wonderful daughters. We had some very good years and some very challenging ones. It seems that when my life was good, I was traveling. When life wasn't good, I wasn't traveling. Fortunately, our family has been able to take some great trips, including going to Europe together. It was a wonderful experience that created life-long memories for all of us. My children have inherited a love of travel and that is a joy we all share.

That spirit of creating memories encouraged me to reconnect with my family. It required a lot of effort and persistence, but I managed to lovingly re-engage with my parents and other family members. Sadly, my mother passed away and a year later, my younger brother took his own life. I made being close to my father and remaining brother a priority. We had a number of good years together before my father descended into dementia and was no longer entirely aware of his surroundings.

On one magical day, my brother and I took Dad up in a small plane for one last adventure in the air. With the good graces of the pilot, he was able to take the helm for one final flight. In that moment, watching Dad at the controls was deeply heartwarming and closed a loop between my childhood and my adult life. As a child, I was able to travel because of my dad. As an adult, I had the privilege to be with him in the air, to witness my dad flying once more.

When my dad passed less than a month later, I knew he had moved on to navigate the winds in heaven. My faith and awareness of a higher place comforted me. I was glad to have been able to spend time with him in his final days, easing his transition.

Now it is time for me to focus on my own journey, take charge of my destiny and fully integrate my ignited, awakened side into my daily existence. There will be new people and places to experience, and my inner work with energy and spirituality will continue. I also look forward to sharing what I've learned with others. This is my life's mission.

Even though air travel may have lost its glamour, I still get a thrill in anticipation of the next trip. I still marvel at the endless lights of a nighttime approach into Los Angeles, or the wonders of nature as seen from my window seat. When I travel, I can naturally tap into my inspired, creative side. Where shall I go next — and who wants to come with me?

You too can find adventure, both by traveling to new places and by seeking out new experiences. Bring an open mind and a notebook. What you see may surprise you; close your eyes (but open your mind) and you may be surprised even more.

IGNITE ACTION STEPS

1. **Follow your heart, be true to your inner passion, wherever it lies.**
   - Do what makes you happy and try your best to ignore the rest!
   - If your passion is unclear, ask spirit for guidance — and keep moving forward. (Meditation helps!)

2. **Life can be filled with ignited moments when you dare to win.**
   - Be willing to try new things and step out of your comfort zone.
   - Go ahead, sample the new food, choose a backroad, bring a friend.
   - Pick a spot in the world to learn about and plan a trip there.
   - Learn to integrate each new experience as a chance to grow.

3. **You can always find a positive outcome, even when it doesn't feel that way.**
   - Some lessons show their true meaning over time.
   - Even a heart attack, family tragedy or dementia can be an opportunity for loving expression despite the challenges.

4. **If you forget who you are, get back to what inspires you.**
   - Travel is central to that. Sometimes the best option is to hit the road.
   - Today is a new day — it doesn't have to look like yesterday.
   - It's your life — no one else's. Honor the gift and go full out!

Scott Owen Harrell
Owner/Founder, LifeTree Prosperity System
www.lifetree.info
ScoHarr
scottowenharrell

KERSTI NIGLAS

"Miracles happen when you greet life with open arms!"

I want to inspire the reader to know that sometimes it's okay to dream small. You have no idea how big your small dreams could become and how much your life could turn around. Be open to the world and don't be afraid to take chances because the only thing you can regret is never trying. I want to inspire you to appreciate the small achievements and small details in your life, and say "Yes" to all of them!

WHEN SMALL DREAMS IGNITE YOUR LIFE

"Dream big," is said a lot these days. Well, I've never had a problem with dreaming of any size. From early childhood, I could spend hours and hours fantasizing. My biggest dream of all was to wake up in the morning and have a room full of… bananas. Yes, bananas! Growing up as a Soviet child, all through my childhood we saw bananas only a few times. I remember my grandmother's birthday, where my aunt cut a green banana into four or five pieces so each of us could taste the exotic sweetness of the fruit.

Honestly, I didn't even dream about traveling and seeing a real banana tree one day; that seemed way too surreal and out of reach. When I was about nine years old, my friend taught me a trick. She told me that when you sleep at night and dream of bananas, try to grab one and hold it real tight so that it might come into the real world with you when you wake up. I didn't think that was too likely, but it was sure worth a try! Unsurprisingly, it never happened. But when I was 12, something truly unbelievable did happen! I had an incredible chance to go to Finland with my music school! Estonia, in 1991, had finally gotten out from under the Soviet Union. Before that, for Estonians to travel, special permission was required from Russian authorities. It was rarely granted.

I could hardly believe it! Finland, our fancy neighbors!!! Living near Tallinn, if the signal was strong, we were lucky to catch the Finnish TV signal. I had seen from TV commercials they have all these colorful candies, sweet desserts and bright fruits that were in the shops! It was like suddenly you were in Disneyland! Of course, we didn't have money to buy them, but that was fine, I had my imagination. It was unbelievable to see that this fantasy world really existed somewhere! I will never forget when our ship arrived in Finland. A guy named Jussi met us there and he gave each of us a ham sandwich and… a banana!!!! I sat in the back seat of the minivan and sighed with joy and the biggest smile. I'm in Finland and I'm about to eat a banana! Life can't get any better, I told everyone!

One thing struck me as funny… the Finnish kids bought candies from shops and then *ate* them… I mean, each ate *all* the candies from their own package… Never offering to others… It was impossible to understand for a Soviet child as when we got something good at home, we always shared so each of the people around us would get a taste (of course, you would choose the moment and the number of people who were wanting a piece of your precious bite). To this day, I still have a hard time eating candy in a public place and not offering it to everyone around me, but I forgave the Finnish kids… they did not know what they were doing.

Just before going home from that trip, our new friends gave us some money (about three to five euros). I already knew how to invest it wisely! I went to the harbor market and bought six bananas!!! The best investment ever! I had two sisters and a baby brother at home, so I thought that should have been enough for everyone. Of course, I had to eat one there, all by myself; one full banana for me! I sat down on the ground right there at the market and enjoyed my beautiful moment eating my banana. After I had the first one, I had a thought, "Could I have just one more?" I knew that I shouldn't; I had to share with my family, but *just one more* should be fine.

This conversation continued in my head until I had eaten FIVE of them! I was a really skinny child so I don't even understand how all these big bananas fit in my tiny body. At first, I was so incredibly happy! And then the guilt hit me — I had only *one* banana left to bring home. Well, at least I had one, right? I took it home (and oh, it was a hard fight not to eat it on the way!) and Mom split it into two. Both my sisters got half. My baby brother was too young to even understand the big secret we hid from him. The part that is hardest to admit is how much pressure I had to put on myself not to eat the last one.

Let me tell you… life was not bad, I had a trip plus, finally… I had bananas! Did I start dreaming bigger then? No. We were so used to dreaming about small things in my country that my dreams didn't know how much more was possible. Interestingly, there was a beauty in this, too. Every small thing could make me so happy! I did appreciate even the small moment, a piece of chocolate or candy, a hike in the forest, a new pair of socks or a blouse — each of these things felt like a *giant* happiness in my life.

You can imagine how I felt when, at the age of 22, after graduating from Technical University and working full time as a project manager, I got incredible news. In recognition of our good work throughout the year, our team would get to go to London! I will never forget the trip! I had a childlike enthusiasm for the underground system. I couldn't believe how genius it was! Such a huge variety of people on the train. I thought, "How cool it is that I can just indulge my curiosity and stare at them as everyone just read their newspapers and didn't pay any attention to anything else."

There were shops full of unbelievable choices. I saw my first musical, *Fame!* It left me in tears and shaking afterward. I couldn't believe my luck to experience something like this. I knew it was a once in a lifetime experience! I took some pictures with my cheap plastic 24-frame film-camera and was so excited to share them afterwards. My boyfriend took my film to the lab and came back with *devastating* news. He accidentally exposed the film and I had lost almost every photo. I wasn't angry at him as I knew it was an accident, but I cried from sadness as I knew it was unfixable. My boyfriend hugged me and said, "Don't cry, one day I will bring you back to London, I promise." I looked at him like he was crazy — no one gets to go to London twice in their lives!

If I only knew how many times he would keep this promise! If I only knew how much more life would have to offer as the Universe started to teach me to dream!

Life was going nicely, we got our first apartment, we were married, had two beautiful children, started to travel. Our younger daughter was a baby when we bought our first Canon camera. I started to read the manual but felt that I didn't understand everything well enough and wanted to know so much more. That's how I ended up in a two-month photography class for beginners. I will never forget my first lesson. I felt like something big hit me in the head and I finally woke up!

Everything started to make sense — my passion for drawing portraits, communicating, my passion for people, beauty, making them happy. This was a hard time for my husband as suddenly all his wife could talk about was photography. He even admitted at some point to being a little bit jealous. I couldn't blame him! Suddenly, a new life was in front of me. I saw EVERYTHING through the lens, and I loved it! I remember driving my car and blinking my eyes... frame... blink... blink... blink. Suddenly I was seeing the world as a wealth of possible pictures!

They say when you find your passion, the Universe starts to support you. Oh, how it did! In the most incredible ways! People just found me and, after a few months, my hands were full of work. I had an offer to work in a photo studio, then in the next moment, an incredible woman who is now one of my best friends offered to open our own photo studio together. All that happened in one year! I couldn't believe it! I had a photo studio, clients just came without any marketing, and me, my husband and our two young kids had opportunities to travel every few months. Slowly, I started to dream bigger.

My career changed completely in the springtime after my 34th birthday. There was an incredible chance to shoot an amazing Mindvalley event in Croatia called A-Fest. My friend had already shot that event for few times before and I knew that they needed someone from Europe for that one event only. I gathered my best work to show them what I could do. I remember getting the news that "I'm in" — I jumped, screamed, laughed and screamed some more! My world just exploded!!

Going to a huge event like that was really scary! I felt I had to take a leap out of my comfort zone. I knew one thing — it's a once in a lifetime experience (yeah, again!) and I was determined to make the most out of it and give it my absolute best. Oh, what an opportunity... those days changed my whole future! I discovered that people at that event were making 'stepping out of your comfort zone' really easy! Everyone was so welcoming and warm, so it was exciting to work hard and give your best! After that week, I went back home floating in a big huge pink bubble. I tried to bottle that feeling! After A-Fest, I believed that I could be so much more in this life.

After a few months, I received unbelievable news. I was officially part of the A-Fest photo team and booked for next A-Fest in Costa Rica! I thought, "How could something like that happen to a small village girl from tiny Estonia?"

I was the first child born to my family. We lived in Southern Estonia but moved to a Northern Estonian village when I was six. That meant I lost all my best friends in the south. At the age of seven, I got a skin infection that caused all my hair (waist long at the time) to be shaved off three times in a row. It was devastating for my self-confidence to be the bald girl at school and have the bigger boys feel there was no better entertainment than to pull the hat off the girl with no hair.

My father, who I learned at 16 was actually not my biological father, suffered with alcoholism for most of my childhood. His drinking burdened the family and during the hard Soviet times when the shops were empty, we had practically no money. Mom did her best to feed us four kids, teaching us to be practical. How could something like traveling to fascinating countries and taking beautiful pictures happen to a person with a background like mine?

I'm the girl whose hair got much thicker after shaving. I'm the one who slowly built up my self-confidence. I was a good student, attended university and did well in life. My father stopped drinking when I was 16 and all the family was so so proud (and still are — I just talked to my mom recently how much they still love each other). I love my sisters and brother all the same, no matter that they are technically half siblings. I am so grateful to my dad for not treating me differently from the others and always being MY DAD. And I'm lucky to have another cool man in my life as biological father. I'm thankful that I have two beautiful daughters, the most amazing, deep and beautiful friendships with people I never imagined would want to become my friends, and clients all over the world… It's all in our hands eventually, our stories… We have the power to redesign and improve them.

And my life was improving! Here I was, seeing magical cities, amazing sites and meeting dynamic people and that was also just a beginning. I stepped into a crazy rollercoaster of my own dreams and I had just one rule — always give your best!

It's interesting… When you do something with so much passion and love, you sometimes don't even notice how much you actually worked for it. I remember explaining to someone that things have just come easily for me. As I started to describe what I have done and how I work, only then did I finally realize how much energy I really had put in to make it happen. So much effort, so many sleepless hours, and so much learning! I was shooting and editing non-stop while raising two small kids and still giving my all to everyone. I was doing everything I could in every area of life, as all mothers do! So no, things don't come easy. But when they came with passion and love, it becomes effortless!

Giving my best each time has continued to be my secret. People *notice* passion and they want to experience it too.

Let me share one of my greatest adventures to date... It was freezing cold and I felt dizzy and weak. I felt like vomiting and I did — in front of 15 people. Giving birth to my two girls was a piece of cake compared to what I felt then. I looked over my shoulder and sat down to take a break. The sun was just about to show its first rays; the world was getting lighter and warmer. I looked down and I saw some thin clouds below me. Through those clouds I saw the massive crown of Africa. It was gorgeous! Painted with light pink, green and blue colors, one of the most beautiful sights I have ever seen. I stopped to take it all in, and appreciate the moment. I was climbing Mount Kilimanjaro.

Two weeks before that, I had received an email as one of A-Fest speakers, Eric Edmeades, was looking for two photographers to capture a trip to Kilimanjaro and a safari adventure. I laughed, thinking, these things don't happen, right? You just don't get offers like that in the middle of a Sunday afternoon! Right? My husband was giggling at the idea of me mountain climbing. So, I opened Google and typed, "Kilimanjaro where?" and "Kilimanjaro how hard?" The answers were, "in Tanzania" and "very hard but doable." I knew I wanted to give it a chance by answering "YES!" So I did. One sentence — "We can do it! Kersti and Karen, two photographers." One small problem... Karen did not know about it yet as she was on a cruise ship. I basically decided for both of us.

Three days later, I found myself facing a not-so-excited Karen, trying to convince her that this was the opportunity of a lifetime. I knew it would be so much better to do this with her, my friend. She gave in and we started to pack for Africa, all the time asking ourselves, "How many 'these things don't happen in my life' situations must one person have until she starts to believe that they do?" Well, I'm getting there! This trip ended up being one of the most amazing adventures I have ever had, and I gained a new loyal client and friend — Eric. He is another person in my life who has changed so much for me and still keeps on doing that. Sitting on my couch and saying "Yes" to something so unreal and crazy opened up next big door for me.

Life started to get really 'oh-these-things-don't-happen-in-my-life' crazy. Event after event, I met new people and got new offers. Each festival, workshop or class taught me much and brought me more gratitude than I can put into words. Suddenly I wasn't an Estonian photographer who *sometimes* travels; I became a photographer who travels the world!

Today, I finally know that there is so much more. Everything is possible with only a few tools: love, passion and work. Next year is about to bring more incredible adventures and I'm grateful, so grateful. Keep your eyes open; say "yes" rather than "no" to possibilities, even if they sound intimidating. If you don't take risks, then you don't give life a chance. Trust your inner feelings. Trust the Universe. When you do the right thing, you will feel the support!

IGNITE ACTION STEPS

Try to find your passion, but don't put too much pressure on yourself. Many people think that passion has to be something creative like photography… but it doesn't! Selling can be your passion! Accounting can be your passion! Cleaning can be your passion! Try to understand what really makes you happy and do it with joy! What others think is not important. When you do what is meaningful for you with passion, people will understand. It's one of the most beautiful things to see someone doing 'their thing' with great joy, commitment and happiness.

Give your best. Never stop pushing yourself to develop and be better! Open yourself to the world with humbleness and wonder; the world will return more than you give.

Kersti Niglas - Estonia
Photographer
www.kerstiniglas.eu
⊙ kerstiniglas

ALBERT URENA

"Inevitably, everything that happens to us, happens in our favor."

My intention in writing this story is to awaken in you the spirit of wonder, to question everything around you, so you can then express who you really are.

MOMENT OF CLARITY

Waiting to board an airplane at the airport has become something familiar in my life. In the span of two years, I have been on 14 trips of which eight have been to countries on different continents around the globe. My network of friends has expanded. I manifested my childhood dream of getting recognized on stage in the City of Angels: Los Angeles, California. All is aligned and getting better every day. I have people in my circle that push me continuously to become a better Albert Urena. It is good to feel like I have it all! Yet, it wasn't always like this.

Let me take you back to a time where it seemed that everything in my life was getting out of control.

I constantly lived with a victim consciousness and complaining attitude all the time, "Why is this happening to me? Why me? What did I ever do to deserve this?" Those were the phrases that constantly rumbled in my mind and came out of my mouth. It all started when I was a little boy with rosy, chubby cheeks, only four years old, and my father pulled on his worn and muddy leather work boots one morning, went to work and never came back. As a small child, I didn't comprehend what was going on. All I could remember is the loud crying and shouting happening in the room and I started crying myself. The next thing I knew, I'm visiting my dad in a cemetery box that has his picture on it. My immediate reaction was to ask my aunt, "Why did God take him? Don't people leave with God only when they're old?" My childhood innocence was robbed by this event and my doubt about there being a higher power began. This catastrophic situation led us to live a humble life, considered by many to be below middle class and my mother had to now play both parental roles in my life and the lives of my siblings.

Traveling had always been a foreign word to me. As a widowed mother of three kids, Mabel Alba couldn't take us or herself around the globe as she desired. We were constantly living paycheck to paycheck; getting on an aircraft seemed like a dream too far to reach at that time. Regardless of the obstacles, my mom did her best to take us to the resorts in our country. I remember enjoying the palm trees and swinging in the hammocks while drinking pina coladas. It was as if I was sitting on a cloud with happiness all around me, a smile that extended from ear to ear, a sensation of freedom and joy simultaneously. Ever since then, I knew I wanted more of this in my future.

Growing up, I've observed that everything *falls* into place for me during the *fall*. New jobs appear, new beginnings… autumn was always a time of rebirth and renewal for me. Right after college, on an October night, in my favorite season: Autumn. This time around, it was quite a different scenario and not what I was expecting at all.

I was sitting next to my critically sick mother as she rested in a hospice bed. Suddenly, I remembered her telling me that her dream was to visit Mexico. Our ancestors came from there. My intuition started whispering to me. It told me I had to honor my mother's desire to visit the land of our ancestors. My stomach started churning and I just knew I had to do it. I leaned close to where her head lay on the crisp white hospital pillow and gave my mother my word that, when she got out of the hospital, we were going to take that trip. I was convinced she was coming home soon, but unexpectedly, a few days later, my mother passed away. I felt crushed and heartbroken. I was filled with disbelief, shame and guilt for all the memories we didn't get to create together, all the promises made to her left unfulfilled. In an instant, I saw the woman who knew me best take her last breath in front of my very own eyes and my faith shattered in pieces like a broken mirror.

I fell down the rabbit hole of doubt and confusion about my place in the

Universe and what happens to us when we die. Do we go to Heaven? Is there really a Hell? Do we just cease to exist? All these questions were like bombs that destroyed the foundations of my life. The months following her death were emotionally intense for me. I had been grieving my father for the past 24 years; now, at the age of 28, I also had to grieve my mother's death. I was officially an Orphaned Adult.

The mere idea of going back to work to only pay bills and deal with regular life was a psychological torture in itself. I didn't know what to do. Frustration crept through my skin. I felt afraid to relapse into drugs again, as I did in my early 20s. For many days, all I could do was stay home and read.

The New Year brought a new dawn into my life. I received a letter in the post box and opened it; there was a life insurance check, the beginning of changes that would allow me to stay off work for half of the calendar year. Checking my email, I noticed a headline that mentioned my all-time favorite teachers would be together somewhere I had always wanted to visit: sunny California. My impulse guided me to book a flight to San Diego.

Travel awakened new thoughts and ideas in me. In San Diego, I had the honor of meeting my favorite author, Neale Donald Walsh. It was a surreal experience. I felt euphoria rushing through all my veins. I took a picture with him, the two of us standing side by side with our smiling faces close together. I also had the honor of meeting the boy with the broken brain, super genius and brain coach, Jim Kwik. We spoke about Alzheimer's disease, how it affected our grandparents and the reasons we are both passionate about Brain Health. I was finally able to speak up about the agony of seeing my grandparents not remembering my name, or who I was. Jim Kwik understood that pain. His empathy was healing for me. I found the tribe I had been praying for my entire existence.

As a teenager, I always felt like I didn't belong. In high school, I expressed that through drugs and fighting. After San Diego, I was on the verge of transformation. I met the most extraordinary people who today I'm blessed to call my friends and who make me feel accepted for who I am.

While in San Diego, I had the opportunity to enroll in the biggest adventure of my life: moving to a foreign country for a month with other students from all over the world. The location... Tallinn, Estonia! It's a cold northern country that used to belong to the Soviet Union and it's one of the most progressive countries in the world today. I thought to myself, "This is crazy man! I don't speak their language and this is totally something out of my comfort zone." I had never lived by myself before. I had never even been to another country other than my native island, the Dominican Republic. I felt anxious and scared, but the enrollment window was about to close and, again, I heard a whispering voice in my gut that insisted I go enroll. It told my Self that this was the beginning of a new chapter in my life, a phase that would push me to become a better version of *me*. Listening to that voice with everything in me feeling on fire, I walked over and enrolled in the program. It seemed like by Divine Appointment. While I was filling out my application, another person was enrolling in the same program. I had no idea that man, Yoram Baltinester, would end up becoming my Life Coach! Or that a year later, he would encourage me to share my story with the world.

Life was giving me a great opportunity to re-create myself anew. While Estonia was still many months away, I was filled with hope and possibility. Back home in the southern heat of Florida, inspired by the promise I had made to my mother, I started a home-based business. In just the first week, I earned an all-inclusive trip to Cancun, Mexico. I'm not a person to believe in coincidences, but I couldn't ignore this synchronicity! It was an attraction to my intention. Filled with a rush of excitement and goosebumps, I went ahead and booked the trip for myself and my siblings.

The Universe kept speaking to me, whispering in my ear that *travel* was the key to my healing and growth. My best friend works for a major airline and he invited me to fly with him to Milan, Italy, for a soccer World Cup friendly match between Colombia and Egypt. Fascinated by the idea of going to Europe, I decided to go early in May. The buildings in Italy were amazing, a huge contrast to the small cement structures I grew up in. My favorite building in Milan is the Duomo di Milano cathedral, which is the largest temple in Italy. It's heavily decorated and I was in awe of the art on the walls and doors. I fell in love with Milan because of the Gothic style architecture that I could see all around me.

The day of the soccer match, I met some nice people from Egypt. The only connection I had with Egyptians prior to that interaction was reading their stories in the Old Testament and the Hollywood movies. It was pleasant to find out they are regular human beings like I am. We spoke about the political issues and the division going on in their territory and we celebrated the Unity that Football brings to humanity. Standing side by side, we took a picture holding the Egyptian flag high in the air. After a weekend in Italy, my intuition started whispering in my ear, "Go to Thailand! Go to Thailand!" Once again, I listened. There, I visited many of their holy temples and experienced the Buddhist religion up-close. It was a beautiful sight, seeing altars all across the city... seeing silent monks walking in their orange robes. Inside the temples, we had to take our shoes off out of respect for the Universal Presence. Meditating there was truly a Divine Experience.

After Italy and Thailand, it was time to go to Tallinn. Estonia was transformative and caused a great shift within me. I was surrounded by people from all ethnicities and religions and we connected in profound ways. I could relate to their stories, even though we each came from different parts of the world. The more individuals I met from different parts of the world, the more I identified myself as an Earth Citizen.

I came back from Tallinn, Estonia with a healed heart and an open mind and ready for the next adventure: the trip I had won to Cancun. It had been five years since I had last been on a plane with my brother and sister and I felt truly excited to be taking them on a dream vacation! We arrived at the resort and were immediately upgraded to the presidential suite. It was like the Universe was saying, "Your dream trip isn't dreamy enough without a little extra luxury!" I was stunned by the glamorous apartment. We had a private pool in our balcony!!!! I thought to myself, this is what we work for! To make a living... LIVING!

Fascinated by the Mayan civilization and their culture, I went to explore the Quintana Roo area. Mexico, like most Latin America countries, comes from two of the major ancient Meso-American cultures, those being the Aztecs and the Mayans. My Adventurous Spirit took me to the Chichen Itza ruins, one of the Seven Wonders of the Ancient World. I was definitely filled with a spirit of wonder!

I found myself standing in the middle of a ball court about the size of a football field with a massive stone border. The ball courts were intentionally placed in ceremonial centers of ancient Mayan cities and the games were serious affairs solving political and social issues. Losing the match meant decapitation, with the heads of the losing team displayed on a skull rack beside the entrance to the courts. Talk about a way to spread fear and obedience!

At that time, I couldn't comprehend how in the world these people were able to play a game like that. The court was enormous with huge, circular stone rings on the top jutting outwards. The objective was to get a round, heavy ball into those rings without using your hands. Those people must have been in great physical shape!

The ball courts are an amazing piece of architecture in the most surprising of ways. When you are standing inside them, you can make the song imitating the Quetzal bird (the bird featured on the Guatemalan peso) and the sound from the northern wall would be heard on the southern wall. Listening to the echoed sound of my own voice gave me chills. It was the most profoundly amazing experience. Being in that space opened my eyes to understand what Steve Jobs said in his legendary interview, "Everything around us was made up by people no smarter than us. Once you understand, you will never be the same again." At that moment I knew I would never again follow life blindly.

On the way to the Cenote (an underground purified watering hole), walking through the jungles of Mexico, we encountered a priest preparing for a beautiful Mayan ceremony. He invited us to participate in this powerful spiritual practice where you go down to the mouth of the earth to symbolically die and rise up again as a newborn believer.

My last stop was the city of Coba where another pyramid stood tall. Everything in my past had brought me to this 'Golden Moment in Time.' Inspired by the Divine within me, I decided to climb all the way to the top. The pyramid is made up of huge stepping stones. Each step demanded that I really stretch my legs to reach the next one. It took tremendous balance and endurance. By half way up, I was wondering if it wouldn't be easier to turn around and go back. But once I reached the pinnacle, I had the entire Northern Peninsula in front of me. I could feel the wind on my skin and the heat of the sun. My body relaxed into the moment with a huge sense of relief. Looking down, I felt like I could see all of North America in a single glance. I felt like I had the eyes of a god, looking down over every building and person on the continent. It was a symbolic climb to enlightenment.

That's my Ignite moment. In that instant, I felt my soul being freed from the bondage of bullshit rules and beliefs I grew up following. In that moment, I became what my mentor Vishen Lakhiani calls 'Culture Hacker.' My eyes could see the Culturescape for what it is, just a web of ideas and systems to live by, a Matrix that I just been unplugged from. I could feel the Love of my parents, honoring the promise I made to my mother. I could feel my siblings by my side. I could feel the support of all my ancestors. I was connected to everyone and everything that had influenced who I was up until then. And in that moment, I knew I was ready to make my dent in the Universe.

I am forever grateful for my mother, being wise with her finances and being prepared for the worst case scenario. Trauma can take years to heal and can take unexpected turns. For me, traveling was the cure for my grief and the means by which I discovered who I really am and unlocked my connection to the Oneness of the Universe.

My Ignite Moment came during a time of *Kensho*. *Kensho* is a term defined by Rev. Michael Bernard Beckwith where he states that we awaken through pain and hard situations. Your life may see many hardships and much pain; it is a part of life designed to uncover your growth. I received an 'aha' moment in the deepness of my soul with a sense of peace in my heart that surpasses all understanding. I learned a fundamental truth of life: Inevitably, everything that happens to us happens in our favor. You can get through anything, no matter how difficult it seems to overcome. There's a light at the end of the tunnel. You are not alone and you exist in relation to all that is around you. There is more that unites us than what separates us. Life is always working for you and aligning people, situations and circumstances to help you express who you really are.

IGNITE ACTION STEPS

- **Honor your feelings.** Listen to the whispering voice within you (Your Intuition) and act on its guidance.

- **Question everything!** All the rules and beliefs you grew up following, you can use the Brule Test by Vishen Lakhiani. Get clear on your Heart Virtues, Super Power and Life Purpose. A Life Coach can help.

- **Travel** as much as you can and experience the diversity of cultures around the world. You are more alike than you realize. Embrace the concept of Unity.

Albert Urena - United States
Transformational Leader
realalberturena@gmail.com
alberturena2transform
albert-urena

YENDRE SHEN

"When you're lost, trust your inner compass to guide you."

My wish for you, the reader, is that you follow the adventures your heart takes you on; that you find the courage and strength to face what you most fear. In coming through to the other side, you'll have discovered more of yourself that you didn't know was there, and you'll find the place that you are most at home.

FINDING HOME

My adventurous spirit was born from exploring the fields behind my father's noodle factory in South America. My sisters, being seven and thirteen years older, worked in the factory. I was five years old and was often left alone to entertain myself. I did so by roaming the vast open field, where wooden racks lay row upon row, holding trays of loosely coiled noodles drying in the hot sun. As a child, looking into the distance, there would seem like nothing but sky and space.

I would venture out beyond the rows of racks, wandering off on my own, studying the grass and plants on my path as I made my way, careful to avoid snakes. One plant, in particular, intrigued me. I gave it the name 'shy grass.' Once I touched its fanned leaves it would close up, folding itself as if in prayer and would not open again for some time. I would play with it for hours, finding one, touching it with my finger, and watching it fold up, then finding another, repeating the game again.

My rambling led me to discover a weather-faded wooden house at the far end of the field. I realized an old man lived there. I don't think my family knew of him. It was only because I went further and further each time that I came across his property. I cautiously approached his place a few times, and once I did so while he was inside an outdoor stall, showering. There were small gaps in the wooden panels, I pressed my eye to one of them and saw for the first time a man's naked body. It startled me and I never went back.

My curiosity has gotten me near danger a few times, but something always brought me back safely. These events would set the stage for my adventurous spirit to grow and expand. They sparked my awe in nature, instilled my urge to roam and ignited the thrill of putting myself at peril. I would be pulled closer by curiosity to the edge of the precipice of danger, often literally. Flirting with the risk of death has a particular appeal to a certain crowd. Mine would be heights, but I wouldn't know it yet.

My first experience on a plane was when I left China with my two sisters to meet our father who had moved to South America to make a better life for us. I was four. We didn't speak any English. The plane had stopped; while some passengers got off, others remained in their seats. My sisters and I didn't know what was happening. I was thirsty and we motioned to the stewardess for some water. She noticed the signs pinned on our clothes indicating our destination: Guyana. My sisters would tell this story about how if I hadn't asked for water we would have missed our stop.

The second time I got on a plane I was nine and I was moving to Canada with my father. Canada is an ideal place for those who are drawn to the majestic beauty of nature. I learned to canoe on the lakes of northern Ontario when I was 16. That summer I joined Junior Rangers and was stationed in Sioux Lookout. My memories of paddles dipping into serene still waters, making the canoe glide gracefully across the lake, passing along endless tree-lined shores will stay with me. My family cannot relate to my love for nature and the wilderness. They cannot understand why I would want to sleep on the ground in a sleeping bag and not shower for days.

Canoeing and camping became my way of exploring nature as I joined the University of Toronto Outing Club (UTOC). On one trip, we paddled on a lake that emptied out into Georgian Bay. Somehow my canoeing partner and I got separated from the group. It was the days before smartphones. In that instant, I remember I became very still and quiet, seeking within myself to sense the right direction to rejoin our group. We may not have been apart for long, but I felt my heightened awareness and I recognized that it turned up whenever there was potential danger.

My love of travel was awakened at 18. It was my third time on a plane; I was heading to Europe with my first boyfriend. We were going to explore England, Switzerland and France on our bicycles. Seeing places by foot, bike, car, train, boat and plane — each mode of transportation offers a different level of intimacy and, on this trip, we used them all. Our perspectives were widened as we were steeped in a different culture. I wanted to take in everything, the streets, buildings, cafes, shops, museums and parks. I could feel the difference of age and history through the art, architecture and people from where I lived. Canada is a relatively young country and in Toronto, being multicultural, I hadn't noticed my Asianess as much until then.

The possibility of getting lost is always imminent when we are in unfamiliar territories. It happened on the streets of London when our bikes got separated at a major busy roundabout intersection. Toronto streets are a grid. If you're ever lost, a series of right turns could bring you back to where you started. This is not how London is laid out, as I discovered; a series of turns did not take me back to where I wanted. In fact, it took me away from rejoining my travel companion.

When you're lost, a good thing to do is to stop and assess your situation. I didn't stop, orient myself, ask someone for help or directions. I kept on riding. I didn't have a physical map but I had a mental one. We'd been staying at a bed and breakfast for a few days and we used it as our home base. My keen awareness seemed to narrow and expand at the same time. I could take in more information and remain focused on relevant details. It was dark by the time I found my way back. He must have been terribly worried and upset that I didn't stop and wait for him to find me. When he saw me, he was so relieved and happy that he just hugged me tightly for a long time.

That trip showed me the richness within different places, people and cultures. The experience gave me the confidence to travel by myself. I went back to England, then Germany, Holland and the Czech Republic: the magnificent cathedral of Cologne, bike riding along the Rhine river, passing by vineyards, the fascinating museums and picturesque streets and canals of Amsterdam, and the magical fairytale city of Prague. These images are filed into my memory banks.

After close to two months away, I began to feel homesick. I was surprised how painful that feeling is, as I had never felt it before. It resembled the deep yearning I had felt.for a person, but the yearning was for a place. Once I landed in Toronto, the feeling subsided, replaced by relief and I knew then where home was for me. It seems we discover something we didn't know about ourselves when we leave what's familiar.

Coming back, my perspective was broadened. I recognized the vastness within Canada to explore. I didn't have to fly over oceans or to another continent to discover things. I visited the east coast and west coast; the diverse characters of the people I met and witnessing their uniqueness helped me understand more of the country I call home.

When I visited the Rockies, despite all the beautiful places and things I had seen, there was something that made my soul sing the moment I saw mountains up close. Their majestic grandeur gave me an almost out of body experience. I wanted to be formless and be able to reach out and touch them. They called to me. This must be how it felt for those early alpinists who were wild at heart, and decided to set out to overcome their challenges to see the world from the top of those peaks. But it would be a few years before I'd be among those who've had that experience.

I wondered if the mountains are an extension of my fascination with rocks. Since I was a child, I would find ones that are special, that would be my favourites and I wouldn't give them up, so I ended up with collections of them. I still have some in boxes, because they came from places I visited and they hold the memories of those moments. Moments like hiking the spectacular white quartzite mountains of Killarney Provincial Park, which are hills compared to the Rockies. And the impressive 100m high sheer granite wall that rises out of Mazinaw Lake at Bon Echo Provincial Park.

However, it was the sight of seeing people on that granite wall at Bon Echo that stretched my imagination. I was canoeing and noticed they were climbing up the rock. A boat with the words 'Alpine Club' on its side was shuttling them across the lake to the wall. I was mesmerized and smiled in delight. I said to myself, "I want to do that."

The first time I went rock climbing was with UTOC at Metcalfe Rock. It was on top rope, like a pulley system, so as you climb a belayer takes up the rope slack to ensure you don't fall if you let go. This setup is possible if the cliff doesn't exceed half a rope length: that's about 25-35 meters. The rock face at Bon Echo is 100 meters high from the surface of the water, which would require climbing 3-4 times on top rope to reach the end of the cliff. I had to learn new skills in traditional (trad) lead climbing to become one of those people I saw at Bon Echo.

I did so and joined the Alpine Club of Canada (ACC). I vividly remember the first time I attended their annual general meeting. I picked up a pamphlet of all the huts they had across Canada. Many of them were in the mountains of British Columbia and Alberta. Looking through it, I felt like a child who's opened up a catalogue of toys I dreamed of having for Christmas. Climbing became my bliss, my passion and addiction. Much of my traveling evolved around it from then on. It challenged me in ways that were exhilarating and confronting. It put me back in places I recalled as a child where I was testing the boundaries of how far I could go before I got into trouble.

Trad lead climbing is not for everyone. It requires focus and a certain head-space to be able to "go all in" when your survival instinct doesn't want you to. It's an intimate confrontation with fear and discomfort. When I reach the most difficult part of a climb, the crux, it's usually where I'm physically and mentally at my limit and a part of me wants to quit. But I don't give in to it. I devise my approach to overcome it. Sometimes, this place is at a roof on a wall and the only way out is to move into the open space, into the void where I feel most exposed and vulnerable, away from what's comfortable. This happens in life too, where we'll remain stuck until we welcome discomfort.

I recognized the call of the mountains was waiting for me. I joined the ACC General Mountaineering Camp (GMC) for my first mountaineering experience. We went into the Bugaboos of the Purcell Mountain Range. Our first day we hiked into base camp. We traveled across spectacular landscapes with breath-taking views of white and pink snow, mountains and turquoise lakes. When we arrived at the top of the moraine, I saw the tongue of the Vowell Glacier, although receded, rolled out like a lumpy carpeted welcome mat, inviting us to embark on the adventures ahead. Looking down near the foot of the glacier, our camp and tents were set up as our home for the week to come.

The next day, I learnt the basics of mountaineering in snow school: how to use my crampons and ice axe, and how to arrest my fall should I slip. We had expert and amateur guides take us up peak after peak each day. I was grateful for their skills and knowledge that allowed me the incredible experience and views from the summits we reached, and I was proud I got there by my own physical abilities being pregnant.

After having my two kids, I returned to the mountains for four consecutive years and I gradually became a more seasoned mountaineer. I was able to ful-fill the dream of staying in alpine huts while exploring the mountains: like the Bill Putnam Hut at Fairy Meadows while at the Adamant Group of the Selkirk Mountains. My favorite is Sorcerer Lodge near the Iconoclast Group of the Selkirks. Flying in by helicopter, I caught sight of the red and white lodge on top of a rock outcrop above a lake. It's surrounded by wild beauty and moun-tains on its outer edges. I had a bed with sheets, blankets and pillows, and the view of the Nordic Peaks from my bedroom window. There was a sauna and we had a cook who made us delicious meals every day.

How spoiled compared to the stark contrast of getting out of warm sleeping bags and unzipping tents at 2 AM in the morning, confronting the harsh elements outside, to leave in the dark and begin your journey to a summit. What is this tug on our heart strings that makes people like me willing to endure the stinging pain of razor sharp winds, crossing frigid cold rivers, walking on knife-edge ridges, making tedious steps on steep ice or snow and finding our way in treacherous terrains? Why put our lives on the line just to touch a part of the planet rarely seen by human eyes?

When you feel you've reached the edge of the earth and you're looking over mountain ranges upon ranges, you sense you're communing with God. In the midst of beauty it's a glimpse into the magical timelessness of creation. Feeling the interconnectedness of all things, the powerful forces and grandness of nature contrasting the smallness of my own existence, helps me acknowledge how precious this life is.

I felt this interconnectedness also during a silent 10-day Vipassana meditation course. Getting to the top of a mountain is very much like meditation, where you don't respond to the pain in your body or mind, but focus only on one step at a time. I had the expansive feeling of being formless like the first time I saw mountains. The Vipassana experience created a quiet stillness in me. It silenced the restlessness, the need to escape; I didn't have to go too far and hard to reach places to experience creation. The Universe within me is as vast and beautiful as the nature I saw outside of me.

I realized then I've been running away from my discomfort since, as a child, going into the fields behind my father's noodle factory. The discomfort of not belonging. I sought solace and refuge in the solitude of nature, as there's no judgement or criticism, only the presence of being. It's at the risk of getting lost in the physical unknown that I found myself. I see now I was never lost as I had my inner compass guiding me, to find the places and people that I belonged to — like the outdoor nature enthusiasts with UTOC and the community of climbers and mountaineers with the ACC.

And recently, meeting JB Owen and fellow authors at the Vancouver Ignite book launch, I experienced the kinship of people passionate about sharing their stories to inspire and give voice to others. Being sensitive, I'd learned as a child to keep my views and ideas quiet. Writing helped me rekindle my own self-expression that was lost. Creativity is the realization that we're boundless. Like climbing, mountaineering and meditating, writing is a process that brings us to knowing ourselves deeply and differently.

Discovering my various soul families felt like finally arriving at the destinations that were waiting for me. My adventurous spirit had been leading me home all along. The exciting part is that the adventure continues, the journey doesn't end here...

There are parts of us that lie asleep, that take exposing ourselves to new experiences to awaken and identify what resonates with our souls. We think we are looking for something outside when we travel, then we realize we're getting to discover what's within us. It becomes a homecoming to ourselves when we push our boundaries and leave our comfort zones. It allows us to shift perspectives and view things from different vantage points. Sometimes these experiences are to reclaim the parts we didn't realize we've lost. Or we think we're lost, and it's just our meandering path to finding yourself. Trust in your inner compass to find your way home and take you where you want to be.

IGNITE ACTION STEPS

Here are some things to practice to guide you in your journey home.

- Connection and Interconnection: Allow yourself to be in nature, as well as with people; relate to all creatures, human or not.

- Belonging: Find your place of home. This can be a physical space or your unique clan of people who accept and support you.

- Meditation: Spend quiet time with yourself and look inside your inner Universe.

- Journaling and Writing: Write down your insights and observations. Become aware of the connections you see in your life.

Yendre W. Shen - Canada
Naturopathic Doctor & Bowen Therapist
Innerguidance.ca

ELENA RODRÍGUEZ
BLANCO

"The purpose of life is not out there to be found; it is to BE and FEEL alive."

This story is an invitation for you to open up to the most significant journey of all: being alive. Imagine if, the next time you travel, instead of *'must-see'* lists, you create *'to-feel'* lists. Think of all the feelings you want to have in a particular day and then simply live them as you go along! Create memories that will BE forever!

BECOME YOUR AUTHENTICITY

My heart was pounding in my head. My feet felt as if they weighed 60 pounds each. I lacked oxygen, and I felt dizzy and nauseous. I was fighting my body to continue this trek up the last few hundred meters to the highest peak I had ever been to. The dialogue, the self-motivation talk and the internal struggle were real. I honestly did not know if I would make it. All I could hear was my own voice inside my head telling me to go on, that it would be worth it, that I could do it.

Hiking more than 16,500 feet (5,033 meters) to the top of Tserko-Ri mountain in the Langtang Valley in Nepal was one of the most challenging physical experiences I've had. I reached the summit, took pictures, saw the incredible view and felt accomplished. I then headed back down the steep, sandy trail, trying to forget my body existed. When I arrived back to Kyangjin, the base camp town, three hours later I went straight to bed to lie down, close my eyes and disappear.

Even though I had grown up in a mountainless region of Central America by the Pacific Ocean, the mountains had become my place of solace. As a child, I didn't have access to these monuments of earth, grounded through centuries, bringing us a different perception of what is below us with every step. As soon as I discovered the joy of hiking, I knew that the Tserko-Ri peak would be my initiation into a lifetime of mountains and trails. The busier my life got, the more I took an interest in spending time in silence and solitude.

I learned how to pack and unpack backpacks, and discovered the subtle differences between different types of rain. I had limited gear, yet throughout the next few years, I would still make it to the mountains in Iceland, Montenegro, Alaska and also the Pyrenees next to my home. At first, I started hiking in search of silence. I wanted to 'unplug' from my busy, city life. I then kept going for the new challenges it offered, the sense of accomplishment, the fact there was a clear goal and a way to get there. I would make myself summit no matter what, literally through rain, hail, snow or shine. I liked the ego boost I got from checking another mountain off the list.

Many mountains later, during the spring, it was my second time hiking the Camino Primitivo of Camino de Santiago (the Way of St. James), known as the original and primitive way. Having done this trek before I had seen people do it for 'penance', prayer and meditation. I had seen the walk done in many different ways, some people even walking on their knees. Something inspired me to try something new myself and I started the day's trek barefoot. I was curious to see what would change. No socks, no shoes, just feet on the ground.

In the Amazon jungle in Brazil, I had seen children running barefoot next to insects that were twice the size of their toes. I was impressed at how fearlessly they placed their feet as they ran, without even looking down. In my hikes, especially when I am getting tired, I look down at my shoes and let my gaze follow the pace of how one foot follows the next, and I focus on that one next step. I completely lose perspective of what is around me. I forget to look up at the birds and trees and any surroundings. I am just focused on making it through. The idea of removing my boots — that protected me from the world and helped me get to where I was going fast — was a little terrifying. At the same time, I enjoy exploring new ways of doing things and this exercise was in line with something that would get me outside of my comfort zone.

I took my shoes off and started walking very, very slowly. I glued my eyes to the terrain all around me and ever so gently put my feet down, noticing how every indent on the ground was a possible hazard. And then it started slowly, but there it was... hello pain! The smallest, tiniest rock was having an immense impact on my body. I was feeling sensations in my feet I didn't think possible, so much so, I started forgetting that at this new slow pace, I would not meet my required walking distance for the day.

I also noticed the chatter in my head — the one that I use for self-motivation and overcoming obstacles and talking my way through things — had gone quiet. I might possibly have shocked it! This simple act of putting my foot on the ground, feeling every sensation that came along with it, breathing through it and taking the next step made me feel more alive and more vulnerable than ever. I felt the natural weight of every step, much like in Tserko-Ri, except this time, I was connected to my body. I was choosing to walk slowly and my destination was nowhere. I was just walking to fully walk. I don't think I had ever done that.

Others on the path greeted me, stopping to check my well-being and possibly also my sanity. I kept going, starting to explore little patterns that were emerging. For example, I noticed the moment I would trust and just place my foot 'wherever' and look up at the surroundings... the pain would ease dramatically. My perception of the 'fear-of-stepping-on-the-ground' would dissipate as I became more in tune and trusting of every step. Because, seriously, what could happen? I wasn't in a jungle; at most I could step on an ant. I realized my fear had absolutely no foundation.

The pain was still there, but I felt I could pick up the pace. With every step, I took long, deep breaths and smiled. My mind was blank. Here I was, walking; an action I took for granted and performed daily, now turned into a whole new, extraordinary, multisensory experience. This one act had just turned my entire trek into a complex and beautiful journey with layers unfolding with every step. My self-talk and internal motivational speeches had also gone silent. I wasn't running or competing to get anywhere, I was just simply walking. It was about walking, about feeling my whole foot on the ground, about not having to go anywhere or do anything. It became about *being*.

For many, travel is a reflection of how to do life and how to measure success. A whole mythos has grown up around that idea. We build our personal bucket lists from what seemed like impossible destinations not more than 30 years ago. And I had bought into that mythos. When I visited a city, I used to run through the 'must-see' places, ensuring I got better pictures and food than my friends. I was 'doing' countries, checking-off monuments, buying the feeling of 'living like a local.' This is just 'doing' travel and consuming 'to-do' lists, to have a local experience. I was hiking mountains to 'do' summits, to check mountains off the list, to have a sense of accomplishment that only comes from having an even more extensive list.

I came to realize I was doing the same in life: setting myself goals, projects and challenges to overcome without looking at the journey. Happiness is the goal, rather than the feeling we have at every full step on the ground. This is a never-ending cycle. I then started asking, every time I accomplished something, how much of my authentic me, really all of me, had been engaged during the journey? What parts had I forgotten along the way? In all the running and fretting, what feelings, sensations, pains and happiness did I ignore?

We see the promise happening at the end, once it is done. But when you actually get there... when you are at the top of the mountain, you are just too tired to enjoy it, especially if you run your way up! All we have then is a picture, yet we realize that we had nothing to prove. The purpose of life is not out there to be found; the purpose of life is to BE and FEEL alive.

In my twenties, I founded a company in the travel space seeking to find the Authenticity of travel experiences. The more I delved into the way people travel and *why* they travel, the more I realized traveling is not so much about going anywhere, but rather about how we want to feel throughout the experience itself. Travel is not about where you are going or what you are doing, but rather, the moment you find yourself in. Traveling is about your relationship to 'aliveness,' to the whole process of travel itself.

The adventure is not about where you go. It's found in every moment of how you get there. The process of HOW we do the planning, the actual hello we say to the air steward, and the smiles we give to the people around us... it's all more significant than you know. Most people travel and come home needing another holiday because they have been rushing, rather than slowly walking and feeling it all. And travel is, of course, a metaphor of how we do life, how we plan and live. I always wonder what would happen if, instead of 'to-do' lists we would have 'to-be' lists, where we would list all the feelings we want to have in a particular day.

Back at Camino, I realized I had been walking for several hours with bare feet. My toes were wiggling with excitement, like they had been let out of a cage and into freedom. I sat down at the next stop, took one foot in my hand and massaged and cleaned it. I also thanked it for getting me this far. Then I did the same with my other foot. I don't think I had ever thanked my feet for allowing me to walk paths and trails and get places. I felt connected, silent, grateful and real.

I wasn't resting because of tiredness; I had stopped because I wanted to thank my feet. Now, that was new! There was no lack of oxygen or urgency this time. This experience was completely different. I could slow down, surrender and receive on this journey. This didn't mean I would never wear shoes again, yet my relationship with my feet, the ground and each step had changed forever. I chose *slow travel*. I then became more curious about the path even when it was foggy or unclear. I wanted to connect with how I would feel or could feel versus those days where I did it just to take a picture or know if I could make it to the top.

I started loving the moments where I could help wash the dishes after a meal with a family in Sarajevo rather than visit the city itself. I would travel to places for the first time and stay in only one of the locations on the itinerary for the whole time. I began reading books in jungles, many times just sitting there in a porch, on a hammock, on the ground. I started traveling in silence and speaking only when necessary. I found silence helped me to take more layers away. Silence allows the transcendent to be heard, seen, felt and lived. I began realizing that in search of the authentic, I had to strip it all down and find the joy of aliveness in the most ordinary of moments.

As you start taking layers away, you realize that what you remember is not a collection of just moments, but instead of extraordinary feelings and sensations. Hearing, seeing, and living authentically in every single instant can make anything extraordinary because it is being *lived*. And in this sense, living life in a constant state of awe comes from your capacity for seeing with new eyes, hearing with fresh ears, sensing with your whole body, everything that you already know. Perhaps the most extraordinary way to travel is to go deeper inside, feeling more.

When you start discovering the depth of being in a place, you can peel off the exterior layers and continue finding different facets of a city and country. This increased depth becomes an immediate invitation to look at the surroundings under different perceptions. For example, that same street you walk on every day is shared with people who make that street their home. What is their perception of living on the streets? What stories do they have to share? How do they view and understand life? As I started exploring and talking to the homeless, I realized that many of my beliefs about their situation were unfounded and I had missed the real gifts in seeing the city through their eyes and experiences. As I built friendships, I knew I wanted to share their stories, offering an entirely new way to see the city and to give back at the same time. So I visited the non-profit associations working with the homeless community in my town and proposed giving them the opportunity to work. I started asking, what if these individuals could learn to tell the stories to travelers in the format of a 2-3 hour neighborhood tour? In turn, visitors would have an authentic, first-hand story of someone with whom they probably may not interact very often in their lives while they visit a city. That allowed me to create employment and empower a person who has been outside of society for an extended period to be heard, seen and valued. This ensures a cycle of good that is very much needed, especially in city landscapes.

This and other similar experiences I co-designed and co-created with non-profits around the world became the foundation for my company *Authenticitys*: a social impact experience platform that connects travelers with humanity and the environment plus experiences around the world. We have partnered with hundreds of nonprofits in cities and designed travel experiences that gives a unique perception and allows one to give back and make the city better. Each and every one of our social impact experiences is mapped out to the United Nations Development Goals. Hundreds of thousands of travelers, students and companies have bought our experiences to impact the cities they live in and while traveling abroad.

Authenticitys is transforming travel. It is about relationships and adding value and doing good in the places you visit. The invitation is for you to think during your travels: How can I leave the city better than I found it? How can travel have a positive impact? How can I build a connection to the organizations that are working to solve this city's challenges? These are the questions you can ask yourself next time you travel to get the deepest experience possible. Having your must-feel list and widening your awareness will make you feel the most alive at all times and will allow you to travel and experience your true, authentic self everywhere.

IGNITE ACTION STEPS

- **Make a 'To Be' List.** Have a look at your to-do list for the week and take note of what feelings come up while you read it. Associate a feeling to each activity. Look at those feelings and connect a positive or negative emotion to each task. Decide if there is a way to connect more positive emotions to each one and how you want to feel throughout your day? Can you make changes to your 'to-be' list? Practice adding sensations you wish to have throughout the day to your list, assigning yourself a task that helps you get to that feeling. For example, 'be peaceful' might be associated with breathing and watching the sunset that day.

- **Take note of your self-talk.** What words, language and tone are you using? When do you use self-talk the most? Are you self-talking yourself through things you don't really like? Can you start 'wanting to do' your life? What changes can you make to ensure your day is full of 'I want' rather than 'I have to?' For example, if you often catch yourself saying, "I have to get up early and exercise." but then never follow through, try changing your self-talk to "I want to have a moment of active physical activity at some point today."

- **Slow down.** Make a list of 10 things in your ordinary life that you could do differently so that you can more fully experience every aspect of the experience. This works best if they are repetitive tasks you know well. Think of engaging more of your five senses every time. For example, when washing the dishes, take a moment to get lost in the scent of your dish soap and to feel grateful for the people helping you with the chore. When traveling, get some local soap and get lost in the scent of that place.

- **Do one thing a day that you have never done before that triggers a strong emotional response.** Gift something to a stranger, give your number to a good-looking human, pick up plastic on your way to the office. Keep challenging yourself to feel more deeply every single day.

- **Plan a slow travel trip.** In the next trip you plan, detach from the destination and the 'must-do's,' and focus on how you want to feel during your days. Enjoy being in the moment and exploring different sides of yourself in the experience. Include deep, quiet moments like a silent meal, a chill-out afternoon reading while soaking in the energy of the place, or perhaps a barefoot walk.

Elena Rodríguez Blanco - Spain
Founder, Experience Designer and Curator
elena.rodriguezblanco@gmail.com
www.elenarodriguezblanco.com
www.authenticitys.com
authenticitys

ALEANU IMBERT MATTHEE

"The obstacles to your dreams are never in your heart."

I would like to show you through my story that life is what you manifest. Anything is possible, even helping those in need halfway across the world. Answer your calling and realize your dreams. The obstacles are never in your heart. All you need to do is clear them from your mind.

LIGHTING SKY LANTERNS

The dirt road followed an emerald green mountain ridge smack on the border between Thailand and Myanmar. We had just left the camp leader's hut that clung to the steep terrain along with hundreds of other shacks in the sprawling Shan refugee camp. From our side path, we stepped onto the rutted red dirt road and turned south. My guitar, in its soft case, hung from a strap on my shoulder. My heart quickened inside my chest as we began walking up the camp's main arterial to the center. I was nervous. I had been asked to perform during the camp's celebration of the Shan calendar New Year. I tried hard not to show I was sweating bullets to the others who were with me. On the right, I was flanked by the camp leader, on the left by two of my colleagues from our aid organization.

How did I get myself into this?

I had brought my Baby Taylor guitar with me on this mission just to noodle around on it in camp while no one was listening, but in a refugee village where the shacks have thin walls or no walls at all, even my quiet picking and singing were noted quickly. Word spread of a tall westerner singing American songs on his bunk. Soon, requests poured in to include me in the New Year's evening line-up. Reluctantly, I relented. I knew at least one tune fairly well. That afternoon, I practiced the song I agreed to play: Bob Dylan's *I Shall be Released*.

But was I ready?

The moment we appeared on the main road, kids came running out of nowhere. They skipped, they laughed, they pointed fingers at us and they ran circles around our little procession in the dust. The camp leader did nothing to discourage them. He just smiled. This was New Year's eve: a time for the Shan to celebrate being alive and to forget, even for a few hours, their struggle for independence, the burning of their villages by Burmese government troops and their traumatic escape from their ethnic homeland. I picked up my pace.

I reminded myself that we here for humanitarian reasons: to support the healing, recovery and mobility of refugees who had been injured by landmine accidents. That was our specialty throughout Southeast Asia, where war had raged for decades in Vietnam, Cambodia, Laos and inside Myanmar. In and near the refugee camps, we set up prosthetics workshops and supported husbandry projects for the accident survivors and their families. Several of them had just visited us at the refugee camp that morning, showing us their new artificial legs fabricated by fellow amputees whose training we had funded two years earlier. Our mission was to get them back on their feet, in more ways than one. As the organization's director and co-founder, I had made many program visits in the region but never with a musical instrument.

We followed the road up the hill, the kids still giggling and milling around us. Smoke rose from make-shift vending shacks and chickens scattered at our feet. My mind was busy chewing on the lyrics to Dylan's famous song. I loved this song. It was so cathartic and so poignant for where we were. But I guessed — and secretly hoped — that very few in the border camp had ever heard it before.

They say everything can be replaced. They say every distance is not near
So I remember every face. Of every man who put me here

The words had so much meaning here: several thousand Shan trapped in no-man's-land, *clinging* to the side of steep unforgiving mountains, *clinging* to dreams of returning home that faded with each year their conflict with the Burmese junta dragged on. They were *clinging* to distant hopes of resettling in another country, *clinging* to their sense of sovereignty, dignity, community. From this prison deep in the jungle and far from the eyes of the world, they wanted to be released.

I started learning Dylan songs when I was a teenager. An older son of our neighbors in the Dutch town where I grew up started teaching me how to play the guitar when I was barely 13. All these years, I had remained a closet musician. I was way too self-conscious to perform even in small groups or at open mics, let alone in front of large crowds. But this evening felt different to me. I was invited to represent those who were far, far away yet cared enough about the Shan to support them through our cause. I was there to bear witness and carry a message of heart, of solidarity, of empathy, of love. I could not escape my few minutes of unsolicited fame any more than the Shan could escape their tragic predicament. This was something I had to do.

We arrived at the camp's center. It was a large plateau just down the hill from the now-congested ridge road. It had sports fields and a large stage where a band was setting up. A military parade and Krav Maga exercises were in full swing on the sports fields. In the golden afternoon light, the Shan watched their young heroes in awe, cheering proudly each time a demonstration wrapped up. The formal festivities continued for two more hours with more displays of military preparedness and fiery patriotic speeches. We were brought here early to be impressed, to see the Shan's survival in exile and to report back to our corner of the world. I began to relax. I took some pictures of the teary-eyed faces in the crowd. I was being a journalist again for the first time since I left that career to start our organization, Clear Path International, with three other young activists six years earlier.

A few years before we launched Clear Path and after several years as a local business news reporter, I worked as the Pacific Rim correspondent for the Seattle Post-Intelligencer. Since the first shipwrecked Japanese sailor beached on its nearby coastal waters in the late 1800s, many Asians have set foot in the Seattle region and stayed. Chinese immigrants helped build the railroads. Japanese immigrants settled to farm. And refugees from the conflicts in Indochina resettled en masse on the West Coast, including the greater Seattle area where I reported on their lives for the newspaper.

I made many friends in our Asian American communities and learned about their heart-wrenching stories of escape from a region in flames. I took their stories and friendships with me when I left the newspaper and joined the Port of Seattle as a spokesman. At the port, a colleague introduced me to three young activists who were helping remove landmines south of the former Demilitarized Zone in central Vietnam. They reported that their de-mining teams were regularly approached by kids and adults who had lost limbs and sometimes their eyesight from stepping on hidden land mines or playing with unexploded ordnance. This instantly brought back memories from my 1970s childhood, watching TV news footage of B-52s dropping their payloads over the Vietnamese countryside. I was sold. After 15 years as a journalist — always the 'neutral' observer on the outside — I wanted in. I knew I could use my writing skills and my connections in the business community to make a difference in these places where the guns had fallen silent but people were still affected by the legacy of war, particularly in Vietnam where we shared such a troubled history.

When the four of us started our small aid group we had nothing except a grant from a foundation in Vermont and a whole lot of heart. I had never started or run a nonprofit, never raised money, never dealt with a foreign government, never interacted with a medical patient, never left the security of a well-paying job to launch a charitable dream. To top it off, we were barely off the ground when 9-11 happened and the world froze in shock. Nothing moved. Nothing other than Ground Zero got attention. No money flowed.

We kept at it, hoping and dreaming. At least I could write, so I started working on a seemingly endless stream of grant proposals that resonated among donors when the country began to breathe again. And I worked with friends in the media to get the word out about this obscure legacy of a war that had long since begun to recede into history. Slowly at first, aid support began to trickle in again and our project began to grow. In the years that followed, our programs spread. We grew our small survivor assistance effort in central Vietnam to include other parts of the long narrow country. We ventured into neighboring Cambodia, then Thailand and eventually Laos and Afghanistan. We held fundraising galas, piggybacking on the generosity of musicians, actors and artists who backed us with in-kind donations, money and attention.

We forged on, determined to help as many survivors as possible in as many communities as we could. Eventually, we secured funding from the State Department and from large foundations. Our work expanded from mere emergency medical care, prosthetics fabrication and physical rehabilitation to micro-lending, animal husbandry projects and support for our younger beneficiaries' participation in regional ParaOlympics. We even built a rice mill near a former Khmer Rouge stronghold in Cambodia where dozens of landmine amputees and their families had taken up rice farming.

All those fundraisers and outreach campaigns gave me a lot of exposure as a public speaker. I took every opportunity to promote our work at potlucks, service clubs, elementary schools, universities, churches, charity fairs and music gigs. The last time I had been on a large stage was at a Natalie Merchant concert at the Chateau Ste. Michelle winery near Seattle. A crowd of 5,000 joined me in applauding her generous gesture to donate part of the concert's proceeds to the mission of another organization for which I worked briefly before we created Clear Path. I was nervous then too. What got me past my stage fright each time I spoke was my passion for our work and the 'reporting' I could do to all those who otherwise had no idea that children in Vietnam were still killed or injured by munitions from a war that ended three decades earlier. Or that Phnom Penn had the highest per capita population of landmine amputees in the world after a quarter century of tyranny, genocide and civil war. Or that here in the emerald mountains on the Thai border with Myanmar several hundred thousand Shan, Karen and Karenni refugees were trapped in their make-shift jungle settlements far from home.

As the sun went down behind the ragged mountain skyline beyond the border camp, families began to prepare their sky lanterns for launch after dark. This is a long-held New Year's tradition in parts of Asia. Legend has it that the first paper lantern was built and released by a Chinese military man in the third century, with a message asking for help against an enemy that had surrounded his platoon. In Thailand and parts of Myanmar, many locals believe that in releasing a sky lantern they can let go of their worries and fears, while Buddhist monks believe releasing the candle may get them closer to enlightenment.

But first there would be music.

In the twilight, the crowd in front of the stage began to grow. The band tuned their instruments. The camp leader went up and introduced the band. Before long, the entire ridge and valleys around it were filled with the sound of pop songs and the Shan's patriotic favorites. Two thousand people sang along with a strength that briefly put their violent past behind them and allowed them to be free in the moment. I had almost forgotten that I would be called on stage soon, basking in the unison of songs to which I didn't need to know the words or their meaning. I simply felt comforted by what the singing channeled. When my moment finally arrived, the camp leader found me in the crowd and invited me to follow him to where the band members awaited me with an electric guitar and a mic. Looking out across the crowd while the camp leader introduced me, a wave of terror crested inside me and then subsided. With a softening gaze, I looked into the crowd and saw a wonder in the eyes that looked back at me. I was reminded that even though few might know Dylan's song, many would still understand the words since English is a second or third language to them. As I struck my first few chords, the band dropped in behind me. I looked over my shoulder. The band members smiled with a look that said, "We have your back." And after the first two verses, the crowd fell in with the song, humming or singing the melody. My voice strengthened. My chord progressions smoothened. The band was totally in sync with my playing. And the song opened up a channel for everyone's yearning to be free. Whatever had separated us before this moment melted away in soulful sonic communion.

Just as I launched into the last verse, I noticed the crowd's eyes looking away to the field beside the stage and I saw a warm yellow light on their faces. The sky lanterns had been released and slowly drifted up past the band and into the star-filled night. Again, I saw *tears*. *Tears* of sorrow. *Tears* of survival. *Tears* of gratitude. *Tears* of hope. *Tears* of joy.

> *I see my light come shining. From the west down to the east*
> *Any day now, any day now. I shall be released*

The band and I pounded out the last chords with a confident flourish. The song was over. Applause, hollers and whistles followed. Then, a reverent silence set in as we all watched more and more lanterns ascend from behind the stage on their way to the cosmos. I had the feeling that our hearts had ignited these ever-rising points of light and that we watched them like reflections of our thirsty souls hoping to be quenched in heaven. We all looked quietly on as the small sea of lanterns began to merge with the dark starry night. A breeze cooled the moisture on my cheeks.

IGNITE ACTION STEPS

- **Traveling for a cause**. If you're inspired to help others in need and you like to travel, consider volunteering for an organization that provides aid overseas. Service clubs, churches and immigrant communities often have aid projects abroad you can inquire about whether you have professional qualifications or not.

- **Starting or joining a cause.** It's always best to consider joining an existing cause first since many of them need volunteers and support. But if you see an unmet need, consider starting you own nonprofit that makes donations to your overseas work tax-deductible. Donors love to see your passion for the work: money follows spirit.

- **Report on your travels.** Even if you're not on a trip for a specific char-itable reason, report about the humanitarian needs you see during your travels to create awareness for those less fortunate.

Aleanu Imbert Matthee - United States
Retired journalist and nonprofit manager
imbert.clearpath@gmail.com

TANYA LOPEZ

"The freedom to follow your heart is the greatest freedom of all."

My personal intention with this story is to convey that all of life is an adventure; all our experiences are part of the great journey back to ourselves to find and follow our heart and soul's desire. Take a leap of faith and follow your greatest excitement; trust that the Universe will support you.

THE GREATEST JOURNEY

I grew up seeing photos of my parents traveling and exploring the world. I was raised in the small town of Palm Coast, Florida. There wasn't much to do in a 30 mile radius in any direction. It was an odd little town, initially developed as a retirement community plopped down into the middle of wild palm trees and swampland. As a child, I would chase rabbits and move turtles out of the road. I didn't question much.

The small town vibes continued when I moved to Gainesville, Florida to attend university. Studying abroad in Sevilla, Spain in my junior year was a major shift in perspective. I don't know where I got the idea to study abroad, but a world of possibility opened up to me.

I fell in love with Spain: with flamenco music (and a flamenco guitarist), with the smell of orange trees wafting in the air, with long, lazy afternoons of Spanish tapas and sangria, with ancient cobblestone streets and picturesque squares filled with ringing church bells. Most of all, I fell in love with the lifestyle. I felt that people there were ALIVE, they were joyful and playful, the streets were full of life and music at all hours. There were endless parties and festivals like La Feria de Abril with gorgeous women dancing Sevillanas in polka dot flamenco dresses, while horses pranced around adorned with vibrant flowers and bells. I dreamt of someday living in Spain and soaking in more of this culture and life that touched and inspired my heart in a way I had never experienced...

Alas, I had one year left to graduate. Sad to leave my beloved Spain and new lifestyle, I went back to Gainesville and, after graduating with the highest honors, I moved to New York. I had no idea what I wanted to do in life and I figured New York was the place where I had the most opportunities to sort it out.

I started as an entry-level junior account exec at a boutique PR firm on Park Avenue in Manhattan and I quickly rose in the ranks. I was making a pretty meager salary by New York standards but I found a room in a shared apartment I loved and I made friends. It was a good life. I had a strong work ethic, a great relationship with my supervisor and incredible accounts and clients. This said, I was still working in a cubicle with a traditional 9-6 workday and had only 10 vacation days a year. I felt a bit trapped and worried that life could potentially pass me by. While I was fulfilled in many ways, I had a yearning to adventure and explore the world.

One year, I spent several months planning a holiday to Argentina with a friend from Spain. That one annual holiday was my only opportunity all year to travel, take time off work and see friends overseas; that was hard to swallow. The dream of living abroad, traveling, exploring the world and having freedom was very much alive inside of me, but at the time, it just wasn't in my realm of possibility. Instead, I started to feel that one day I wanted my own business. My father was an entrepreneur and I saw him working from home and making his own hours. I thought that having my own business would be my ticket to freedom (of course I found out years later that wasn't at all necessarily the case).

Despite the limited opportunity for travel, I was happy with my job and I felt inspired in New York. I had spent three years there finding my flow, friends and favorite places, when one of my clients brought me an incredible job opportunity: to become head of a newly-formed corporate communications department at a national TV network focused on music and lifestyle. It was based in Los Angeles and was more than triple my current salary. It was my dream job! I knew from the incredible excitement I felt inside of me when they made the offer that it was one I *had* to take.

So, I moved to Los Angeles, once again not knowing anybody there. Very quickly, I felt I was in way over my head. I was the youngest (by far) on the executive team in a high-profile and demanding role. Fortunately, I loved the work, my colleagues and my boss, so I was motivated. I hunkered down and met every challenge, working crazy hours, learning and growing tremendously in the process, and seeing the fruits of my labor pay off. When I faced self-doubt, which was often, I reminded myself of how much progress I was making and how far I had come.

About three years into working at that company, I was pulled into a meeting to give a presentation to Nike and was then recruited by them to my complete surprise. As head of communications and spokesperson for the West Coast for one of the biggest and most-loved brands in the world, I would be working with some of the top athletes and have the chance to travel. My mind and heart were dreaming of global opportunities. As much as I was thriving in my current job, I knew this was an incredible step in my career I had to take. And so I did.

Working for Nike was extremely demanding. Trying to understand the structure, systems and inner workings of a global company like this was overwhelming, not to mention the work itself. I was again greatly expanding professionally but there were many weekends spent working and nights that I went home crying feeling overwhelmed.

Then, something very interesting happened, which I now see was a major crossroad in my life. At a time of economic challenges in the U.S., Nike underwent a restructuring and laid off a significant amount of employees. In my case, they offered me a position to relocate back to New York, giving me less than 24 hours to decide. I was shocked. How could I possibly make such an important decision so quickly? Obviously this was an extremely hard choice to make. I had never lost a job during my career and I felt scared of being jobless. However, when I was completely honest with myself, I also saw it as an opportunity to take the leap to pursue my dream of travel and to start my own business.

After a sleepless night, I told them I would take the severance package and go my separate way. As risky as this decision was, I now see this experience helped set me on a different path that was more aligned with my heart and soul's calling. It turned out to be a major blessing in my life. Sometimes the Universe gives us the little push we need...

With a deep desire in my heart to explore, I packed all my things into a storage unit (again) and I set off to Africa with my boyfriend. I spent three months having adventures there that included a month-long road trip in South Africa, Zambia, Botswana and Namibia. We camped on the roof of our Land Rover for two weeks in the bush, waking up at sunrise to follow animal tracks and making a fire at night so they wouldn't eat us. An African safari had always been my absolute dream trip. I savored the quiet and stillness of being in nature and the opportunity to slow way down.

After my travels, I landed back in Miami where I reconnected with a few prior employers who were excited to work with me. Overnight, I registered a business and started a social media and PR consulting firm. Very quickly I had more work than I could handle. This is when I learned that having your own business does *not* necessarily equate to making your own hours with plenty of freedom and flexibility!

About a year into launching my own business, I saw a Facebook ad with the headline "Is This the World's Most Awesome Job?" I clicked on it out of curiosity. I wasn't looking for a job, but it caught my attention. That click led to my entire life changing overnight *again*. After excitedly shooting my video submission, I woke up to an email from HR, had a call with the CEO and was offered a position the very next day. The company was called Mindvalley, a personal growth and education company; the position was Events Director for their signature event, A-Fest. It was based in Kuala Lumpur, Malaysia. I had never heard of Mindvalley before, I hadn't worked directly in event production and I had never been to Malaysia.

I took the job.

I had no idea what I was getting myself into. Logically, it didn't make any sense, but I was following my gut and my intuition was telling me, "YES." Seemingly overnight, I phased out my thriving business, emptied my house, packed up my things once again and took off with a one-way flight, this time the furthest I had ever been. I had several sleepless nights in the weeks before leaving, second guessing myself and my decision to embark on such a major transition.

What reassured me in the midst of my deep doubt was the incredible feeling of excitement I felt when I saw the video announcing the position. The video gave me goosebumps, the hair on my arms literally stood up and I just *knew*. It was as if some deep part of me felt, without any doubt, that despite all the unknown factors — a major move to a new country, a new role in a new industry, a massive pay cut and more — that everything was going to work out. I was going to allow the excitement I felt in my body and heart to guide me and just *trust*.

My time at Mindvalley was transformative. I found my absolute passion, my art and a key source of creative expression in organizing transformational events and experiences in the space of wellness and art. Being able to deeply and positively impact people and create what they called 'the best experience of their lives' left me more fulfilled, inspired and motivated than in any other job I'd ever been at. I was also traveling all over the world, organizing events and visiting over 20 countries in just a few years. I was kicking ass because I loved it, I felt so inspired. I also found some of my best friends in life. I found my Tribe.

While I have always been into personal development, working for Mindvalley and being exposed to some of the biggest teachers, authors, ideas and events in personal growth led to greater self-exploration and a catalyst for deepening my spiritual path. I studied many different healing and spiritual modalities all over the world with various teachers and healers.

There's something about threes in my life though. Three years after living in Kuala Lumpur and exploring most of Southeast Asia, my next leap of faith appeared. I felt I was ready for a new chapter. I was ready to leave Malaysia. Mindvalley was very supportive and we worked out an arrangement for me to continue to organize its events while working remotely. The thing was that I didn't know where I wanted to relocate to. I just knew in my heart it was time to go. I gave away most of my belongings, left a suitcase with a friend and took off to Croatia where I was organizing my next event.

I had no plans, no home, no hotel bookings, no *stuff* to hold onto… nothing. I gave space for things and plans to emerge and trusted that the path would unfold as I began to travel it. I ended up living out of my suitcase for three years (there's those threes again!) exploring the world.

When my heart began to tell me it was time to find a place to settle, a series of synchronicities happened that led to me moving to Ibiza, Spain. It wasn't until a few weeks after settling into my new home on the island that it sank in that my heart had led me back to Spain. The dream that I had held deep inside since that trip to Sevilla in my junior year of university had now come true, nearly 15 years later.

Today, based in Spain, I work remotely and still love to travel and explore the world. I've started my own event design and production company that I'm consciously structuring to give me the space and freedom to do so. My life is not perfect or without its challenges — I am always a work in progress. I'm in the process of creating a new dream, and through all my adventures and leaps of faith, I know the Universe has my back.

What I have found is this: if you leap, the net will appear.

And I have definitely leaped! I've thrown myself into all sorts of adventures as they've appeared. I've camped in the bush in Africa and slept amongst lions, bathed in the Dead Sea and in sacred waterfalls, and danced with Flamenco gypsies in Spain. I've had my palms, cards, Akashic records, dreams and charts read by mystics across the world. I've sat for weeks with plant medicine in the Amazon, hiked to Machu Picchu, visited the sacred sites of the world and traveled through oceans and deserts seeking peace and truth.

I've worked with healers, shamans, sangomas, medicine carriers and tantrikas to heal my heart and understand my purpose and true essence. I've sat in Temazcales, temples, ashrams and caves contemplating consciousness and my existence. I've danced, cried, breathed, traveled, prayed, meditatated, screamed, shook, sung and fasted to get to the core of it all.

I have left everything to start all over again. Several times.

In the end, the freedom I was looking for was the freedom to follow my heart. Through everything I was doing and everywhere I went, I was looking for *myself*. I'm much closer to that now than I ever was, and I also know this journey deep into myself will be forever.

The greatest journey is the journey to find oneself. The greatest treasure we can find, all the world over, is that in our own heart. I encourage you to learn to understand the whispers of your heart. To trust your intuition and to make decisions that bring you joy. Even if you don't have all the answers or can't fully see the path ahead, at any given moment you can follow your highest excitement. If something looks good on paper but you're not excited about it, it's a no. If something is a maybe, it's a no. If something seems like a crazy idea that doesn't make sense at all but you're super excited about it, it's a yes. Take that leap of faith and trust that the next steps will appear.

Ignite Action Steps

Get clear on the life experiences you want to have and cultivate your connection to yourself and your own inner wisdom. When these things are strong, you have greater self reliance, greater trust, and you can feel and follow your highest excitement.

- **Get clear on what you want.** Fuzzy targets don't get hit. Feel, see and write what you want in some key categories like health and fitness, love and relationships, home, career and financial. Write what you want in travel, bucket list adventures, social life and creative expression, too. Be as specific as possible. Think of how you want to *feel* rather than the specifics of the thing.

- **Dream up what you really want** and desire in life, without any limits or restrictions. Putting visuals to whatever goals you put on paper helps supercharge them. Cut out photos in magazines to put on a vision board or create a digital vision board using Pinterest. Check in often and keep it updated.

- **Cultivate your self-reliance and inner wisdom.** When times get tough, talk to yourself — the higher Self that has a deep inner wisdom and all the resources and answers you need. There is often no better coach than your higher Self. Trust this inner wisdom and find your own way to cultivate and nurture this connection, it can be different for everyone.

- **Build up your trust in yourself and the Universe.** Try this journaling exercise: Think back to some times when you thought something was 'bad' but with some time and space, you could see the lessons and benefits that it brought, and that it actually was in your best interest. Write about at least three times this happened and keep this updated.

Tanya Lopez - United States Expat living in Spain
Event Designer, Producer & Facilitator
www.tanyalopez.com
tanyacristina
tanyacristinalopez

JOHN D. RUSSELL

*"Leverage your pain and suffering and make
it your 'why'— not your demise."*

**My wish for you is that you read my story and become inspired to harness
your pain to make it your strength so that you are able to live the life you've
always dreamed of living.**

MY PAIN IS MY STRENGTH

One late summer day as I was getting ready to go on a job interview I
received a phone call from a family friend, "John, you need to come to your
mother. She's dying." In shock, and having no time for lengthy explanations, I
hung up the phone and I immediately booked the next flight out of Los Angeles
to be by her side.

After two days of being by her side while she was incapacitated, I finally
learned my mother had tried to kill herself. She had ingested 100 pills of Aspi-
rin, dissolving them in water, drinking it and laying around the house vomiting
blood, and writing me suicide letters until she felt like there was no return.
Finally, she called her nurse practitioner to pick her up and check her into the
hospital. She even tried placing a Do Not Resuscitate order on herself so that
nobody close to her could interfere. But why? What happened? How did she
get to that point? What the actual fuck?

Let's go back in time a bit. When I was 21, I asked my mother to find my
father. I wanted to meet him, to figure out why I had certain traits and ultimately

fill a gap in my family tree. I wasn't looking for a father figure. I simply wanted to meet the guy. Surprisingly, my mother found him and even more surprisingly, the two started dating almost immediately. I just kept thinking, "This is insane — I only wanted to meet the guy."

Shortly after they started dating, my father moved in with my mother. He moved to another state to be with her no less! That year on the fourth of July, I found myself standing in my mom's long gravel driveway with my mom, my dad and a handful of sparklers. I felt uncomfortable to say the least. I told my mom at one point, "I'm not looking for a father. I just wanted to meet him. If you're doing this for me, it isn't necessary." But my mom *wasn't* doing it for me, she was doing it for *her*. I told her as long as she's happy and being supported, I support her and that I was willing to simply move forward. Life is short after all. Truth is, he is an interesting, smart and talented man who had accomplished a tremendous amount in a relatively short time. I am proud of him for those qualities.

But their newfound relationship wasn't without its own pain and suffering. About a year later, it became clear to me that my father was being mentally and emotionally abusive toward my mother. He would threaten to leave, leave for a few days and then come back. Repeatedly. My father wasn't working; he was ill and was also on medications. My mom was now not only dating my father, but she was financially helping to support him. I also learned that while she was trying to make their relationship work, my dad was meeting other women online and having intimate connections with them.

I was furious. When I found out, I gave my mom two choices: 1. You kick him out or 2. I'm going to come and do it myself. This ends now.

Shortly after, my mom kicked him out and my dad left and moved in with one of his females across the country. It broke my mom. Roughly two weeks after that happened, I later learned my mom jumped on a plane and went looking for him. They needed to talk. They ended up driving 1400 miles back to my mom's house across multiple states and when they arrived days later, she gave him an ultimatum. An ultimatum my father climatically declined and he left… again. Later that same day and in so much pain, my mom decided to take her own life.

After saving her life, my mom woke up and she was furious. I had ruined her plan and now she had to face her loved ones and answer for her actions. Unfortunately, my mother's stunt had put her in end-stage liver failure and she needed a liver transplant. For the next several years, I served as my mother's primary caregiver with some help from her sister and a few family friends (thank you). We got her on the United Network for Organ Sharing (UNOS) transplant list and waited. And waited. And waited.

As time ticked away, my mom slipped into a coma. I begged the transplant coordinator to transplant her. It was now or never. Her body was shutting down and her health was deteriorating rapidly. This was it. She was only 49, held two Master's degrees, rarely drank and didn't smoke. Aside from her clinically (and newly) diagnosed depression, she was a solid candidate for a new liver. Thankfully, they obliged and proceeded with the liver transplant.

This was rare given the short supply of organs and the high demand for them. Ultimately, there are more people that need transplants than there are organs available. To be granted an organ, one has to be pretty sick but not too sick. It's a fucked up game of test scores and timing. The transplant coordinator and transplant team agreed that she was an excellent candidate and the probability of survival was still high even though she was in a coma. They proceeded with the intense operation and the transplant took close to 12 hours to complete. Amazingly, my mom woke up the next day. The transplant was a success and the transplant team felt confident she would survive.

For the next 31 days, I visited my mom in Intensive Care virtually every day. The physicians on staff liked to joke with me that I was at the hospital more than they were. Truth is, I was. I told myself that if she didn't make it and I didn't put in the time and effort that I would regret it for the rest of my life.

During recovery, she was ventilated and unable to speak as a result of her transplant and a pesky lung infection that doctors couldn't get rid of. For the next month, I communicated with my mom on a dry erase board. She would point to letters and I would form sentences for her. It was heartbreaking to see her in that state but I was hopeful that my mom was going to pull through. Every day seemed brighter and brighter. After all that we'd been through, she was going to make it.

And then one cold, early Sunday morning, around 2 AM, I got a phone call, "John, you need to come to the hospital immediately." My mom was gone.

I knew it without even having to ask. An emotional wreck, I rubbed the sleep out of my eyes as I began to panic. "Fuck! Fuck! Fuck!" I uttered under my breath while I frantically struggled to get dressed. One of my roommates woke up during the chaos and offered to go with me (thank you Adam Miller) and we hauled ass on an empty 405 freeway to the UCLA Medical Center. When I stormed into the ICU, I asked the doctor on duty if she was gone and he confirmed. I was devastated.

He sat me down and told me that her breathing tube had punctured her lungs and lacerated her pulmonary artery. She bled out of the mouth in under a minute. It happened so fast, there was nothing they could do to save her. My only immediate family, my best friend, my mom — had died.

I sat next to her cold lifeless body and cried for what felt like an eternity. For the next few months, I was in a dark place. I was alone. I was angry. I was sad. I cried often and heavily. I didn't know what to do or how to handle the massive amount of pain and suffering I was experiencing. As a young man in high school, I lost a friend, my aunt and both of my grandparents in a very short time span. Sad to say, I was used to death by the time I was 15. This, however, wasn't even close to the same feeling. This was way, way worse.

But I made a pact with myself. I wasn't going to let this destroy me. I wasn't going to crawl under a rock and play the victim. It would have been easy to do so given all that had happened in the last several years. Fuck that.

I wanted to live a happy life, pursue my dreams and do right for me while also honoring my mother. That's what she would have wanted. It was the right thing to do for my own well-being and for humanity as well. I was hell bent. I had made a choice. But I was scared. I was alone. I would often ask myself, "What's next?"

You see my dream was to travel the world and take photographs. I had always been interested in photography. I had taken a photography darkroom class in high school, but after getting a grade of 'D', I turned to sports instead. When I became my mother's caretaker, photography became an outlet for releasing my stress. I would grab her Olympus SLR camera and take it hiking in the mountains of Montana. I'd let the landscapes I captured be my escape from being a full-time caregiver.

Given my mom's condition, traveling the world wasn't a reality and I instead opted for stability. I worked as an underwriter for an insurance company in Los Angeles. I was good at my job and climbed the corporate ladder very quickly. Even quicker, however, I had reached a ceiling. Not having a degree was hampering my ability to be promoted even higher within the company and I felt stuck. Furthermore, I didn't truly love my job. There were days I simply didn't want to go to work. I had a great boss and enjoyed being with my coworkers, but I yearned for something more. I wanted to follow my dreams, but I couldn't because I had to take care of my mother. I needed to be close to her in case anything happened. I was only 27 when she died.

About a month after my mother's death, I was going through her possessions when I stumbled upon several boxes stacked in the corner of the storage unit labeled in large block letters "Family Photos." Overcome with emotion, my progress came to a standstill. That's when it hit me.

As I was going through our old photos, I realized the true power of a photograph. I knew *immediately* that this was my life's calling. These photographs were all I had left of my family aside from my memories. I was meant to do this. For the first time, I felt purpose in my life. I knew what I wanted, but I was deathly afraid of failing. I thought, "What would happen if I dedicated my life to something and failed?"

I struggled for a few months with my decision on how to proceed with my life. Ultimately, I decided that I needed to focus on something *positive*. I chose to go back to college and earn my degree and, while I was attending school, I would also pursue my passion for photography with drive and purpose.

I opted to abandon security and quit my job working as an underwriter and went back to college full time. I chose my degree carefully, thinking that developing my business acumen while pursuing photography made the most sense. It would also give me something to fall back on if photography didn't pan out. I graduated with a Bachelor of Science in Business Administration with an emphasis in Accountancy. While I was studying, I started working as an apprentice for an up-and-coming lifestyle photographer in San Diego. I worked for her for free, learning as much as I could. Upon graduation, I was faced with a new dilemma. I could return to my old job and rise through the ranks, or, I could try my hand at being a professional photographer full-time. This was a big struggle for me... security versus the unknown... I had no money and nobody to lean on, but oddly, I felt extremely empowered to be in a position to make this decision. I had the freedom to choose to follow my passion even though it meant being broke and homeless for a while, living on a friend's floor (thank you Perry House).

It was a monumental decision and I had no idea how it was going to turn out. I positioned myself as a portrait and wedding photographer and started to promote my business and my newfound mission in life. Shortly after, things started to take off and I was able to find more suitable accommodations and support myself. I was doing it.

Fast forward to today (14 years later) and I've been on assignment as a photographer in over 30 countries. I work with some of the largest companies in the world and several of the world's biggest celebrities. Now I primarily shoot Commercial, Lifestyle, and Event Photography. I've also worked with nonprofits around the globe to help them communicate their missions, and raise awareness and funding to continue helping others.

I've served with my camera over and over again to help make our world better for future generations and will continue to do so.

I started a local photography group in Los Angeles and I also teach a class called 'Photography for Social Change' locally, whereby I teach aspiring photographers how to work with nonprofits and help make the world a better place through visual storytelling. My love of adventure led me to start a division of my company called PRSPCTV. It combines the three things I love most — adventure travel, photography and philanthropy. I take my clients on adventure photography trips to exotic locations in The Americas, Asia, Europe, Africa and India. I now truly live an adventurous life.

Photography is my calling. What started as an escape is now so much more than that. One of the things that I love the most about photography is that I equate it to mindfulness. You have to be *present* to capture what is in front of you. It just doesn't work if your mind is in the past or the future. Photography allows me to slow down and really notice the world around me — finding beauty and, as a result, gratitude in everyday life. I now look at the world through a different lens.

My mother gave me so many gifts in her short life. She took me skydiving for the first time (I'm now a skydiver), river rafting, skiing, rock climbing, backpacking and so much more. She was an adventure junkie and I loved it. My passion for travel and adventure is no doubt due to her showing me what was possible when I was a young man. I owe my mom everything. I am forever grateful for all that she sacrificed and did for me.

For a few years, I battled with guilt. By asking my mom to find my father, I felt that I had caused all of this. I realize now, however, that I didn't *cause* any of it. My mom made some bad choices. I'm not responsible for that. God knows I've made plenty of bad choices myself. I don't judge her for hers. I love her unconditionally and in some extraordinary way, this has all been a gift. But, I had to make that choice and so do you. We all have pain. We all experience suffering. My hope is that you leverage your pain and suffering. Let it fuel your passion. Harness that pain and turn it into your motivation. The world needs you to do just that.

I love you mom. Thank you so much for giving me life, teaching me to follow my dreams with intensity, live a life full of adventure and for showing me what's most important. Today and every day, I honor you.

IGNITE ACTION STEPS

Ignite your life, your actions, and turn your pain and suffering into your strength.

1. Get focused and commit to something. Pursue training or learning something positive. Take that class, get that degree or go on that retreat. Invest in yourself.
2. Don't be afraid to fail. It's okay. As the saying goes, "If you're not failing, you're not trying hard enough." If anything, try and fail more often. Growth will occur naturally.
3. Take ownership of your pain and suffering and be proud of your story. Often times when people hear my story they reply with, "I'm so sorry.", etc. I always reply with, "Don't be." It's my story and it has shaped me into the person that I am today. I'm proud of that. You should be proud of your story too. Own it!
4. Change your PRSPCTV. It's easy to become self-absorbed and play the victim. Don't. You're better (and deserve more) than that. Reframing your thoughts and your views will help you feel more positive and appreciative. Find another lens.
5. Help others and give back. Selfless acts of service heal. If you're feeling overwhelmed, strive to help others. This will reposition your life and make it more about serving than suffering.
6. Forgive. Lead with love and trust that those around you are doing the best they can. Practice forgiveness and you'll find life is much brighter and happier. We all come up short sometimes. That's okay. None of us are perfect.
7. Practice gratitude. Determine what you're grateful for and make sure to express it loud and often. We all have people and circumstances we can be grateful for even in the darkest of times. Remember that.

John D. Russell - United States
Professional Photographer & Creative Director
www.johndrussell.com
⊙ myeyescapture
⊙ john.d.russell

RAVI MUTI

*"Ignite what your heart already knows and take
the path to live the adventure!"*

**My personal intention is for you to know that we are all spiritual, conscious
beings in a human experience with the ability to shine bright and do anything the heart desires. We are not to be constrained by the expectations,
words and insecurities of others. By adventuring out of our comfort zone,
learning about our world and figuring out where we fit in, we can individually live the life we want while at the same time collectively making the
world a better place for all. We are unique, special beings here to live out
our passion and enjoy this life experience. Make now the time you start!
Create the life you desire. Ignite your Adventurous Spirit!**

THE MAVERICK DO GOOD BOY WANDERER

I was 23 years old and I had never seen anything like it. I was walking down
a dusty dirt road in Thailand, pulling my luggage behind me on the way to my
hotel and there was a prostitute calling out to passers by in a bored-sounding
monotone. She was not alone. Everywhere I looked, I could see women just
like her repetitively trying to solicit customers in tired, robotic voices. To most
people, the ready availability of cheap sex would be a thrill, but for me, it just
made me sad.

In my circle of family and friends in the west coast of Canada, travel was
something no one had experienced. When I decided to travel, my parents kept

asking what I was doing with my life. Why travel? Why do you need to go to Thailand and Vietnam? Young as I was, I didn't know how to answer them. I just knew I had to go. I was curious… nervous… anxious… and I was not the most prepared for the trip. The hotel my cousin and I had chosen was not the most suitable place and the jet lag caught me by surprise… We were total amateurs!

Growing up in a Sikh family, in the East Indian culture, there are various expectations of how to live life: get good grades in high school, go to college, and oh man, if you got into university, you gave your parents a ticket to brag about you tenfold! Personal development? What the bleep is that? Travel? Jeez, you are wasting your life! Become a doctor, lawyer or accountant, find a life partner, settle down, have kids, and — oh yeah — work, work, work and make lots of money. Well, I just never got the memo, nor did I understand that way of living. I chose to follow my heart and my desires, and it all began with questions.

As a child, I was extremely shy and didn't say much, but I wondered. Something about the way I'm told to live or how people lived around me didn't feel right to the child I was. I witnessed selfishness, hate, violence, abuse of drugs and alcohol, and uncontrollable vices; I did not want to be a part of this. I did not express what I felt or how my thoughts were not aligned with the understanding and beliefs of others. Trusting my gut instinct, I decided that I would carve my own path. More importantly, I would explore the nature of life and what it means to be a decent human being.

With curiosity, I set out to wonder about the world: who I am and how do I fit in? High school was a time of pondering and I spent many hours thinking deeply, unsure how to translate those thoughts into action. True awareness and alignment to who I am only started to be possible after high school. Initially, I wasn't sure what I wanted to do with my life. I threw around the idea of becoming a firefighter or police officer, fighting organized crime, before finally deciding on going to university to become a lawyer. My dad always wanted me to be a lawyer and in the stoic way he had, he expressed his happiness with my choice. My motivation was not the status or money. I wanted to help others and make the world a better place, fighting criminals and providing counsel to those in need. The commonality between the above disciplines was simple: service to others.

I chose Criminology, a wonderful discipline, but it soon became repetitive. Scrolling through a list of programs, I stumbled upon something that really caught my eye. Sociology! 'Study of the world.' At this time, I had this curiosity about our existence, eager to learn more about it. I decided to add Sociology to complement my legal studies. "What will that even teach you?" people asked.

Sociology requires a lot of critical thinking and analysis. Academically, it was challenging; but more importantly, it turned out to be a key aspect of my personal growth as a conscious human being. I was able to learn about how society has been shaped by the interaction between societal institutions and individual agents, us human beings. More importantly, that various groups of human beings exist. On the surface, we may come from different backgrounds and cultures, but at the root, we are all one. It was time to discover others and their way of being.

My adventuring into the unknown, to get to the known, had begun.

My friend Nick brought my attention to a pretty successful fellah by the name Richard Branson, a global, maverick-like entrepreneur and daredevil, world traveler. I had always desired to be a part of something bigger than myself, global, connecting the world and helping others. I wanted more from life and with Branson as inspiration, saw travel as a way to broaden my horizons. Safe to say, I wanted to emulate his lifestyle.

I tapped into my Adventurous Spirit. My first significant travel took place at the age of 23. After taking my last Sociology class, I packed my bags and set off to explore Thailand, Vietnam, Malaysia and China. At this point in my life, I was pondering over graduate school decisions. I wasn't quite sure of my direction. There was this niggling question of how do I want to impact the world? I will be honest, I did doubt myself as to the possibility of this occurring and could I do it.

So I kept following my intuition.

My trip to a Vietnamese countryside village would prove to be the answer to this question. Vietnam was still struggling from the effects of the Vietnam War, especially the dumping of chemicals over the Vietnamese people during Operation Agent Orange. I witnessed this impact first hand during my tour of the city, war fields, cu chi tunnels and craft shops. In the shops, the children of those who endured the chemical attack were working in an assembly line. These youngsters were born with deformities and were incapable of performing anything more than basic assembly line tasks. My stomach churned with nausea to see it, but people seemingly ignored it, saying, "This is life."

In that moment, watching those children, it all became clear. This was *not* how things should be. This was not *life*.

I instantly became even more grateful for *my* life. For the bone-deep knowledge that I was healthy and safe. That was a knowledge I had become aware of when an individual I went to school with was gunned down execution-style in a gang kidnapping and shooting. I learned from that experience that life is short and full of unexpected surprises. We need to spend our time both enjoying life and making the world a better place.

Before that time, I worked side by side with my father in our family's real estate business where I got my first taste of entrepreneurship. It taught me that I wanted to work for myself and in doing so that would allow me to pursue my passion. Instead of following a generic path, I wanted to work diligently towards creating ventures that would have a positive impact on more people than just myself.

Witnessing those children unable to live an optimal human life, this was an 'aha' moment for me! I finally knew what I was going to do with my life… sort of…

Some internal work still remained. It was clear to me that my childhood thoughts that something is wrong with the world had come full circle and that my life experiences had given me the entrepreneurial know-how to do something about it. What a revelation! This was the inception of social entrepreneurship, a definite significant Ignite moment in my life.

That first trip was just the beginning. I had not planned to become a worldwide traveler, but here I was… I had skydived in New Zealand for my 30th birthday and driven from the top of that country to its bottom. I had bungee jumped at the mountain resort in Whistler, Canada, white water rafted in Croatia, ziplined in the jungles of Costa Rica, hot air ballooned over Angkor Wat in Cambodia, hiked countless mountains, and snorkeled the Great Barrier reef. WOW! But the most truly life changing adventure was yet to come.

It's December 2017, and I'm off to Nicaragua for an adventure, planning to visit a couple of cities there, laying over in Los Angeles beforehand, hanging out with friends, biking, catching a sunset. I love sunsets! This is important. My sister, Poonam, decided it was time for change; it was time to ignite *her* Adventurous Spirit! She proposed we stay at a village, like a retreat. Never having been to a retreat, I said "Yes!" Okay, it wasn't an immediate yes, but indeed, yes.

Maderas Village is tucked away at the end of a dirt road in the jungle off the coast of Nicaragua and it is one of the most beautiful places I've ever been to. Our first day there, I decided to check out the sunset. The water, illuminated by the setting sun, was glorious and I walked in up to my waist. Five minutes later, I felt something go into my foot and I immediately yanked my foot forward. Immediately, I knew something was terribly wrong! Despite my inner panic, with a calm voice, I immediately told my cousin, Sandeep, who was there with us, that I needed help. Once out of the water, I could see how I was bleeding uncontrollably from the back of my foot. It's bad! My heart raced and I starting thinking, "I'm going to die!"

I honestly did think my life was over! Luckily, paramedics were on site. They told me I had been stung by a stingray and quickly patched me up before things could turn for the worse. Stingrays inject poison into your body and you can die due to bleeding or infection. As I sat there being tended to by an entire cluster of paramedics, a gentleman walked by. Sarcastically, he threw out, "Need any help?" which made me giggle.

Now patched up, I headed back to the village with the help of a local and his 4x4. Coincidentally, the individual who offered his assistance was staying at the same village. Nothing is ever a coincidence, because over the next three days, we spent endless hours sharing food, drink and our most deeply desired goals and aspirations. He shared his unique eating style and inspired me to become a Vegan. He told me his life story and I told him mine. In that short time, we became family.

It was such a powerful connection, the commonalities we had, and the more we talked over the months that followed, the more it grew. Eventually, he pitched me an idea and a few months later, we joined with 40 others from 20 countries to start creating a concept called *Imiloa,* a place where people connect, learn, become themselves, align with nature, and heal via plant-based food. Also where they can immerse themselves in other cultures and perspectives, cure their dissonance, and ultimately, taking home what it means to be an evolved human being, spreading a positive message across the globe that we can all co-exist. How did this happen, 40 strangers coming together? We don't know, but we think we Ignited something even before birth! Powerful, unbelievable, mind blowing!

We have lots planned, more locations coming, and have started working with the United Nations as well. It's a convergence. People with the same adventurous spirit from all around have Ignited it! I thought I was an oddball, but it turns out not at all! There are many more like me and I see that now from people who are visiting *Imiloa* and Igniting from within. Working on themselves, using imagination to create solutions. It's a movement!

Never has there been such a time where we have been in such a need.

With that, my life path was set. I am a social entrepreneur who develops, funds and implements solutions to social, cultural and environmental issues. Motivated by my father's hard work, Richard Branson's adventurous spirit and business acumen, Nicola Tesla's ingenuity and the Ignite experiences in my life, my life has come full circle. I couldn't have imagined the opportunity I'd be presented with, not just the travel adventures, but projects and relationships in subsequent years to follow.

Tapping into my Adventurous Spirit has led to so many opportunities and so much fulfillment!

My genuine desire to learn about the world has brought me to where I am today. I know that I cannot fix every problem in society. I also know that I am not perfect and have things to work on, just like any other human being. But what I'm aware of now is that if I — and we — continue to Ignite that Adventurous Spirit and curiosity, there is no limit to what we can achieve and do for this world. You are here to live your life and carry out your passion, so go do exactly that! Adventure: it's the place to start! Go for it!

Ignite Action Steps

- **Practice True learning.** Realize we are all indoctrinated. Accomplish this by traveling, reading, and meeting others. Essentially, learn about the real world.

- **Take the necessary time to figure out who you are**. What is your heart and gut (intuition) telling you? They say the soul lives in the gut!

- **What do you want from life?** Make a list of what makes you happy.

- **How do you fit into this world?** Learn about the interactions between institutions, individuals and humanity's needs.

- **Realize that we all are one.** Every one of us is individual and special and we all have a role to play, we just have to find it. Igniting your Adventurous Spirit is a good way to figure that out!

Ravi Muti - Canada
Director- Maverik Endeavors & Muti Properties,
Founding Partner- Imiloa Institute, Founder- The Mazlow
www.mutiproperties.ca
www.imiloainstitute.com
www.themazlow.com
⊙ ravimuti527

HANNA MEIRELLES

"Every trip takes us somewhere; there is a purpose to it."

I wish for you to discover your purpose for traveling and for living an adventure. I wish for you to never stop your free spirit and let it run through the future you are destined to have. Be grateful for the place where you come from and you will enjoy the adventure of a lifetime! And while you are on your journey, always do something that makes you feel good about yourself.

THE PLACE WHERE I BELONG

One of my housemates once asked me, "Why do you like to travel?" To this I answered, "I don't know." I turned the question back to him, "Why do *you* like to travel?" and he said, "Because I want to find my place in the world." I was 21, living for the first time outside of my parents' house, in a foreign city located 33 hours away by bus from my hometown in Brazil. I had never left my country at that time but traveled extensively within it. I found his answer intriguing and for many years I asked myself if that was the reason why I was so passionate about traveling. Unsure of my reasons, I kept planning for future adventures.

It all started with the author Sidney Sheldon.

In my school, it was expected that in the year that you turned 15, your parents would gift you a trip to Miami and Orlando so you could have fun with your friends in Disneyland. As I was very aware that I was one of the few in my class that could not afford such a trip, I didn't entertain that dream. While my friends were going to the United States, I was in the school library reading my favorite writer.

Each of Sheldon's books told me stories that were happening in a different continent, and sometimes in multiple countries. He would describe with perfection the details of cities like New York, Paris or Sydney. I devoured them all. As a teenager, I had the impression that I knew the entire north of Spain without ever being there just by reading his book, *The Sands of Time*.

Dreaming through Sheldon's novels was part of my daily life. I loved the idea of living abroad. I even thought of leaving my country as soon as I had money and never coming back! I wanted to travel the world so much that I would look at the world globe my parents had at home and would spin it very slowly to observe closely the smallest names written on the map with curiosity and the determination to go there sometime in the future.

Born in Brazil, I would dream about going to those places that sounded very different and far away; such as India, Turkey and South Africa. I wanted the mystery, the unexpected, the unknown. Those were countries that my friends at school never thought about going to and maybe because I loved to be the different one, those places attracted me.

The very first one I moved to was Nelson Mandela's home country. I was 24 and totally inspired by his story and how he was changing the world with his perspectives on diversity and education. I dreamt about meeting him one day. When a work opportunity in Johannesburg landed in my lap, I grabbed it. I wanted to get to know the nation where the Apartheid regime had made him a prisoner for 27 years.

Living in South Africa was one of the greatest gifts life has ever given me. It was three and a half years of pure joy, challenges, friendships for life and exploration. I changed projects and companies, moved to Mozambique in between, learned how to become a vegetarian and lived a passionate romance.

South Africa was definitely my initiation to a global world: 11 official languages, three capital cities, ten Nobel Prize laureates, a multi-ethnic society, a country with another one inside and a land where two major oceans embrace each other. I was constantly experiencing conflicting values due to so many cultural differences and diversities.

My first trip to Guinea, another African country, was a true adventure. I did not know anybody who had traveled there and I was going by myself with not much information. My mission was to stay there for a week, conduct meetings and learn about the country's education system.

Getting to Conakry, the capital, was a journey by itself. Arriving in Paris from Johannesburg, I had an eight-hour wait for my connection before departing to the final destination. I was feeling excited and nervous as I had no idea about where I was going. The adrenaline in my body was telling me to enjoy the ride, but also be careful and aware so as to stay safe.

When I entered the Charles de Gaulle airport's business lounge to wait for my next flight, my ears immediately identified my home language, Portuguese, being spoken. I approached the two speakers and asked, "Where are you going to?" And they said, "Conakry!" I instantly felt relieved. Speaking with them, I discovered those two gentlemen were working for one of my company's competitors and they had similar interests in Guinea as me.

Whenever I travel anywhere, I do whatever I can to not listen to what other people say about my destination. I want to discover it through my own eyes, without the influence of others' opinions. But sometimes, even if you don't ask, people will tell you their perceptions and it is up to you to decide what to do with that. Parts of what those gentlemen shared with me in the next few hours were helpful, but other parts were just their fears and judgments. After we boarded to Conakry, I noticed I was the only woman among more than 100 passengers. One of the gentlemen said, "You better say you are with us when we land, as you are alone!"

When I left the plane and walked down the stairs, an immigration officer stopped me and asked, "What's your company?" Without even allowing me time to answer, one of the gentlemen said, "She is with us!" I am an independent woman, but in that moment I trusted those two men, blended with them and surrendered to their guidance.

Days before this trip, my colleagues advised me to not check-in my luggage because the statistics showed that, there was a high risk of a bag to be open or lost during such a long trip. I also heard that in some airports in Africa, people would '*throw*' your suitcase from the carousel and try to negotiate a price for you to pay. Trying to avoid that discomfort, I put everything I needed for a week in a small backpack that I took as a carry-on luggage.

Crossing the arrivals section, I witnessed one of the funniest scenes I saw that year. I saw the baggage claim area was crowded by people who were not passengers. These luggage 'supporters' would carry a suitcase from the carousel and, as if they were juggling bags in an auction, throw them high through the air from one person to the next, all screaming in French, "Who is the owner of this one? And this one? And that one? Catch that one! Who gives more for this one?" While the first-time travelers were desperate watching their bags flying above everybody's heads, I couldn't stop laughing. I was grateful for my colleagues' advice. At that moment, I realized that I shouldn't worry too much and life didn't need to be so serious. I had the feeling I was about to have a lot of fun!

On that trip, as I was driven from the airport to my hotel, I faced reality. It was late in the night and the city was very dark. Not much electricity around, except for a few gas lamps along the streets where hundreds of people, including kids, were still awake selling a variety of products by the road. The driver explained to me the tough reality the country had been going through... the unfavorable economic scenario, the lack of job opportunities, food, healthcare and education, the political conflicts, the extreme poverty in most areas... and in contrast, the vibrant tribal beliefs, their love for soccer and their rich soil full of minerals desired by most of the developed nations. It made a perfect equation in my head: natural wealth + inequality = creativity.

This equation was often repeated in my adventures. Whenever I went to a place naturally rich in precious resources and high in social inequality, people found ways to be extremely creative to survive. It was fascinating to see that many things I grew up thinking were unacceptable, in other countries were accepted and part of life. My concepts of right and wrong were challenged constantly.

I spent a wonderful week working in Guinea. I met a lot of fantastic people, tried the local food and defied the 'rule' that said, "Don't walk around." I traveled in between cities and had to frequently wait for negotiations between our driver and the different militias for what was supposed to be a toll. I watched boys with t-shirts full of holes playing soccer in the mud barefoot and became emotional when they scored a goal and shouted: "Brazil, zil, zil..."

The time for me to go back to South Africa was arriving. I checked-in at the airline office in the center of Conakry and, hours later, went to the airport. One of the people I met during my trip insisted I should carry at least one dollar in my pocket just in case anybody would try to stop me from boarding the plane. I told them that would never happen and that paying somebody for something I didn't have to was totally against my values. I thought I had already gone through everything I could possibly go through that week. Then, something happened that not only changed my trip back home, but changed me as a person and my views about traveling forever.

At the airport with check-in done, I walked along a passage that was supposed to take me to a security check and immigration. The passage looked like a maze with high walls, so I couldn't see what was coming. As I turned the next corner, the three tallest and strongest men I have ever seen stood up. Two of them yelled, "Passport, passport!" The third one asked me to put my backpack into the broken x-ray machine for a search.

I felt scared. The size of those men and the way they were speaking to me was totally intimidating. My mind was trying to get me worried again about what could happen next, reminding me that I was by myself with no money and just my personal belongings. Suddenly, I remembered I was not alone. I had my principles with me. I had my character. I had a powerful passport with stamps from many countries in the world showing where I have been as a proof that I was an experienced traveler. And even though I was afraid, I was also ready to fight with them — *God knows how would I do that!* — for my integrity. I would never corrupt myself!

The first officer looked at my passport and immediately called for the attention of the other two. I was internally shaking in fear. He asked me, "Brazilian?" And I confirmed with an enthusiastic "Yes!" The men responded, "Pelé! Romário! Bebeto!" And continued to say all the names of the most famous Brazilian soccer players in history with so much joy and pleasure that I immediately felt relaxed. When they said, "…Ronaldinho…" I joked, "He's my cousin!" They laughed and so did I!

The queue behind me got longer and longer as we kept talking and laughing. They forgot about searching my backpack and never really looked inside my passport. Seeing my country on the cover was enough for them to create a connection with me. They forgot their hardships and difficulties, and instead remembered that life doesn't need to be a struggle, and that we can appreciate each other and treat one another with kindness, no matter where we come from. At the end of the day, we are all human beings. We are all people traveling through the journey of life.

After much pleasant conversation with my poor French, they wished me, *"Bon voyage, mon ami,"* and I boarded the airplane. It was only later during my trip home that I learned the two people after me in the queue had had their belongings and money *confiscated* by those very same men.

Those men who had been so friendly to me had pulled apart bags, searched through belongings, took batteries out of cameras, creating fear and a sense of violation in my fellow travelers. I felt profoundly shocked. I also felt profoundly grateful.

I realized so many lessons from that special moment with the immigration officers.

First, it wasn't where I had been in the world that mattered, but who I was.

Along with where I was born and where I grew up. It was the fact that being a Brazilian was part of my identity. Some of the habits of my culture has benefited me as a person, making me happy and relatable. By winning five FIFA World Cups, Brazilians have touched the lives of people worldwide. That connection has been endearing with others and helped me maintain my integrity in different occasions, including that one.

Secondly, making judgments and worrying is never helpful. Worry is either past or future based and doesn't allow me to fully live in the present. Making assumptions about *"what happened to others may happen to me"* just made me worry about being forced to pay a bribe, have my belongings taken or not being allowed to leave that country… Fears I could overcome with humor and connection.

Another important lesson was about creativity and flexibility. In a place where people are striving to survive, the rule of law may not be strictly observed. I had to relax and be creative, make a joke — which I was not used to — and break the protocol to prove to myself that I don't need to be that serious. It is a message I seem to be getting many times in my life. Brazilians are known as masters of flexibility. We even have a special name for it: "The Brazilian Way." As with everything in life, there are positives and negatives about it. We are so flexible that we tend to break rules or find another way of doing things. On the flip side, we are extremely adaptable. If a situation requires change, I will adapt myself and go with the flow. In that moment with the immigration officers, it was great to be reminded that I am Brazilian.

After that moment, I realized the reasons *why* I travel. When I choose a place to visit for the first time, most of my interests are focused on history and culture. When I choose somewhere to revisit or to live, my focus is on weather conditions and cultural behaviors. No matter where I have been during the last decades, it has always boiled down to the place and its people — the feelings and the connections that bring joy to my soul.

I once heard from a mentor: "Always do something that makes you feel good about yourself," and that is absolutely the reason why I travel. It doesn't only make me feel good, but it also opens a space for me to contribute to the people around me; to lift up my spirit and touch the hearts of others. And, when I give something like that of myself, I feel good about the person I am.

Traveling is part of who I am. The journey by itself is my way of living. I travel to value my place in the world and my history, wherever it might be. I travel to honor the place where I belong, the people, the heritage, the culture and the *Maravilha da vida!*

You may ask yourself sometimes where do you belong; wanting to find that spot where you fit in. Know that you were born in your place for a reason. You grew up in your country because it was meant to be that way. There's a master plan working in your favor, guiding you from one destination to the next. Life would never give you something without a purpose; you may discover along the way that finding yours becomes the travel of a lifetime.

IGNITE ACTION STEPS

- **Collaborate and trust your intuition:** When living and adventuring, share any valuable information you have with others around you. Sometimes you will need support and you will have to trust and let people help you. Collaboration is always better than competition – and can save lives!
- **Look at the world with a child's eyes:** Remember that even if you know many things, you don't know everything. There is a lot in this world to be discovered. Be open to experience with genuine eyes what life has to offer you.
- **Use Humor:** Even if you think you are not funny yourself, you have a sense of humor! Look for opportunities to make jokes to lighten up situations that can be perceived by others as difficult. Make those moments (from packing to unpacking) easier for everybody who is in that journey with you.
- **Be Grateful and go with the flow:** While the neighbor's grass might look greener than yours, there is a reason why you were born where you were born. That reason is always there to serve you. Your roots are part of who you are and they contribute to your life without you being aware of it. If you ever wake up thinking, "Why is this going on with my country?" remember to be grateful for where you come from, not only for the places that you have been traveling to.

Every journey guides us somewhere life-changing if we are open to embracing the opportunities as growth and learning.

Hanna Meirelles - Brazil
Global Trainer and Development Facilitator,
Leadership Specialist and Founder of Life Level 10
www.hannameirelles.com
🖪 *lifelevel10byhannameirelles*

MARIFLOR ARCOIRIS

"Everything is possible as soon as you believe it;
an intention made with love is an act of magic."

My intention is that you feel inspired to trust and go through whatever path your heart is showing you. That you reconnect with your Inner Child, rediscover who you are, love yourself, awaken your magic and dare to live the life of your dreams. *Believe to see.*

BE YOURSELF

"What are you waiting for? What are you doing with your life? Who are you?" It was early morning, I was looking at my reflection in the mirror asking myself those three questions. I don't know what happened in that moment six years ago; I just know that that day started a new chapter in my life.

I was living in Chile, next to the beautiful ocean with the most glorious sunsets I have ever seen in my life, doing 'very well' with my personal goals. I studied business and was running a vegan start up, giving entrepreneurship lectures at the university, and doing business mentoring in a company recently founded with both my partner and a friend. Everything was apparently running smoothly with many opportunities ahead.

The problem was I was not satisfied. I was feeling empty with a lack of inspiration... depressed... I had everything and nothing at the same time.

I never had time for my color pencils and white paper that were under my bed... or any other creative expression I enjoyed. Looking in the mirror with tears in my eyes and a compressed heart, I saw that my whole life was only about working hard, making goals, achieving them and starting again. Always looking to the future... running... The more success I had, the more afraid I was of not having enough freedom to live my life.

I had been in love with someone for almost five years. When I was a teenager, I never cared about getting married. However, a few years into that relationship, I changed my mind, but from the beginning, he told me, "If you go and travel for a long time, we are not going to get married." He was willing to travel with me for up to two months but that was not enough for me, I wanted more. I wanted to feel I had all the time in the world and the freedom to choose to stay wherever I wanted, for however long I chose.

I had been waiting for two years for his marriage proposal... until that day in front of the mirror when I realized that there was nothing to wait for... I was not going to beg for love anymore and not going to let my heart wait to explore!

On that morning something miraculous happened. It was like the reflection in the mirror was talking to me and challenging me to SEE! To see what? I still didn't know... and here the adventure began.

I still can feel my heart beating stronger than ever, willing to do whatever was needed to be happy and to find my way. I felt I wanted to fly away, to open my wings for the first time in my life. I knew I had to make a drastic change and travel by myself.

On the one side was my heart saying, "Go!" while on the other side was my structured and old-schooled mind telling me, "You can't travel and do nothing; traveling for pleasure is for lazy people! You have to invest your time working or studying."

With this idea in mind, I desperately tried to find a good 'excuse' to travel, something that could be acceptable to other people. How I was going to express this to my family, relatives and partner? I did not know.

Synchronicity has always been my best friend. One of my businesses was needing a 'business coach' so I offered to go and fill this role myself. This was the gateway I found to start the most adventurous story that never ended. Quickly I signed up in a 'coaching training' in New Zealand (NZ) and four months later, I was scheduled to travel from Chile to NZ for three months.

My family was used to my short trips so it was nothing new for them and, as grandmas always see beyond our words, she asked me very curiously, "For how long are you leaving?" looking to me with an 'are you sure?' expression. I answered her, "No worries, I will come back very soon..."

Before I knew it, I was one day away from taking my 24-hour long trip, only worrying about what clothes, beauty care products and other superficial stuff to bring. All the rest could be left behind as I was coming back in three months. One part of me was afraid of being alone in another country, the other part was full of excitement.

At the airport, I said goodbye to my family and to my partner, knowing he had a ticket to visit me in NZ in just a couple of months.

When I arrived in Auckland, the change started. After realizing that I was crazy enough to bring two huge pieces of luggage plus one backpack and a few bags to carry by hand, for the first time, I saw how much weight I was carrying in life.

The study program began! When you study a coaching program you experience inner self-therapy as it is not only theory. It was so powerful that I completely transformed my life! I discovered that I was very good at connecting with the deepest side of people despite the barriers of language (as I had only basic English skills). I had to allow my intuition to flourish and to trust in it to have a clear understanding and resolution. I succeeded in completing the first part of the training program despite not exactly following what it was teaching me. The director told me, "You are a very colorful soul! Follow your intuition! You are not a rule follower as many are." I realized that there was much I didn't know about myself. My only goal in that moment was to FULLY live in the present as I never had before. I needed time for myself to rediscover who I was.

Without knowing it first, the Universe delivered an amazing opportunity. I discovered the 'Work and Holiday Visa Program' that allows foreigners to travel and work in NZ for one year. It was a huge opportunity for me! The tricky thing was that the applications are only open once a year for only 20 minutes, and that process was going to start in two weeks! I had to hurry.

When I found out my application was successfully approved, I was shocked and ecstatic! NZ visas are one of the most difficult to obtain compared to this kind of visa from other countries and I was one of the winners! I decided I would take it to only extend my trip for three months. I still had to go back to Chile to keep running the family business, and Love was waiting for me. It was so exciting to continue traveling and discovering the country. I did lots of hiking and camping and loved every minute of it.

On the other hand, I had to start working in NZ because I had big responsibilities to pay in Chile and I also had to pay for my 'extra life.' On top of that, the feeling of wanting to stay and live there was growing every day. I knew there was no way back. I was never going to be the same again. I wanted to explore completely new things so I started to do seasonal jobs that I had never done before, those where you signed out at the end of the day and you are able to be completely disconnected from work. This was new for me. In Chile, I was working even in my sleep and dreams.

My first NZ job was being a cleaner in a resort. Yes, cleaning toilets, making beds, washing dishes, among other things. My family was in shock! They couldn't understand my decision. Despite what people thought, I was extremely happy with that... The 'Master in Marketing' had become the 'Master in Cleaning Toilets' and it was completely right for me. I had no prejudice; the only thing that counted was the happiness and the moments after work, on the beautiful beach with friends, with 'nothing to worry about!'

Yes, I wanted to stay... I was still not brave enough to say it!

During the first months in NZ, I mentioned a few times to my partner that he could take a break and join me in my adventure. He is a successful professional in Chile, so I thought that it would be easy for him to find whatever job he wanted in NZ. I never got a positive answer. I was starting to worry and at the same time happy to know I would see him soon. The moment to decide had arrived; he called me one week before his arrival to NZ and asked me the most difficult question: "Do you want to stay to live there?" At that moment, my heart started beating stronger and stronger. I knew I had to say it to be true to myself for the first time.

I replied, "Yes, I do. You could also try to come and stay for at least three months." He said, "I'm not going to take the plane only to go there and say goodbye to you. I don't like any of the things that you are doing now; nothing." I can still feel the sensation of that moment. I was in a free fall from a high cliff. I saw the ocean below and the sensation of falling with no end, with not knowing what to do, what to expect. The relationship ended and my heart felt squashed flat with the pain of it.

I was afraid. A few times, I felt that I had to go back to Chile. Fortunately, I didn't. I had nothing to lose now, that was clear. The happy person that I was becoming was not vibrating with him anymore, so I used all of my energy to go forward. That moment was crucial in my life as I started wondering what was Real Love and if I ever felt In Love... Then, the big question began: "WHAT IS LOVE?" That day, a new chapter in my life started, called "Why not?" that quickly changed to "Why yes?" I wanted to explore everything! And in parallel, a voice from my heart whispered, "Did I ever feel in love?"

I always had a tendency to spirituality, despite my business studies, so I already had a strong connection with Mother Nature and all of its creation. One night in Waiheke Island, NZ, I was looking to the stars, listening to the waves and with all the power of my heart, I asked the Universe, "Please show me. I want to know what Real Love is. I want to feel it." I didn't ask for a man; I asked for Real Love.

As usual, Universe listened and I started having completely new experiences. I found connection with new passions, things I never experienced before. I started to paint, to play music, to play circus games, to give yoga lessons, to share life coaching sessions, to heal others... and discovered that all of this was the starting point of a new career. My life was making a 360-degree turn.

My priorities changed and I was not focused on superficial things anymore. I gifted all of my clothes and started living in a more light and natural way. I learned to live as a nomad with no attachments, sometimes living in a tent (one of the best homes I had). I felt so free! My personality was changing to the point that I no longer identified with the name my parents gave me (Maria Francisca) and I found many new nicknames that made sense to me. Today, I'm Mariflor. It could change in the future as I understood that life is a game and that everyone is free to choose how to play it.

For me, NZ is one of the most beautiful places in the world, especially Waiheke Island, with its magical rainbows, the song of crickets and the dolphins. This place touched my heart. Swimming naked in the sea with my friends and feeling the joy of drawing our fluorescent bodies through those waters full of plankton, I can still see the stars shining closer than ever under the full moon. This new deep connection with Mother Nature increased the sense of Unity in me and I understood the great impact on The Whole from every little action we do.

Even though I was starting to live my freedom, I still had to learn an important lesson... On the one hand, I was rebirthing myself with completely new things I discovered that I loved. On the other, I was submerged and blind in a violent relationship. I had found a new partner with whom I experienced the most painful relationship that I ever had. I needed to love myself more than ever to leave him and recover from that experience. It was crucial in my journey. He was a tremendous life teacher; he came into my life to teach me about Real Love. The Universe was in charge of letting me know what is Love. Through pain, I understood that Self Love is essential to feel any other Love. So, I made a *Love Commitment* with myself and today I feel deep gratitude to him and to ALL the experiences that made me explore *Love* in all its facets.

As a result, the more I started to be myself, the more I knew that going back to Chile was not my way... and I never lived there again.

Those past experiences blossomed in my heart the courage to do whatever I want, accepting and daring to be myself, a shiny rainbow star, even if sometimes it doesn't fit with the social paradigm. I realized the importance of respecting the authenticity of each one of us and that I'm the only one responsible for who I am.

For me, fear was a catalyst to go forward. I saw how that feeling contracts our Being and how important it is to cultivate Love to reconnect with ourselves and expand our essence. Becoming a citizen of the world, I realized that the whole of life is an adventure. Traveling became my lifestyle.

Now I practice self-love as a basis for living, knowing that the best thing I can do to change the world is to stay in a high vibrational energy level, and this is only obtained by doing what vibrates in my heart. I am motivated to discover who I am constantly, to accept changes, and to know that I can always be reborn, transforming myself into another person. That experience encouraged me to explore more my unique talents and I'm sure that this is the key for living a successful life. I know that what I believe, I create; and I believe I deserve the best, so that is exactly what I'm getting now.

It doesn't matter how big the challenge or the uncertainty, I just have to jump towards the path that my heart points to and something better will come. There is always something I can do to affect the change. And I wish to have the will to put this into practice. The change starts within, so I dare to be the change I want to see and live in the world.

During the trip, I discovered that my main color (talent) is to inspire others to 'awaken their magic.' I felt a strong call in my heart to help people realize each of us holds a MAGICIAN ARTIST OF LIFE that is constantly creating their realities!

Everything starts with a dream. I learnt how to manifest the life of my dreams and I became aware of how reality is created. Now, I stand up for Love and Unity. This is my life purpose and the core of my life project 'Co-LOVEvolution.' Through it I'm inspiring people to improve their quality of life with educational tools focused on conscious living, creativity and universal Love. All of this is based on my deep belief of a world with a new conscious humanity, free human beings vibrating in LOVE, reconnecting with their essence, understanding their potential to create the life of their dreams... in peace... in respect... in harmony with ourselves... with each other... and with Mother Nature.

Love is the way, the most powerful energy; it is pure creation. I hope you see how this frequency is here for your evolution. We all can access it if we connect with our Inner Child that lives in our hearts — and this is exactly what I did. My Inner Child was asleep. Now that I have reconnected to her, she is always at the center of my awareness and I feed her regularly, letting her be free and play. Your Inner Child is inside of you, too. Get ready to play and shine your colors!.

With Love and Togetherness Everything is Possible.

Ignite Action Steps

Use this magical formula: Imagination + Feelings + Action = Reality Creation

- Ask yourself each day while looking in the mirror, "Who Am I? How will I love myself today?" Tell your reflection how amazing you are and thank yourself for being a loving presence in your life. This is a beautiful practice of Self Love.

- Every morning, gift yourself at least 15 minutes to be with yourself. Take this time to awaken your body and soul. And later in the day hug a tree.

- Practice daily gratitude. Think about five things you are thankful for.

- Dream out loud. Imagine things you want and give thanks in advance that they came true.

Mariflor Arcoiris - Chile
Magician Artist of Life
www.co-lovevolution.com
co_lovevolution
co-lovevolution

KATE WITHEY

"Connect with joy."

Learning even a little of the language, customs and unspoken traditions of the places you visit – whether distant countries or new communities of people – will help you to connect more deeply and have richer experiences.

SECRET CODES OF CULTURE

Language codes

"Scheisse!" I dropped my coin purse, scattering coins all over the floor of the bus and the word popped out of my mouth without conscious thought. I was a 20-year-old on my first solo trip abroad and I had just said, "Shit!" loudly on a public bus in Germany. I was mortified, but the driver and passengers started to laugh. A moment before, I had been stumbling with my German to ask the driver the fare, an obvious tourist, but somehow a colloquial swear word had come out automatically. Several people helped me pick up my money and the driver plucked the right coins from my hand. When I sat down, the people around me teased me about it, wanted to know where I was from, and suggested local places I should visit: the best hidden restaurant and a club where I could go dancing. Without even meaning to, by swearing in another language, I had broken the ice and made a connection!

Language is the most fundamental 'code' that can help unlock a culture. Even if you're convinced you're not good at languages, stretching yourself to learn some basic phrases will pay off in goodwill as well as helping you communicate. I don't, however, recommend starting with swearing!

My father learned this in Paris a decade after my German experience. My whole family was sitting at a sidewalk café when I saw a language code connect for him for the first time. "Un bier, s'il vous plaît," he said, prompted by my sister Gale and me. We both spoke fluent French and were experienced travelers by then, but Dad was resolutely monolingual and had never been abroad. The first time he said the phrase, it was as if he was joking or saying nonsense syllables: his response to not feeling in control in an unfamiliar situation.

Dad was a brilliant physicist, but was bad at languages (he told us he had never received his PhD solely because he couldn't learn Russian or German to read foreign technical papers). As he drank his beer, we coached him again how to ask, and the second – or maybe the third – time he said "Un bier, s'il vous plaît," to the patient waiter, it was as if a light went on. He got it: he wasn't just making funny sounds, *he was actually communicating in a foreign language!* I was so proud of him for making the effort to experience a little of what his wife and daughters all loved about travel: connecting with other cultures by doing things in a new way.

Food and drink as codes

My father had his moment over a Parisian beer; years later, my mother and I had ours over tea in Japan. Kyoto was beautiful in April – we had hit cherry-blossom season perfectly – but it was also *cold*. We were on a guided walking tour of Zen temples and gardens. We were learning more about Buddhism and Zen design principles than we had ever imagined, but we were spending much of our days outside and weren't dressed warmly enough. Until we found a uniquely Japanese solution to this problem: hot green tea in a can from sidewalk vending machines! My first thought was how weird that was – who's ever heard of a *hot* drink in a can? – but I quickly found that it warmed my hands as well as my insides. We think nothing of walking around with a take-out hot coffee in America, so why not a can of hot tea in Asia?

Green tea is much more than just a drink in Japan; for centuries it has had a position of great importance and respect. Like many things, from calligraphy to flower arranging, the preparation of tea had been raised to a ritual and an art. We had experienced the higher end of this spectrum by taking part in a tea ceremony at a Zen temple: kneeling on *tatami* mats at a low table, with sliding screen panels open to the beautiful simplicity of a Zen garden, we drank the powdered green tea whipped by a monk in a precisely choreographed ritual. There we were at the other end of the spectrum, appreciating the depth of the Japanese passion for tea by drinking it from vending machine cans on the sidewalk!

Although each small taste of a popular food or drink in another place might not unlock the whole culture for you, sampling many regional specialties in the same way the locals do will give you a deeper feeling for the ways that people live there. Eating octopus in the Greek islands or drinking tiny espressos every day in Italy won't turn you into a native – any more than experiencing a tea ceremony in a Kyoto temple turned me Buddhist – but doing things the way the locals do will give you more appreciation for the myriad ways that people live. That's fundamentally why I travel. Isn't that worth passing up the comfort of eating and drinking only the things that you're used to?

Parisian cultural codes

I've visited Paris more than anywhere else – I fell irrevocably in love with the city the first time I was there with my high school French class – so I know many subtle codes that most tourists never learn.

For instance, every customer, entering every shop, every day greets the shopkeeper, and is greeted in return. Marketing begins with a polite repetition of "Bonjour, Madame," "Bonjour, Monsieur," and ends with "Merci, au revoir," "Au revoir, merci." To many foreigners, this seems absurdly formal or unnecessary, but to the French, politeness – 'La Politesse' – is extremely important. What's more, if a foreigner just walks in and asks for something without saying this ritual "Hello," it feels rude to the proprietors. They, feeling slighted, may respond abruptly, leading to the foreigner thinking that it's the French who are rude. The foreigner never realizes that he or she was the one who broke the code of politeness in the first place. I love this code: every time I buy my daily baguette, successfully performing this simple ritual, I feel a little more like an insider.

It's not only what you say, but how you say it, and your clothing and body language, too. Tourists in Paris can be perceived as crass for speaking 'too loud.' In a restaurant, people are seated at intimate tables right next to other parties. The French speak softly, giving each other privacy, and are annoyed if the boisterous volume of their neighbors' conversations drowns out their own.

"You're not going to wear *that* in Paris, are you?" My California boyfriend's jacket looked like something he should wear hiking in the woods, not visiting Paris at Christmas. "It's a sophisticated city; you have to dress up. To them, it feels like you're insulting the beauty of Paris by being sloppy." Like me, he had spent a lot of time in Paris, but it had never occurred to him to follow the not-so-secret dress code! No French woman would so much as run to the bakery in the morning without being totally put-together; seeing tourists in shapeless T-shirts and loud sneakers makes the locals cringe. I dragged my skeptical boyfriend to a department store to get a good men's overcoat and cashmere scarf. Once in the stylish coat, he noticed the difference in how he felt and how he was treated. On previous trips, he had only been *visiting;* this time, by following the local code of dressing up, he felt more like he was *taking part* in the culture.

Even French parks have different codes. In the United States, we love walking on the grass, but in France, you're supposed to stay on the paths. I got scolded like a naughty child by a park official when I chose to break this code. I just *had to* get close to a Henry Moore sculpture in a park, to caress the sun-warmed bronze, even though it was surrounded by grass. The problem wasn't that I was touching the sculpture; it was that I had been so rude as to walk across the precious grass to get to it!

The tango code

Parks in Buenos Aires had a much more uninhibited feel. I had come across a charming little square by chance and of course when I saw the couple dancing tango to a portable stereo, I had stopped my meandering to watch. It was a sultry, late-summer afternoon. Most people were inside escaping the heat that radiated off the cobblestones, though a small crowd had gathered. The man was wearing all black with a long-sleeved, western-style shirt – classic tango attire despite the sun and the heat – and the woman had a blue dress that twirled around her knees. I had watched them dance a couple of songs before they took a break. I could watch good tango dancers for hours, hoping to improve my own dancing through the osmosis of feeling their steps as if I were doing them. This couple's dancing was playful and fun to watch: not world-class, but worth my lingering to observe. The woman walked off, probably in search of coffee or a bathroom, and the man sat down on a low stone wall.

Everything felt upside-down in Buenos Aires. It seemed as if I'd been disoriented for the whole time I'd been there: I was strangely aware of being in the Southern Hemisphere; I couldn't seem to get past jet-lag from the 16-hour flight, and my sleep schedule was completely backward from dancing tango all night and sleeping half the day. Although there were lessons and practice sessions in the early evenings, the real dances didn't start until 11 PM or midnight, and ran until 4 AM, after which people would go out for breakfast! I was feeling even more adrift exploring the city on my own as the group tour I had come on with dancers I knew from home had just ended. I was also hot and tired – definitely outside my comfort zone – but I was getting in all the dancing I could, and wasn't going to give in and nap the day away.

I was crazy about the tango. This was a decade before its international resurgence but I had been taking lessons for a couple of years and was now on a pilgrimage to its birthplace: Buenos Aires. Tango is the soul of Buenos Aires. Although it had first developed in the brothels and bars around the ports in the late 1800s, it became hugely popular in the early twentieth century. Now in 1997, however, while younger Argentines were familiar with the music, very few knew the dances. Like big-band swing in the US, tango was the dance of their parents or grandparents. Most teachers and experienced dancers were in their seventies – with the smoothness and grace that came from dancing this style all their lives – but a growing number of younger dancers around the world were reviving it for new generations. Although there were certainly other 'dance tourists' in Buenos Aires, the local dancers I met – and more so the non-dancers – were often astonished that I would fly 7,000 miles to study the tango in its native habitat.

I have always loved partner dancing: salsa, swing dance, Lindy Hop, even American square dance and contra dance (a version of the dances you see in British period dramas with lines of people opposite each other). I was *not*, however, one of those little girls who danced her way naturally through childhood; instead, I've learned the codes of different dances as I have foreign languages. Like different countries, each dance has its own unique language of non-verbal communication, as well as its own music and steps. Tango, however, takes this to a whole new level.

Back in the square in Buenos Aires, I am staring fixedly at the tango dancer. He looks a little bored without his partner. He glances over at the people standing around, his eyes flitting over me – just another tourist – and then they click back to me. My heart beats faster as I hold his gaze. He raises his eyebrows and gestures with his chin; I smile and nod. I feel triumphant as he starts to walk over to me, because I have just successfully communicated in the secret language of the Argentine tango that:

I am a tango dancer.
I am good enough to know the non-verbal request to dance.
I would like to dance with you.

And he has said, "Yes!"

This subtle communication, called the 'cabeceo,' is used at tango dances around the world. In the tango culture, a woman doesn't just walk up to a man and ask him to dance: it feels pushy and is the sign of a beginner. If she is then hurt or huffy if the man says No — which is perfectly acceptable — she has compounded the problem by not understanding that she is the one who was rude. On the other hand, if she graciously accepts the refusal, he might ask her later, after watching her dance with other people to see if he thinks their styles will work together and if he wants to lead her. Tango is a very intimate dance, and the sets are long.

When the dancer in the square walks up to me and we exchange a few words (my Spanish is shaky, but I can manage, "What's your name?" and "Where are you from?"), my nervousness almost overwhelms my excitement. What have I just committed myself to? Am I really going to do this? Even my toes tingle with trepidation. We walk over to his stereo and he turns the music back on. I notice that my hands are sweating as he takes me in the tango embrace, but I close my eyes and breathe deeply, connecting to this moment: this familiar song, this unknown man, this sunny square in Buenos Aires, *this tango dance.* I become more relaxed as he leads me confidently through a few songs, though I'm still self-conscious, worrying that I'll mess up, or that my street shoes will catch on the uneven paving stones. And yet, here I am performing the tango in public, however informally, and I feel a deep sense of belonging.

Unlocking codes

Sitting in a sidewalk café, I try to guess the nationality of people walking by, then to figure out what gave them away. That woman who carries herself as if she is beautiful could only be French. That man who walks like a cowboy, taking up a lot of space, is clearly American. Only a German would wear those sandals with socks, whereas those exquisite hand-made shoes must be Italian. By being a curious observer, I can tease out some cultural codes — whether to use them, avoid them or simply to notice them — though some codes need to be learned explicitly.

I love being mistaken for a local when I'm abroad. This isn't about denying my own culture; in fact, I like being a counter-example for people who have negative beliefs about Americans. Sometimes I feel like an outsider, even in my own culture. When I'm somewhere else, feeling like an outsider is okay because I am one. I'm more conscious of looking for the codes of cultural communication and have a greater sense of satisfaction when I unlock one. Being mistaken for a local is proof that I'm using the codes correctly, and this gives me a surprising sense of achievement.

By using the local language, taking part in a cultural ritual, making an effort to fit in through your dress and behavior, or using non-verbal codes, you will have more experiences of mutual understanding. Even in a transient moment, that authentic connection can break down barriers and melt away any sense of 'otherness' — in that instant, you've become a citizen of the world.

IGNITE ACTION STEPS

- If you're traveling, **get a cultural guide** to the place you're going, in addition to any regular travel guidebook. Two good series are *Dos and Don'ts...* and *Culture Shock!...* (with the destination name); an online search will find many other titles.
- Whether you're traveling or joining a new group of any sort, **ask people** there what common mistakes newcomers or foreigners often make, or things they do that people find rude. Not everyone knows these secret rules consciously, but often they can figure them out by thinking about what seems rude.
- **Listen** to what these people or books tell you instead of arguing about why your way makes more sense! Customs are not about logic; they are about tradition and respect.
- If you think that someone else has been rude to *you,* see if you can **figure out** if what you just said or did isn't how the people there are doing it. This is often the sign of a cultural misunderstanding.
- **Try out** your new skills, even if — or especially if — they're a little outside your comfort zone! Sometimes you can ask, "Did I do/say that right?" if it seems appropriate. Most people are very willing to help you understand their culture.
- **Notice** that you feel more connected and that people seem more polite to you. Be proud of yourself for going beyond what most people do and mastering a secret code!

Kate Withey - United States
World Traveler & Global Citizen
kate@katewithey.com
f *katewithey*

JANIE JURKOVICH

"Soul Connections are not only possible but life-changing."

My intention is to create a story that opens the reader's mind to the possibility of connecting to other Beings on a soul level.

THE POWER OF SOUL CONNECTIONS

"No, we want *two* beds," I stated to the three hotel staff members while checking in. My son, in his thirties, was giving me the 'look' that said, "I'm not sleeping with my mother for a week!" The staff glanced at each other and then at me, their disbelieving expressions saying, "Sure, lady. We know you are here with your young lover. You aren't fooling us." So, I responded with, "He's my *son*." I am not sure if they believed me or not, but they did give us a room with two beds, much to my son's relief!

This is how our trip to Egypt began. My son and I were on a great adventure. While married, I was never able to put such plans into action, but now that I was divorced, I wanted some bonding time with my son and, tired of staying home, we decided to go somewhere far away and exotic.

In learning to travel on my own, I let go of long-ingrained money worries and found ways to afford to go on adventures. Friends had timeshares and air miles. I asked for what I wanted and trusted a Higher Power. Funds became available miraculously.

Little did I know that on this trip, I would learn more than historical facts about Egyptian life and culture. I would be embarking on an adventure of a lifetime, one that would challenge my status-quo and propel me closer to my future mission in life.

The five-star Cairo Marriott, the former home of King Farouk, was undoubtedly the most exquisite hotel I had ever stayed in. Just walking around, we felt like royalty! The regal coffee-bar near the entrance greeted us, as did the attentive doormen. The staircases and furnishings were fit for those well above my social standing and were an indulgence I was quite happy to enjoy.

The complex was huge, encompassing seven restaurants and more than one bank! Between the buildings, there were lush gardens. Gold, marble, beautiful artwork and statues surrounded us and the responsive staff met our every request. It was like everyone and everything was in tune with our needs.

From the first day, we were at ease mingling with the locals. I used to live in Turkey where my former husband and I adopted our son. My son's olive skin made him look like a local. Hoping to fit in even better, my son had grown a beard to enhance his experience. The country felt very much like other eastern European countries where the shop keepers happily engage you in conversations to buy their wares. I was delighted to find the people most congenial.

My son noticed a local woman and her two-year-old daughter begging on the street. I sensed he was thinking that possibly, he, too, could have endured the life of a street urchin. Being adopted by an American family profoundly changed the trajectory of his life. He was quite smitten with the little girl and asked permission to take her picture. The mother obliged and he paid her handsomely in return, glad to have an excuse to share his wealth with them.

Often, the locals spoke to my son in Arabic. It was only by our quizzical looks that they knew we were foreigners. One curious young shop girl asked my son a question and they used a translation app on his phone to communicate.

I, too, worked on my communication skills during our visit using a method not requiring any equipment, just an open mind and a willingness to connect.

On our second day in Egypt, the formal tour began. Our able guide gave us a quick glimpse into the history of Egypt on the way to the Egyptian Museum of Antiquities. The current facility, although huge, only contained a fraction of the country's treasures; the rest were in storage. Visiting the museum was literally a step back in time. It held the most amazing artifacts and historical items. The intricate details and the workmanship were just stunning!

Our next stop was Muhammad Ali's Mosque. He was quite a revered person in Egyptian culture, having ruled the country for over 40 years. The famous boxer, the former Cassius Clay, changed his name in honor of him.

This association certainly sparked my memory, but what occurred *inside* the mosque is what I will remember forevermore.

We learned from our tour guide that Muhammad Ali had been raised in Albania. His parents died when he was young, wherein he was raised by an uncle. After his uncle passed away, Muhammad joined the Egyptian army. He was loved by many people and known for his fast decision making. Muhammad reached the high rank of Pasha - an exalted Lord and later built the exquisite mosque. Supposedly, he is buried in the tomb there, although many believe his body was returned to his homeland.

Outside, a large marble fountain adorned with multiple columns sits in a huge courtyard. It was originally built for people to wash their feet prior to entering the mosque. In Egyptian times, the enticement of free water also encouraged villagers to attend the religious services inside.

The alabaster walls of the mosque are 70 feet tall, a beautiful, massive sight to see. It impresses one with the feeling of just how special the venue really is. When you enter, you are required to remove your shoes or wear paper booties. I wanted to feel the carpet beneath my toes in this sacred space so I removed my shoes.

My mind traveled back in time to my vacation the previous summer when I went to South Carolina. I remembered jogging on the beach one morning and passing a woman walking along the shore. She was rather thin and had a head covering, like those going through chemotherapy. Her long sleeve blouse blew in the wind. She was thinking. Intently. *Very* intently. And I could hear her thoughts, which was both startling and emotional. She said, "I'm not ready to die. There is so much more I want to do. I want to live!" It felt as if her heartfelt cries were being absorbed into my body, into my soul.

Admittedly, I could have just conjured up this notion of what the woman was thinking. But the feelings were so intense, I knew it was not my imagination. I was *certain*. This feeling of certainty Ignited my awareness and opened a whole new chapter of my life. There in Egypt, I wanted to test my theory. I wanted to see if it was true that I could connect to others on what I call a 'soul level.'

I approached the gold railing surrounding Muhammad Ali's tomb. I quietly asked for him, and he immediately responded, "I am not here. I'm in Albania, but you can talk to me anyway." I thanked him for building the mosque. He said, "Please tell others about Egypt. This is what I want you to do, dear."

"Wow, pretty amazing," I thought. My feelings encompassed both awe and disbelief. I remembered the tour guide had told us of the controversy about the location of Muhammad's body. Was I imagining it? I wasn't fully convinced I was truly capable of connecting to a long-dead soul.

I walked across the vast mosque to the corner facing Mecca, the Muslim holy city. I knelt down to pray. I asked what I could do. The answer was clear: "Tell others to have more grace, understanding and love for each other. Spread the word. We know it's a tall order, just do the best you can. Return now to your son, for your little Janim (a Turkish word meaning 'loved one') needs you."

At the door of the mosque, I heard, "Thank you my dear. Do your mission with pride. We love you." I felt excitement and chills at the same time.

I started to embrace my connecting ability to other souls. It seemed I could hear and sense the thoughts of others. I could not have known such sentiments on my own. It was a bit surreal and hard to believe. Luckily, I was given another chance to better understand and I used it as an opportunity for growth.

Once outside in the heat, I couldn't find my son. He had been conversing with one of the many 'salesmen' selling wares in the courtyard. I started to walk towards him, but the security guard who was accompanying our tour group told me to stay put. He would retrieve my son. I sensed he thought there was a bit of danger, but my son certainly felt none because he returned to me eager to display the bartered items he had procured.

A few days later on our Egyptian tour, we were traveling the Nile in our new floating home — a large passenger boat with all the amenities. It was quite something to experience; going to the top deck where there is a bar AND swimming pool. You can lean on the railing and feel the breeze while you gaze at the villages along the Nile. You can see children playing, men working the fields and oxen grazing along the shores.

Every once in a while, a tiny boat with men would come close to our large boat with wares to sell to any passengers willing to pay them. This was actually quite entertaining one day when my son engaged the men in conversation and then it was he who tried to sell their wares to other passengers. He fit right in the Middle Eastern culture of deal-making. He helped several of the guests purchase clothing or table linens. It was quite a sight to see the men toss plastic bags of items up to my son on the top deck for inspection. He promptly bartered a deal between passenger and vendor and sent the money back down to their small boat.

One morning, we boarded a tour bus for the Valley of the Kings — a huge exhibit with approximately 57 magnificent tombs at the site. The sheer number of tombs meant we had to travel by bus just to observe them. The colored hieroglyphics intricately etched on their walls told stories of Egyptian history, wars, kingdoms and family life.

Ramesses II was originally entombed there. He was one of many kings named Ramesses, and later became known as Ramesses the Great. Our tour guide pointed out several columns in other locations where Ramesses had his workers chisel *out* the engravings of former leaders and chisel *in* his name! When you actually see these huge columns in person you have some perspective of what a monumental task it must have been and the enormous ego that accompanied one who demands history be re-written in his favor!

Just before heading back to Cairo and then home, we took an excursion to Abu Simbel, which was in effect the 'cherry on top' of the trip for me, for this is where my soul connections could no longer be denied.

I had heard some individuals, known as Mediums, who are well-connected to other realms, lament that they hear souls chattering in their heads! This seemed a bit extreme to me, for in the past I had found the ability to summon the ones I wished to connect with upon request. I was careful not to 'think' or 'ask' anyone into my intuitive sphere, lest I have some unwanted visitors. In Abu Simbel, this is precisely what happened to me!

The day was very hot, over 100 degrees. We started out early for Abu Simbel to see another collection of temples built along the Nile by Ramesses the Great. Before the Aswan Dam was built, flooding was a regular occurrence on the Nile. Many temples were destroyed. Some were moved to higher ground and preserved. This was the case for Abu Simbel, named for the Nubian boy who first led Italian explorers to the temple.

The architect at the time recommended they save the main temple and reconstruct the hill on which it was to stand after restoration. The most magnificent thing about the site perched high on a hill was the immense panoramic view of the Nile River, mountains and the desert. To say it was quite impressive is an understatement.

Outside the temple, there were several HUGE statues of Ramesses. Inside contained even more. There were several rooms inside the temple adorned with intricately colored hieroglyphics showing important scenes.

Many of the scenes depicted Ramesses' victories. The most notable one showed him on his chariot. Most chariots had a driver *and* a warrior, but not Ramesses! He rode solo, tying the reins around his waist to be able to use a bow and arrow. He led his troops into battle like this! According to history, he told the people he was friends with the Gods or God-like himself. He was well-loved, as was his lovely and beautiful wife, Nefertari.

At Ramesses' temple, while I was alone exploring one of the rooms, I was startled to hear a deep, booming voice without any provocation on my part. It said, "I am Ramesses, the King-God of Egypt. I am the greatest!" Although a bit frightened by this unexpected message, I calmed myself and continued to explore the temple.

As I explored more rooms, I could clearly hear deep moaning. I felt it down to my core. It was the many ancient workers who, although they were proud of their accomplishments, felt it had been a very treacherous and painful task. Working so hard and being treated as slaves... I could literally *feel* their pain. It hurt me emotionally and almost physically just to hear them! I felt as though I was absorbing their feelings!

At the same site in Abu Simbel sits a smaller temple which Ramesses built to honor his wife, Nefertari. She was most likely of Nubian descent and darker than him, although in all the pictures of them, he is shown as the darker. In their culture, a darker complexion was more prestigious. He didn't want to be out-shone by anyone.

When I entered her temple, I heard a voice. This time, it was a softer, kinder voice saying, "I am Nefertari, beloved wife of Ramesses, Queen of Egypt. Thank you for coming my dear. We love you and the visitors. Come again, please."

This experience made me realize I have a gift — a real gift — which can be of great benefit to mankind. I am able to connect with souls and use what they share to help us grow as a species. I felt empowered to know without reservation that great things lie ahead as I travel on this journey through life AND I am willing to finally accept this ability in myself so I can move humanity forward.

You, too, can decide to be authentic and move through apprehension to 'come out' and embrace your gifts. Even though many people will not believe such a connection is possible, I am no longer afraid to say *it is*. Whether others believe or not is of no concern. Although, like I was, you may be hesitant, but be open to explaining your abilities to others. To truly embrace your gift, you need to step up and share it.

Many believe we are all connected so it only follows that such a 'soul connection' could indeed be possible. If you are open-minded and curious, I believe *you* can do it too! The following guide will be helpful for you to explore all the possibilities you can imagine.

IGNITE ACTION STEPS

- Believe it's *possible* to connect to another Being at the soul level. Realize this is a process. With sufficient dedication, you can connect as easily as a cell phone.

- Learn to meditate in your own way and be fully present in a relaxed state. The key is to remain calm and positive, keeping your vibrations high. If we aren't on the same frequency, we cannot connect.

- Ask for the person or Being you wish to speak to. Know your question, something you want to understand that they are equipped to answer.

- Ask your question with an open mind. Listen to the answer. Write it down as soon as possible using the exact words. Thank them for connecting and guiding you.

- This capability is not to be taken for granted. The purpose is enlightenment, so we can learn, grow and understand while on our life's journey.

- Soul connections serve as an example of how we are all truly and deeply connected, which is the most important lesson we are to learn while here on Earth.

Janie Jurkovich - United States
Author, Speaker
www.JanieJ.net
 JanieJAuthor
 JanieJAuthor
 JanieJ

KAMELIA BRITTON

"Memories make the best souvenirs."

By sharing my story, I hope to inspire you to book the bucket list adventure that you've been dreaming of, even if it means going on your own. To understand that you don't need anyone else to become a citizen of the world. Embrace the unknown as you explore. Release your fears and experience the freedom of solo travel.

SOLO TRAVEL: A TICKET TO PERSONAL GROWTH

I didn't step foot inside of a plane until I was 18 years old. My first flight was full of turbulence and I found the whole process to be quite terrifying. In fact, I didn't board another plane for almost seven years after that. After a few more experiences I got over my initial fear of flying, but if you had told me back then that one day I'd be traveling across the world for a trip to Bali on my own, I would have laughed out loud.

The thought of traveling alone, much less to a foreign country, had never even crossed my mind. It wasn't something that I had aspired to do or was even curious about. The whole idea seemed pretty daunting to me, especially as a young woman.

Who would I talk to and share the experience with? Would I be safe? Who would I turn to if I ran into a problem? These were all of the questions on my mind when I accidentally fell into a solo getaway to Bali.

Little did I know that this unexpected trip would end up being a first class ticket to the destination of personal growth.

Once I got the hang of flying, I became a total travel fanatic and learned all I could about gaming the system through travel hacking. Finding incredible deals on international flights quickly became my specialty.

I'd discovered a way of finding mistake fares and had figured out how to get these amazing deals sent straight to my phone. It all started when I found an around-the-world ticket for $325. After that I was completely hooked on roaming the globe for pennies ever since.

When I got an alert while at lunch with a friend, we both jumped to see what kind of deal would pop up. A roundtrip flight from LA to Bali for under $500 appeared on my screen. Our eyes lit up! Neither of us had been to Bali before so we bought our tickets as fast as we could before the deal vanished forever. We wrapped up our lunch with a toast of champagne and couldn't wait for the trip to come.

A couple of months passed and it was time to prep for our getaway, but then I got a text from my friend that completely changed the entire plan. Some personal issues had unexpectedly come up for her and she had to cancel just two weeks before the trip. I understood her situation, but I was incredibly disappointed. I had never planned on going to Bali by myself and I really wasn't mentally prepared to do so.

I frantically tried to find a replacement travel buddy with absolutely no luck. I must've called every single person in my entire phone. Unfortunately, the ticket was non-refundable, non-transferrable, and the dates couldn't be changed. Plus, since the flight was only two weeks away, prices were way too high for someone else to jump in at the last minute. I began to feel defeated, like maybe I was forcing it. The overwhelm of traveling to a new country alone started to settle in. My gut was feeling very uneasy about it.

My excitement for the trip started to wane and I considered not even going at all. Maybe it was a sign that I should just stay home. What else was going to go wrong once I got there? Was I even cut out for this? I started to wonder if I was crazy for even considering going through with it. Maybe I should just forget the whole thing and try again another time.

With much hesitation, I made a last minute decision to go for it. I had no idea what was going to happen, but I was ready to take the leap. How bad could it possibly be to explore on my own? I could do anything for 10 days, right? Plus, it would be a shame to waste such a great deal. I decided to fully commit and make the most of my time.

I arrived in Bali, all alone. It was after midnight and I was utterly exhausted from the long flight. As I sat in the cab on the way to my hotel, I felt so alone and completely lost. Reality set in. I started to feel anxious and overwhelmed. That's when I immediately realized that I had no idea what I was doing.

I checked into my room with the palpable realization that it was too late to turn back. My stomach was in a knot and I tried with all my might to push back the fear. I felt incredibly vulnerable being in this new place all by myself. There's a difference between solitude and loneliness, and I wasn't quite sure which one I was in. Feeling disoriented and confused, I made the choice to go with the flow, taking one day at a time.

The next morning I woke up to the sun shining into my room and onto my skin. I felt the promise of a new day begging me to discover it. It was quite warm outside. I was surrounded by the humid jungle with scooters whizzing by on the dirt roads and everything was so green. There was a magical feel to it. The air was moist, sparkling in the sunshine. It felt intimidating yet inviting at the same time.

My first two nights were booked at a cute little hotel near the beach in Seminyak and I hoped the rest would fall into place as I started to explore. I wanted to make the most of the full experience and didn't want to be tied down to a schedule. I liked the idea of being free and seeing where my journey would take me. Slowly, I began to embrace the freedom.

I ventured out of my room and made my way to a beach club in Seminyak for the day. I had to start somewhere, and I figured this was better than sitting in the hotel room. My plan was to get a little taste of this area and then head to Ubud for a change of scenery the next day.

When I got to the beach club, I went straight to the bar for a pineapple juice. I surveyed the area and saw happy couples and groups of friends having a great time together. It made me feel even worse and I didn't want to crash their party. Then I noticed there was a woman sitting at the bar a few seats down from me who also seemed to be alone.

At the risk of being completely rejected and then feeling terribly awkward, I took a chance and introduced myself. Her name was Virginie and I felt so relieved when she met me with a smile. We quickly realized that we had a lot in common. She was a healer and I was a Reiki master. We connected over our common spirituality and became instant friends.

After chatting for a while, Virginie told me that she had been traveling around as a nomad for the past several years. She was single with no children and worked as a healer who saw clients at luxury resorts.

She was currently house sitting at a friend's second home in Ubud and was just visiting Seminyak for the day. I told her that I was actually planning to go there in the morning and asked if she had any hotel recommendations.

Since there was an extra room in the house she was in, she asked me if I would like to stay with her for the three nights that she had left. I gladly accepted the offer and was so happily relieved to have found a new travel buddy.

On the first day, we explored Ubud together, renting scooters and shopping for deals at the colorful markets. We both felt a genuine friendship; it was similar to being with a long-time friend you'd known for years.

The next day, I convinced her to go white water rafting with me. She happily accepted. She had always wanted to try it but didn't want to go alone. Neither of us had done it before and so this was the perfect opportunity. We rode down the rapids screaming with glee. It was another adventure we could both check off our bucket lists.

On the third day, she asked if I'd like to join her in a hunt to find the Bali high priestess, Ida Resi Alit. I'd never heard of her, but I was quite curious and intrigued. Virginie, as a healer herself, had heard of her through word of mouth.

It turned out that Ida Resi Alit was not an easy person to locate. You wouldn't find her in any tourist books and, at the time, she had no presence online. She stayed in a village off the beaten path. There was no address listed for her village and there were no maps to be found anywhere. You basically had to ask your way to her village and hope that she would see you when you arrived.

We set out on a mission to meet her, hoping that she would agree to see us. We drove past several small villages, asking the locals for help to guide us on our way. We kept searching for hours, completely unsure if we were on the right track. Something inside me told me to keep going, even though it felt like we were on a wild goose chase.

We still had no idea if we would even find her at this rate, or if she would even be there when we arrived. After speaking with dozens of locals, our persistence finally paid off. We'd successfully discovered her village and crept slowly into the entrance, all while trying to contain our excitement.

I felt like such an intruder, sneaking onto private property in search of a mysterious healer. My heart was racing and I was a ball of nerves. We gave each other sideways glances questioning our decision to go there. My mind was now thinking, "This is crazy!" but we hadn't come this far to turn back now. As we entered the compound, we both realized that we were the only Caucasians there.

The village was quiet and full of Balinese people. They must've found their way, just as we did, and had come to see the high priestess for healing. We silently gathered around the altar, which looked like it had been used for a ceremony many times before.

Together with a group of about 40 other people, we spent an hour in meditation while the high priestess blessed the water and spoke in tongues. The rhythm of her voice never wavered as she continuously chanted, using a leafy branch to sprinkle the holy water into the crowd.

Once the blessing was done, we lined up one by one to receive our own personal healing. Virginie and I approached the priestess together, standing just below her where she sat in lotus pose at the altar. With a large carafe, she slowly poured cold holy water all over my body. She kept chanting in tongues and then said sternly in English, "Release it! Release it!"

At that moment, I felt a release. A huge jolt of energy shot right out of my left hip, making me gasp. As my body spasmed, I tried to let it go. I felt emotional, but most of all, I felt free. The cold water continued to drench my body and I realized just how powerful I truly was, all on my own. I realized I should have more courage and faith in myself, and trust in the Universe to provide all my needs.

After everyone had their turn, we completed the ceremony by meditating together. What a beautiful experience that I never knew I needed.

Virginie and I both felt the true power of this sacred ceremony. This was not something I could've ever planned for and I felt so grateful. I was so glad to have found her to share this journey with. Together, it held so much more meaning than if we had experienced it alone.

To think that I almost passed up what was there waiting for me. The fear of the unknown had almost held me back. I knew I was rewarded for trusting the process and keeping an open mindset about the trip.

Once I realized I could jet off to a foreign country alone and still thrive, I felt like I could do anything! It's quite empowering to go through a challenge like that and find that you can overcome it.

I never thought I'd be a person who would come to love traveling solo. As I look back, I see just how far I've come, from almost cancelling the trip to creating magical memories and discovering a new friendship along the way. Virginie and I are still friends to this day and we both know that our paths were meant to cross in our travels.

Since that trip to Bali, I've gone on to explore eight more countries as a solo adventurer! Even though I have a fiancé who travels with me sometimes, I still really love the feeling of going by myself. It's a very different experience than globetrotting as a team. When you discover new places with people you already know, there's no reason to make new friends. You'll stay comfortably in what you are used to, but there's so much more waiting to be revealed!

One of the best parts of traveling is the unexpected people that you meet along the way. These friendships enrich your whole experience and might even influence your life. Think of them as secret treasures to be uncovered that are hiding within your journey. The memories you make are the best souvenirs of all. You must try it out at least once in your life so that you can see for yourself.

Always remember, you're never alone unless you want to be. People are everywhere; most are friendly and happy to help. Just ask. Allow life-changing opportunities to cross your path by keeping an open mind. A solo journey gives you the time and freedom to learn more about who you are when there are no distractions. The alone time during those in-between moments can be an unexpected gift.

IGNITE ACTION STEPS

Now that I've traveled on my own, I know how amazing it can be. Use these steps to take action and start planning your next getaway!

- **Get out there and live your adventure!** If you have the urge to travel, then I say DO IT! Start by creating a bucket list of your top ten, must-see destinations.

- **Do it now!** Don't give in to the little voice of fear that wants to hold you back safely in your comfort zone. Don't wait for the right time because it'll never come. Pick a date on the calendar and start planning.

- **Go solo!** Don't wait for the perfect relationship or the ideal travel buddy. Relying on yourself is an empowering experience. You can start small by checking out group tours or maybe even a cruise.

- **Take a chance!** When the Universe throws an opportunity in your lap, follow your excitement! Join a meetup group of like-minded travelers in your area. You never know when you'll meet a new travel companion.

Kamelia Britton - United States
Travel Blogger, Entrepreneur, Coach
www.Hackerette.com
⊙ TheHackerette

TARA HEINZEN

"Rarely do we know how a single decision will affect our lives."

Wounds do not define you. You can overcome those experiences that contributed to inner disconnect, suppression and the inability to hear your own heart voice to become the highest expression of yourself in the world. Despite external voices, conditioning, pain or fears... there is a path back to YOUR truth, it does not rest in your mind but in your heart, you are not alone in your travels.

A BEAUTIFUL SEED

Rarely do we know how a single decision will affect our lives, the chain reaction it can ignite. On a cramped ten-hour flight to Barcelona, Spain, this thought tugged at me. Was I really going back to that country?

Fifteen years prior, our young family moved to an air base outside Seville. A bubbly and heavily pregnant military spouse, hiding a dark secret of an abusive marriage and severe depression. Although I had a small group of supportive friends, I kept my secret well hidden behind my smile. A few months into the move, I gave birth to my second child, a beautiful son. It should have been another highlight of my maternal role, yet I was dying inside. It was a miserable two-year assignment. We returned to the United States where I continued to live a disconnected life for several more years. I had no desire to ever return to the country that held such painful memories for me.

On a plane speeding over the Atlantic Ocean, now forty and divorced, I unexpectedly found myself on a soul journey — back to Spain, despite my time there, almost erased from memory. A struggling artist and single parent since leaving a toxic marriage, I had been on a painstakingly slow journey of self-discovery, facing fears of inadequacy and self-doubt. I was committed to finding my true path and purpose.

It was a mad rush, making that trip to Spain happen. I had just ended a two-year relationship with a stable, successful engineer right before our planned trip to Norway. I spent my time with him trying to be logical about my choices. I believed the *shoulds* and *should nots* pressed onto me by others, because following my heart seemed to lead me down non-traditional paths — the very unknown. The heart was fallible as far as I understood; my heart created trouble repeatedly. A stable life was being offered, but my artistic soul was out of balance, once again dying. I had lost connection with my heart.

With a fresh heartbreak, and no idea how I was going to afford a solo trip barely a month away, I changed my flights from Norway to Barcelona, joining my kindergarten bestie, who happened to have planned a 40th birthday trip with her husband to Spain. The timing was perfect. Ok heart, I did it, a choice not based on logic. What was next?

With my limited funds swallowed up by the flight change, I turned to the couch-surfing community my adventurous 20-year-old daughter told me about. A global network offering free lodging by hosts all over the world, with thousands in Madrid alone. I began planning my adventure, ignoring fears from family and friends about staying with strangers, yet terrified to be a single woman traveling alone. With no idea what to expect, only knowing my heart was pounding YES. Logic and stability stepped aside, my heart was taking over. She said, "Go back to Spain, stay with strangers, it will be OK." I felt the spark of connection within my soul. It was familiar. I felt trust.

From the moment I landed in Barcelona, I could feel a shift. An awareness every step brought expansion. I felt the offering of closure to unresolved parts of my adult life. Breathing in, exploring through the city helped me close old doors, creating space in my heart to open, for so much more.

My friend introduced me to the Barcelona art world, as she'd been there many times. I fell in love with it all. My favorite memories returned — the smell of the markets, tasting favorite tapas, the lilt of language merging with sounds of hurried motorists and pedestrians. I began to feel confident. I *could* travel alone and navigate foreign grounds. My girlfriend offered training wheels.

After a few days, I took time to explore solo, quickly faced my fears of getting lost, allowing myself to *be* lost. Wandering with my heart became a space of comfort instead of fear. Filled with inspiration, not only from incredible art, but empowerment, reveling in my abilities to walk my own path. So many breakthroughs, emotional and physical scars were not defining me. I felt joyous in my skin, especially the topless beaches! It was beyond liberating.

Challenges existed; loved ones questioned my choices and motives. But just like getting lost in the city, I eventually found my way back where I needed to be — where my heart guided. It was the perfect first step, relaxing into what is. My sad past in Spain felt more distant every day.

On the train, heading to my first couch-surfing experience, self-doubt began to creep up. I should have known it would not be easy. I knew my recent ex-boyfriend was in Norway, hurt from my choices. Our limited correspondence was troubling. I wondered about my kids back home; was I really doing the right thing? In my head, external voices were telling me this was unwise, hurting people I care about by taking risks. I resolved to keep my guard up, cautious of strangers. As my inner voice, my heart was getting stronger… she said, "No. Be in the Yes… keep going. Trust the process and growing reconnection with Source… it's all you need."

Valencia welcomed with a warm coastal breeze. A stark contrast to the busy city I just left. Near a park a few blocks from the train station, I waited for my host, an artist himself but in furniture restoration. I did not wait long before a robust and cheerful Italian man walked towards me. I felt an ease and trust immediately; my fears melted away. Over the next few days, I explored Valencia, letting go, opening to soul connections.

As I explored that magical town, I let my heart guide me, flowing without agenda or expectation. I felt my soul connect… growing, expanding. Over beautiful meals and wine, a few tours of his favorite parts of Valencia, we found shared alignment in interests and life philosophies. A memorable friendship emerged. I felt sparks of an inner truth that would never be silenced. Connection is not something to fear, but is everything that truly matters, and everything that gets lost in this world.

With new ease, I let my heart guide every step. She led me to powerful awakenings, and oh, adventures! My days ebbed and flowed from inner stillness to a rhythm of conversations that led me to the next place I needed to be. I marveled at the synchronicity of the Universe. Lingering just a few extra minutes at the beach, taking a different street back, or meeting the gaze of a stranger at the stoplight, any change in any given moment could create a potential connection.

I was slowly waking up. Learning that being present in the NOW would in turn give me gifts of greater connection with myself, and others. Looking back

I see how each place I visited served as a brick in my foundation, in perfect order, prepared me for the next step. The most powerful of those realizations, that have since become a point of gravity in my life, arrived in fullness at my final destination. A city I had once visited with a broken soul.

The train ride to Madrid was different this time, full of trust and confidence. I knew I was on path, exactly where I needed to be, every step. Highs and lows, I trusted the lessons in both, because they were authentically mine.

As resolved as I felt, the moment I heard the announcement we were approaching Madrid, I could feel nerves triggered with old wounds. The past rose in a new way once the train entered the city; it held specific pains that were threatening to swallow my heart. I needed to focus, as finding my way once getting off the train was an adventure on its own. My host lived near the Atocha Station, larger than some commercial airports. Doing my best to navigate, memories of family conflict from years past flooded back in.

My then-husband dictated how the trip would go, due to my inability to be of any use beyond caring for children. I was a depressed and insecure shell of a woman that followed him, dutifully caring for our six-year-old daughter and one-year-old son. As an artist, my dream was to see all the art I could, visit the Prado Museum, see the classic and famous works I learned about. It was the one thing I wanted to do, the only thing I had asked for. We attempted it; caring for children was not his strength. With a toddler in a backpack and one child in hand, we tried to get through the incredible halls of the Prado as quickly as I could. Kids have a time limit. I remember tears as I stood for mere moments in front of art I never thought I would see with my own eyes, the precise brush strokes the artists made, feeling the powerful expression and voice through their art. After an hour, barely to the second floor, the children gave out, and we left the museum. It was one of the few memories from my past in Spain where I felt a connection to who I am inside. The passionate artist somewhere deep, just a moment, a taste, and then I was reminded my life did not have room for her to exist in the open.

That heartbreak, with other crippling memories, surfaced, but I knew I had to figure out how to get through the train station and to my host's apartment. One can not see exactly where a host is located until the request is accepted. I knew the alignment was real, when out of 75,000 hosts in Madrid, I was received by a man who lived two blocks from the Prado Museum. My heart guided me to a host perfectly located for my healing.

He lived at the top of an old apartment building, beautifully renovated with rustic hand-cut beams exposed next to modern decor, stunning art from his travels, and views looking down onto narrow stone streets bustling with people and motorbikes. Immediately upon meeting, I sensed the soul connection with this Spanish brother. He and his sweet dog welcomed me wholeheartedly. He was a mirror, reflecting much about myself I thought I had lost. We talked endlessly, discovered shared views, he reflected everything that was truth for my heart... a positive spirit, seeing lessons and gifts in every experience, especially painful ones... How priceless: openness to Source, connection to the earth, ourselves and others truly is. He reminded me of the power of meditation and breath to center for clear guidance. What an amazing feeling, recognizing the self-expression, self-discovery and healing power within *myself*. Oh Heart, I get it, connection.

My first days in Madrid were a setup for the sparks I had felt, to become a burning flame. I experienced closure and healing, creating space to fully see and feel my life purpose. I took my time, did not rush. I was not there to sightsee, I didn't know what I was there for, not exactly, but I knew I was going to the museums!

Elation barely describes how I felt entering both the Prado and Reina Sofia art museums. I went slowly, sitting in front of magnificent artworks, losing track of time. I wept, journaled, felt inspired, and stood in awe. I felt the closure of a chapter, an unfulfilled desire soothed years later, but at the perfect time. Such a simple act, in a world full of heartbreak, it's just a day at the museum... but it symbolized so much for me, freed a tremendous amount of space. The next steps felt lighter already.

My days began and ended with deep awareness and gratitude of connection. I wandered the streets, connecting to the mini-orchestra of sounds in the city, the ever-changing scents in the air as I passed potent cafes, businesses, people and just life. Every moment a gift. Stunning visual images at every turn may have seemed ordinary, but my new eyes saw each frame. Noticing the way light hit the stone streets, long tree-filled neighborhoods, narrow yet busy alleyways, old or modern buildings with incredible architecture, a kinetic landscape. I felt at home, not because anything was familiar, but because *I* was familiar. I fell in love with *my* life. Feelings blossomed of privilege and honor to have lived in that country previously, bringing my son into the world there. I realized another core truth is that connection heals anything.

New experiences I couldn't have planned for were flowing in at a constant stream. My long wanderings around Madrid led me to art-filled neighborhoods, community gardens and parks, funky cafes, unique local shops and markets, all sprinkled with random connections with strangers.

One evening nearing the end of my visit, my soul-brother shared a healing meditation practice he began implementing years earlier. With yoga mats on the floor, soft colorful lighting, beautiful music that hit perfect frequencies for healing and energetic flow, I fell into complete surrender to my soul. I moved through the guided meditation, feeling my body connect deeply as roots to the earth. I saw my soul; she was a beautiful seed. A simple seed, not yet sprouting, my awareness sensed I was one of billions a part of this life. I curled up into a ball on my yoga mat and cried. A feeling of gentleness and self-love washed over me, so grateful for this journey. Grateful for every moment, even the seasons of intense pain, they all led me to the place I was right then.

Curled up and releasing emotions without shame, I knew I didn't need to be anything else but myself, no one could make me crack open and sprout early, only in my time. I knew I would never again let anyone force me to open or be something I am not. My roots in the earth tapped into the collective knowledge, wisdom and healing of all that exists. By the end of our meditation, as my 'brother' began softly playing drums in line with the gentle music, my emotional release softened. There was this deep sense of inner connection unlike I have ever felt in my life. It was Divine connection.

I felt my soul had been Ignited. My guiding truth and life purpose orbits around one point of gravity, CONNECTION, in all forms of its meaning. Each pain, wound, conflict and question in life can be healed or answered through connection. Every aspect of my life as an artist, mother, unique being on this planet, centers around connection. I had to start within.

I left Madrid shortly after, with ease, feeling complete — whole. Sad to say goodbye to my soul-brother, but with a knowing I would return. I came home to find my two sons had faced their own challenges, resulting in unanticipated growth and lasting changes. My then fifteen-year-old son discovered a new vision of his role as a big brother, of communication and connection. He continues to be a loving example of the developing masculine in spite of an absent father, a shift that's created an unwavering bond with his younger brother. Although my daughter was long on her own expanding journey, our connection deepened as I stood confidently in my heart. She joyously shared in my feelings of closure. All three children admit my trip to Spain 'changed everything.'

Connection grows a powerful heart, it knows *your* soul. Trust your heart, it's all you need and will guide you to sprout, opening you to your highest authentic potential. Identify and release what is blocking your soul from ultimately thriving in your full expression. Keep awareness that change is rarely comfortable, often companioned by an intense fear of the unknown. Yet, this is the space where, if we listen to our inner voice, our heart takes a leap into the unknown, only to find the beginning of great change. In that life's redirection is generally where we discover our strength, break old patterns, heal, find inner freedom and true connected living. Avoid escaping the uncomfortable edge, instead look into it, walk through the fire, you will be amazed at how you emerge.

IGNITE ACTION STEPS

The path to self-reconnection, realization, and self-trust is a process, many baby action steps of discerning between external influences and the higher internal voice. Be gentle with yourself, you are exactly where you need to be at every given moment, you are a gift in every step of that process, and on your own timeline. The biggest lesson I learned is to get out of my mind, and into my body, listening deep within my heart. Whether my heart speaks soft as a whisper, or loud as thunder, trusting the heart-body connection for truth is the ultimate guide.

Try Pausing: Remind yourself to pause whenever you feel your mind analytically overthinking. Get out of your head and look around you. Play soft music without any words. Physically touch your heart/chest to bring yourself back to your body. Speak words of kindness and compassion to yourself. Breathe deeply. Feel into your heart and calm any uncomfortable sensation. From that place, your heart is free to adventure.

Tara Heinzen - United States
Ceramic Artist, Women's Art Circles,
Facilitator of Communication and Intimacy
heinzen.studio@gmail.com
heinzen.studio
heinzen.studio

EVA KETTLES

*"Life is a magical carpet ride — your heart is the magical genie
— and you are the miracle that connects it all."*

**I invite every reader to jump into the Unknown with complete trust. Allow
infinite freedom to enter your heart and inspire the dance of your life's
adventure.**

ADVENTURING INTO PURE STILLNESS

I perceived my life as regimented, organized and was in desperate need of
something different. Knowing that I was the creator of my life and that I had
lost passion and courage, I was in need of a miracle. I had to get off my old
script and create a new storyline. I started to meditate even more and released
myself from torturing old limiting beliefs that had created this 'boredom.'

My soul was yearning to flip the coin. I knew I had to say *"Yes"* to things
that come along, that feel a bit out of my comfort zone, to bring back that
spark, that aliveness.

On a call with my friend Victoria, an idea popped into my head. She told
me about a shamanic retreat in Prescott, Arizona. I was instantly taken by this
idea to go with her. Shamanism was definitely not something I felt called to in
the past, but it would certainly be just the thing that would interrupt my stag-
nation. What better opportunity than to dance with Mother Nature and ground
my whimsical nature into my body.

Little did I know that this would truly shift my life.

Victoria and I have been friends on and off for a long time. The off times are always due to our souls merging us for a deep mission and then separating us when we needed to venture on our own. When we are walking together, we tend to be hyper-aware of the cosmic messages in every moment and are incredibly harmonious in our ability to track each others' thoughts. We are able to give each other insights into our individual creation moment to moment. It is quite a fun duo — we joke — as we are probably the most unlikely couple out there.

Victoria has brown hair and beautiful hazel eyes with a rubenesque figure — is not very tall — soft and gentle to the touch but energetic, fierce, witty and incredibly smart with words. I, on the other hand, am the exact opposite — blonde and tall. Victoria gave me the incredible label 'spiritual Barbie.' In any case, we are a very unconventional pair.

Our little adventure started with a few hiccups — I hadn't received the packing list — and Victoria suggested that I needed to buy sneakers for our activities in the National Forest. I don't like to wear sneakers; I am a boot girl through and through. But I ended up buying them to 'have what's on the list.'

We received the locational pin on our phone and felt like we were on a scavenger hunt piecing together a puzzle on how to get there. Spirit and GPS rerouted us miraculously that morning, as we would discover a hidden, secret road that led into a neighborhood directly connected to the National Forest parking lot. It literally sent us to the exact parking lot, but on the other side of a gate. This gate was marked NO TRESPASSING.

At that time both of us were aware that what had just happened was for a reason. We were meant to find out soon enough that this 'run around' was no coincidence. Now being a bit behind time, we started rushing — trying to make up for the time lost. We were taking the long route, driving now another 40 minutes on a rough dirt road through the forest trying to find the correct spot.

We jumped out of the car with our backpacks on and me in my sneakers. Literally three minutes into a rocky riverbed, I twisted my ankle, so much so that I heard the pop three times. Victoria turned around in shock. I looked at her with a face of "don't say anything" — I went down and became completely silent. In my mind, I reversed the tape. I rewound it, rewrote the story of what had just happened and collapsed time — telling my ankle it was perfectly alright and I was stable and balanced. Slowly I came up and was delighted to feel not much pain and the ankle felt realigned, yet it still started swelling and bruising.

Victoria looked at my feet and said, "You have your sneakers on; I realize you didn't need them after all. You probably would have been better off in your boots." We both were in shock but also greatly aware of the eerie energy around us. This was the wrong riverbed. We jumped back into the car and drove some more, finally recognizing the same gate. We drove 40 minutes only to be on the exact opposite side of this mysterious neighborhood. Very interesting indeed. Now we only had to cross a riverbed to the other side to find ourselves at our seminar location. We walked up a steep driveway and knocked on the door.

Soon after meeting everyone we were prompted to go out again to find specific items in nature. We were trying to take off little branches from the juniper tree. We just couldn't — with all our prayerful gestures and mighty pulling power — there was a trick — we had to become one with the plant and truly connect and ask permission; only then it allowed us to pick it off like magic. It was reacting feisty, rigid and non-compliant. When our energy went into anger, it even stung us. After being shown by a shaman the difference, we were amazed by how we were able to get the thickest branch with our bare hands off the tree in a delightful and easy way. In only a few hours, we could see what miracles this forest held for us — soon to be one of the biggest adventures of my life.

The weekend seminar was almost over — after an amazing ritual that was very sacred. In this ritual, each person was able to receive a message from the energies beyond. Victoria came to me with huge eyes, so excited announcing that she got the message to go back to the forest that night — in the middle of the night — alone! OH my goodness, I couldn't believe my ears as I was confused about her excitement. For my taste — going back into the forest by midnight *alone* didn't sound like anything I would ever want to do. I became worried as she was determined to do it. Since I was the driver and knew that we had to get to the forest gate before it closed at 8 PM, I heard myself saying, "I am coming with you to protect you!" OMG did I really just say that? I must be out of my mind. One of my biggest fears is being out in nature in the dark. For some reason, I have this intense fear of being attacked by wild animals and eaten alive.

One of the other students was amused by our naivety to go into the forest by night and asked if we had even a flashlight or were prepared in some form or another for what might arise. There are a lot of wild animals and big creatures moving around at night and we shouldn't take this lightly. We might never come back alive. His concern triggered the last parts in me that were trying to control my terrified feeling. I was focusing on staying in peace in my mind and my heart. I practiced the ONE breath, connecting myself with every particle around me and keeping myself calm. I started thinking about my family, my daughter, about the consequences this crazy adventure might have. I knew that this forest was full of wild animals, panthers, mountain lions, wolves and bears. A part of me was starting to feel numb.

Victoria, full of adventurous spirit, didn't notice how silent I had become. Our otherwise joyful dynamic suddenly shifted and nine hours of a dreadful energy battle began. I had no idea whatsoever at first on why this occurred, in my perspective, at the very worst time. I had declared to stay in my peaceful place as I was emotionally preparing for the big adventure. Victoria took on the role of an accuser and interrogator. It made no sense why my friend tried to get into one emotional subject after another, trying to trigger me as best she could. It felt so out of context. It occurred to me that this must be a test and that I had to stay calm no matter what was going on. She even asked me, "Why do you let me bite off your head time after time, and why won't you stop me?"

Exhausted, physically and mentally, I collapsed in the tiring accusations and answered, "I don't need to DEFEND, I don't need to be RIGHT, I don't need to be HEARD, I just want PEACE." It felt like I had been given poisonous venom for hours and still survived the process. So I declared, "We can go now! Thank you for getting me ready!" I recognized it was all about surrender and accepting that every moment was perfect the way it unfolded. Victoria had stripped me of my defensiveness. I became *Trust*.

It is such a blessing when we become aware that all moments are led by a higher power, that this power is motivating us daily into a bigger capacity of ourselves. This power is coming through every single being, moving them, speaking through them, acting through them in ways we can't fully understand while it is happening. But if we trust that in that moment — even if it's uncomfortable — that this force is wanting our grandness and that exponential growth is just around the corner. If we trust that in every instance, we gain so much momentum towards freedom.

We went up into the hotel room and gathered our few things, like water, a blanket and a few nutritional bars in case we got hungry. We were given a flashlight in the afternoon by our friend and so we took it with us. I recorded a good-bye video for my family as I had to completely and utterly make peace with the possibility of dying that night. Only by doing that could I be fully present with what was going to happen.

Once I made peace with all of the possibilities I became complete *Clarity.* I felt such strength settling in; I remembered everything I had ever learned from my priestess training and all the other training I had. I created a container of safety for us. I summoned Beings of light and asked for protection in every level of our expression. I was determined to live and felt excitement and joy sparking up inside of me. Something in me had shifted. On our way to the forest, the hiccup of the first day came in handy. It was already midnight and all the gates were closed — we had to sneak in from the side.

We parked the car and seconds later my calmness was again put to the test. Two neighborhood dogs were alarmed by our nightly visit and ran after us barking and baring their teeth. Their owner gave them the sign to check us out! I kept my inner focus on my breathing, thinking nothing but love and oneness. I didn't allow my emotions to get triggered by the scary barks. Victoria and I in pure silence — telepathically connected, stayed centered. The dogs gave up.

The amazing adventure began. We activated consciously the future timeline, spoke our intention of a safe and marvelous trip into being and remembered that moment as we hugged gazing at the sky, loving the moon and the stars, feeling so free and so alive. We took in the air, the smells, everything was so palpable and breathtaking.

Being it was Victoria's mission, I gave her the lead. Right from the start, we had to make sure we followed one direction. We learned how to communicate with each other telepathically and also used sign language to stay in silence. We went into a bigger awareness field, accessing the one mind and one heart. For a moment we tried out the flashlight but were both turned off instantly by the unnatural light source. Together we felt like a lit-up billboard for our wild friends.

National Forest, here we come, without a compass and no light. Every step of the way, we consciously placed our steps, fully aware of the ground and the surroundings. Our eyes adjusted to the moonlight. We were able to practice right away the valuable information from the shamanic teachings and spoke to the trees, asked them for protection and guidance, and felt that the entire forest was watching us. Our surroundings became alive and we felt like the creatures in the movie Avatar — connecting with Mother Nature. We were playing the lead in our own blockbuster but without a script. Every molecule in my body was alive and awake as my ears became larger, my eyes wider and my skin like a sponge, open to feel and sense with antennas beyond my mind. I sensed Beings around me, but I couldn't see anyone. I heard silence — nothing but silence. It was incredible. I wasn't frightened of the dark!!! Quite the opposite — I was feeling held and supported.

By now we had passed through three gates. It felt like we overcame an inner limitation each time, almost like an initiation for each chakra — energy center in our body. Every time we were tested to leave behind a part of us, to listen and understand the other, and give up our own need to be right and surrender to what seemed more important, which was to stay together and connected. We had to become absorbed in the consciousness of the one breath and the one mind.

I found a tree and I felt called to hug it. I started crying uncontrollably, feeling nature hugging me back — all around me, all the energy was focussed on me single-mindedly — just me. It was overwhelming, so much love was there for me — for just me? What? The entire Universe is just here for me? How could this be? OMG, I realized I created all of this — all of this is showing up for me — so I could realize what I am not — and can start learning what I am instead and simply allow it to take me over. I had a fantastic cry, letting nature love upon me and release my shame about not taking time to meet nature more often and in a more adventurous way. Nature forgave me instantly — *She* doesn't hold grudges. It just is.

One and a half hours Victoria and I were walking in trance, in one direction, completely 'synched,' just stepping and soaking in all sounds, still a little bit curious if we would find a species of some sort. Anything was possible and Victoria's mission was to meet something or someone out there. We weren't sure anymore where we were and why we were here. Looking up and around — we had gone so far inside the forest — we now were on the edge on the very top overlooking the entire 360 degrees, seeing the little mini lights from houses far far away. It dawned on us that if something were to happen to us here, nobody would ever find us. We had totally gotten lost and nothing looked the same. We never found the ritual site we wanted to go back to. We imagined ourselves crossing through the entire forest to the other side and jokingly taking a taxi back. But where was the other side and which direction?

I was committed to walk on until whatever happened had to happen — pretty much until my body would give up. Victoria looked at me and saw how tired I was, remembering that I had been walking all weekend in what turned out to be a hairline fractured ankle. I wasn't going to say, "Let's turn around." I was determined to see it through. We walked on some more and then Victoria turned to me and said,"Eva, I think this is the moment where I have to make the decision to take us back. I appreciate you giving up control. Now I need to take care of you and I think it's better for you if we turned around." And she was right. I was lost in the energy of the mystical place, captivated in the deep meditative walk — trancing out without any medicine. I was in ecstasy in every one of my cells. I couldn't believe the amazing silence and was absorbed in the stillness of the vast dark foliage. We had not even heard one peep from any critters. It was almost fable-like, no animals in sight. Only one bird circled us and in the dark, a white butterfly led the way. We took a drink from our bottles and decided to turn around.

The path downhill was much harder now; everything was pitch black as the moon had disappeared on the other side of the mountain. It was steep and rocky and the energy very mysterious. I felt a shower of fear testing me and I had to convince myself all I needed to do was to stay in synch and union with all beings. Victoria guided me gently down the hill, passing through another four gates, which meant we were guided a different way back. We ended up walking through seven gates — what a breathtaking initiation. Three hours had gone by and suddenly we found ourselves miraculously in the parking lot, as if we were teleported in a time capsule. Time felt irrelevant and not real. We felt frazzled, but clear and alive like we'd never felt before.

I realize I am always safe — if I release the fear — as the experience follows the thoughts and the emotions that are sent out. The entire Universe is literally creating the movie scene that matches that inner image we project. We left our turmoil in the car so we could set out for a magical, effortless and mind goggling adventure. I am forever grateful as I feel I have never since left that National Forest. I feel the energies around me have shifted and I see with new eyes, hear with new ears and feel with new senses. Life is magical and we all are the magicians that make it so. We are all connected, and in absolutely every moment, the whole world looks upon us to awaken.

IGNITE ACTION STEPS

- Ask yourself what you are missing.
- What are you longing for?
- Describe to yourself what it would feel like — if you already had what you dream of.
- Start embodying the 'feeling of what it is' that you want.
- Relax into the knowing that what you desire is already on its way to you.
- Get excited and celebrate the magic that is all around you.
- Welcome every moment without judgment, knowing it is truly bringing you exactly where you NEED to be.

Eva Kettles - United States
Business owner, Infertility and Addiction Coach,
Bestselling Author, Spiritual counselor
www.divinealchemy.co
www.evatar.world

DEBORAH CHOONG

"Live life on your terms. Curate your own experiences. Ten years from now you will be more disappointed by the things you said you wanted to do, but didn't, than by the ones you did."

It is my hope that my story will encourage you to travel the world to discover your true self. Experiential traveling can help you re-evaluate and reinvent your life. Traveling is a manifestation of something deeper. It is an expression of our core desire to experience more meaningful and fulfilling lives. Travel trains us to reignite our attention muscles and start noticing the light and good that is all around us.

SEEK YOUR TRUTH

From the outside, it looked like I led a charmed life, from a typical Asian upbringing standpoint. I was comfortable, held a good job in a financial institution and led a lifestyle of my choice. I worked hard, spending more than 12 hours a day at the office trying to make a name for myself in the industry. I was determined to be the best. After slogging it out for four years at the same company, I was finally vindicated for my efforts by winning a coveted industry award.

I had dreamt of that moment where I would beat all the veterans in the industry at a fairly young age. That feeling of triumph only lasted for an hour at best. I expected elation. But what I felt instead was hollowness. Was this what all my hard work, all those late nights was for? Right there at the award ceremony celebration, I had the feeling of being out of sync with my true calling.

For days following that eventful night, I pondered the meaning of life. Most people in my circle didn't think about their life purpose. For many of them, life was doing what they are told and living out a pre-defined existence. Life is about studying, working, starting a family, having kids, going for a holiday once in a while and then dying from sickness or old age at some point. This has been the life path defined by society. When I was a child, I was constantly told by my parents, peers and teachers that our objective in life was to be successful and financially abundant. I was conditioned to follow this path. No one spoke about happiness or living a conscious life. That concept was alien to Asian society.

There I was, in my early thirties, for the first time in my life questioning things. Up to that point, I was pretty happy with the daily routine but winning that award caused something inside of me to shift. I didn't want life to be just… life. Eat, sleep, wake up, go to the office like an office drone, rinse and repeat. I knew I was meant to do bigger things and not lead a 'conventional life.' I had to find my life's purpose as a first step to living a conscious existence.

Within a week, I was frustrated. I decided it was time to throw in my resignation letter. I was going to explore the world and do the things I had always wanted to, like ticking off my bucket list, without being bothered by work commitments and deadlines. I felt so relieved the day I handed over my resignation letter and Blackberry phone. I noticed the burden being lifted off my shoulders for the first time in a long time. I didn't need to look at my Blackberry every time there was a red light blinking. I just felt so free. I realized that I had been having a mental breakdown, overworked and overwhelmed. It was hard to understand, especially when I was thriving in the job. But the pressure took a toll on my body, mind and spirit.

My parents and friends were shocked at my decision to leave my career at what seemed the height of it. They must have thought I had lost my marbles. Why would I take such a risk? But it was something I had to do. Deep inside, I felt dead. I knew I needed a break to contemplate life. In my early thirties, I made an unprecedented move and took off on a sporadic jaunt without warning or in-depth planning. It was an unexpected emotional wake-up call to make some changes in my life. I realized that almost all the career goals that I had been working towards were pointless in the grand scheme of things.

Jobless by choice, I decided to take my journey to the other side of the globe. I eagerly chose South America. My parents and friends were worried about my safety as I was embarking on this journey of self-discovery on my own. The one thing many people fear is solo travel but solo travel didn't bother me at all. Given that youth was still on my side, I figured I should do this before I had a change of heart. Not one day went by during that self-discovery journey where I regretted giving up my cushy job to see the world.

There I was, this little Asian girl, wanting to discover herself in a land far far away. All on her own. Some people think of 'doing things alone' as being weird. It either means you're anti-social or you're a loser and this social stigma is wrong. I must admit I was one of them, and now I realize that I missed out on so many things because I did not want to do them alone. Once I changed my mentality and started to live my life as I pleased, I found this astounding feeling of freedom, freedom to be me and freedom to do whatever I want to without asking for permission. And let me tell you that there is no better feeling than enjoying your own company.

Given my abrupt decision to leave my job, I did not have a friend who could spontaneously go on that crazy journey with me. It was a self discovery trip which I was going to do on my own. I had to learn to become my own best friend. I am the person who chooses to do fun things alone, doing things by myself feels normal to me now. The truth is, not everyone will want to go where you want to go, not everyone will have the same interests and not everyone is willing to step out of their comfort zone.

For many, the idea of venturing out alone sounds daunting, perhaps even a little bit embarrassing. Embarking on a solo adventure isn't anything to be ashamed of. It is somewhat liberating, rejuvenating and extremely good for your soul.

When I was traveling the world by myself, I didn't need to compromise with anyone. I could do things in my own time and at my own pace. When I was feeling sociable, I would talk to strangers and meet new people.

When I ventured out solo, I could feel my senses being heightened. Suddenly the world seemed more interesting, and I was more aware of my surroundings. Going out into the world on my own also gave me the opportunity to gather my thoughts, analyze my life purpose and make important decisions. When traveling solo, I became more self-sufficient, did not depend on anyone to make myself happy because I realized that "I was enough."

The first stop on my self-discovery journey was Brazil for the Rio Carnival. White sandy beaches, mountainous treks, samba parties, Rio de Janeiro is the paradise for beach loving tourists. In Rio, I ticked off my bucket list by visiting the Christ the Redeemer statue and the beautiful white beaches of Copacabana and Ipanema. At night, I managed to get tickets to Carnival and felt so lucky to catch the samba competition finals. I watched as people came together from all corners to see the parade, listen to samba music, dance in the streets and party for days. The city comes alive as thousands of people celebrate in bright, exotic regalia. Carnival is a celebration of colors, of dancing, music and pure energy. The costumes are so extravagant; everything has to be exaggerated since the performance has to be visible from a distance. Up on the stadium stands, everyone was dancing. I was dancing too, without a care in the world.

The other enriching experience for me in Rio was a visit to the favelas. Favelas are Rio de Janeiro's slum areas and they have huge cultural significance in the city. Up to 20% of the residents in Rio live in them. I joined a walking tour so I could embrace the local culture. Favelas are always visible wherever you go in Rio and have a huge cultural importance. For example, the famous dance, samba, was invented in these Rio favelas. Rocinha Favela is one of the safer ones to visit. People seek help from the mafia first if anything happens in a favela. It is an interesting world to see people trusting the mafia and disliking the police. This was a bit of a strange concept to me but I accepted it as a way of life for the people living there.

The Rio favela looks like a jungle and maze of concrete houses. During the visit in Rocinha, I did not feel threatened by any of the residents. Most of the time, the locals walked past us, ignoring us as they were so used to seeing tourists around. I was happy that our tour guide directed us to a voluntary daycare center for kids, funded by donations. The kind lady that greeted us at the door had big brown round eyes that sparkled with kindness. I believe the eyes are an insight into the soul and I was drawn to her story. She decided to open a daycare center so that kids of all ages would have a safe place to go after school and would not stray away or be involved in drug dealing. That center provides a safe place for them to do their homework and learn new skills. I have the highest respect for this lady as her mission is to take women and children out of poverty by providing a safe place for them to learn and grow. She also wanted to keep young girls away from the street and protect them from being groomed for the sex industry. I saw how one person's will, even limited, could change the lives of many.

I stood there listening to her every word. It struck me that she was so self-less. Making a difference in the world begins with the belief that you can do something that impacts society one step at a time. The step that many people miss when trying to make a difference in this world is the action part. Most of us get stuck in overthinking and never get started.There's no need to aim for millions of people to impact when one person can be the catalyst for change to happen. This lady saw the issues at hand and did her part to help the next generation. I was empowered by her actions. I believe empowering girls and women is a powerful tool for the future. It is the key to economic growth, political stability *and* social transformation for any society.

Change doesn't start with being ignorant about these issues and I do believe tourism is a good medium to start showing people around the world that these places exist. More help and funding is needed to make these favelas a better place to live. To me, the visit to the favelas was an eye-opening experience and there is much to be grateful for in our daily lives. Sadly, there are so many people in the world who are praying for the things we take for granted. My lesson from this is to live life every day giving thanks for the blessings I have because there are millions of people in the world who have a fraction of what I have been blessed with.

The main reason for my South America trip was to visit Machu Picchu in Peru. Cusco, once the capital of the Inca Empire, is, of course, the starting point to the famed Machu Picchu. Getting to Machu Picchu was undoubtedly the highlight of my Peru trip. I am not much of a hiker so I did not plan to hike the Inca trail. Instead, I took the pleasant train ride from Cusco to Machu Picchu operated by Peru Rail. Swaying with the rhythmic motion of the train and watching the picturesque meadow around us like a slideshow, I felt so blessed to be alive to take in all the sights.

Machu Picchu is believed to have been built by Pachacuti Inca Yupanqui, the ninth ruler of the Inca, in the mid-1400s. It was a religious sanctuary and sacred place for the Incas as well as a royal retreat. Tucked between Machu Picchu Mountain and Huayna Picchu with the Urubamba River hundreds of feet below, it is safe to say this was a difficult place to get to, thereby easily protected. In fact, the Conquistadors, in their attempt to find this perceived golden treasure, were led away from Machu Picchu, and much of the trail that leads there was intentionally destroyed. This is the reason the city is still relatively intact today.

There is so much to take in at Machu Picchu; it is easy to be overwhelmed. I started the walk around the houses and proceeded to the royal compounds. Consistent with other Inca settlements, Machu Picchu was built with dry-stone walls; the most important structures had polished stones. The Temple of the Sun, built on top of a large and important rock next to the Royal Palace, is the only construction of its kind in Machu Picchu.

It has a unique semi-circular outer wall called a Torreon, a rarity in Inca construction, through which only priests and higher nobles were permitted to enter. The Torreon marks one of the city's highest altitudes, being appropriately closest to the sun. I spent a few hours walking around with my guide and touched the stones which had the ancient tales written all over them. Some stones were so large, I was amazed and intrigued at how they managed to lift such heavy stones, haul them there and build this magnificent fortress in the clouds. The trip there fulfilled another site on my bucket list and I am forever grateful for the opportunity. I captured the moments through my eyes and through my senses and tattooed it in my brain.

As we were leaving Machu Picchu, I looked up in awe and with renewed respect of this once great nation. Seeing the genius of the high altitude terraces used for producing large quantities of potatoes and corn to feed over 1,000 people is an amazing testament to the ingenuity of the Inca. These people were not educated in the western sense, and yet had created a system expertly engineered to build and sustain a community.

With my head full of wonder I walked silently out of the Inca city in the clouds, joining the rest of the travel-weary group to line up for the bus that would wind back down through the jungle clouds to Aguas Calientes. I was glad for the quiet time to reflect on all that I learned, all that I experienced, in that day to remember for a lifetime.

What I've learned from all of my travels and experiences around the world is that we are all alike. Regardless of where we come from, we share the same fundamental needs, desires and dreams. What we bring home with us is an earned appreciation for the factors that connect, rather than divide us as human beings. Through this journey, I learned what it means to live for daily vibrancy and what this means for the life story we want to create.

We should all take time off to reflect and recalibrate. The world is such a big place with much to appreciate, learn and enjoy. Taking time to relax and travel is both beneficial and nurturing for the soul. When you do this your mind will be at ease and your spirit will feel recharged, allowing you to achieve the life of your dreams.

Ignite Action Steps

• Do not be afraid to step out of your comfort zone.

In order to grow, one needs to take the bold step away from the daily routine. Travel allows us to step outside our well-worn, self-constructed realities and provides a platform to explore ideal visions for ourselves — who we are if we were not tied to our fears and anxieties about security and status. Traveling allows you to introspect on life and the meaning you give it.

- Introduce self-love and incorporate 'me' time.

Our breathing space is often lost in our usual day-to-day existence. Travel helps revive that space. By being in the moment and enjoying our surroundings, that 'me' time spent allows us to let go of stress and tension. Travel shows us a fuller form of ourselves to which we can aspire to be.

- Have more gratitude.

Being away from the things we often take for granted (family and friends) makes us appreciate them more. Travel trains us to focus more on quality human connections and be more mindful of who we include in our life story.

Deborah Choong – Malaysia
Citizen of the World
f *deborah.choong*

HANIT BENBASSAT

"Connect to your heart to remember who you are."

Sometimes we go through entire days without tuning in to the beauty of nature that surrounds us. In sharing my story I invite you to allow yourself to wander and rejoice in it. I encourage you to live your most meaningful, connected life as a human being living on planet earth. When we live from the heart in a spontaneous and honest way, we raise the level of joy and synchronicity with the Universe and then we experience magic and amazement as a way of life.

WHEN THE MOUNTAIN CALLS YOU

It all began with my vision board. I thought it would be interesting to travel to new places with my husband and three children, but I didn't have any idea of where to travel to, or when. I remember it like yesterday; I found this specific photo of a tall sign with arrows pointing in different directions, naming many cities and countries around the world. I felt, "Yes! we can travel everywhere we want; I just have to choose." I pasted the image to my vision board, the intention in the Feng Shui philosophy uppermost in my mind as I did. The power of my vision board soon manifested my traveling around the world. It happened so quickly!

The first trip I manifested was to Peru. Specifically, Machu Picchu, the ruined city of the Inca. It is spectacular with its backdrop of steep lush mountains, often with clouds covering their top. The landscape there was absolutely stunning and completely unique from place to place. I loved everything about it:

the friendly people, the fresh rich food, the adventure, the culture, the art and learning about the Inca. It was so fascinating, rejuvenating and heart-opening to be in this majestic place, somewhere I had never visited before. It was a totally different experience compared to where I grew up — Israel, and where I moved to live my adult life in the USA.

This was the beginning of my spiritual awakening. I started learning more about my spiritual self on a deeper level. I learned and practiced rituals to further my connection with my higher self and to nurture a relationship with the reality beyond myself, to live a meaningful life. When I was a part of the weekly meditation group, it was a particularly joyful day of celebration with my friends, my spiritual family. The more I meditated, the more synchronicity and awe moments I experienced. Being connected to the field of consciousness for me was a joyful and important commitment.

A few months before my trip to Peru, while at my mom's house, I saw sticking out of the pile of papers on her desk a white page stating 'the seven sacred flames.' This sparked my curiosity. I pulled it out and read it quickly with a sense of excitement; it felt like this information was waiting for me.

I knew it, it made sense, I wanted to know more, so after I returned home from Peru, I began searching. The practice of the sacred flames involves prayers; it was important for me to have it in Hebrew, my native language, because it is a holy and powerful language. I researched until I found the representative of the Telos organization in Israel who translated the prayers to a small booklet. It opened a door to a new adventure.

I learned about Mount Shasta, known to be the location of the hidden city Telos, where advanced beings from the lost continent of Lemuria reside. I was astonished. I didn't know what to think or feel about this information. But I had a deep knowing that I tapped into the ancient knowledge and wisdom of humanity. I felt a very strong pull to go there. Everything happened so quickly from the moment I had the booklet to starting my journey with a group of strangers, heading to Mount Shasta. It all happened naturally.

Making a decision to travel with only myself was out of my comfort zone. The kids were very young and my husband didn't support me leaving them and traveling alone. But, when you *have* to do something or be somewhere, the whole Universe supports you.

I learned that the seven flames were the main active flames on our planet that preserved the evolution and life of humanity. The flames helped to nourish our mental, emotional and physical bodies with its unique energy. Reading the books and using the flames invocation was a powerful combination for transformation. My body transformed in such a way that I didn't need as much sleep and food consumption was different — I stopped eating meat and dairy products not because of certain beliefs, but because my body demanded it. Only in retrospect did I understand that the changes were part of the preparation for the journey I was going to experience.

The most profound change I felt was discovering my own freedom. I saw some eyebrows raised, heard some comments regarding me being away from my family for 10 days to be with an unfamiliar group of people traveling to a very strange place. It created a conflict within me. I started doubting and judging myself. Fortunately... not for long. The calling to immerse myself in all aspects of Mount Shasta was stronger. You're not on the planet to always meet the needs and expectations of others. You're here to explore, expand and step into your extraordinary self.

The night I arrived in the town of Shasta, I had a very special reception. One of the town's residents told me that it was the first time in a while that there was a party in town. People danced in the street, adults and children; a band performed on stage and everyone was happy, singing and laughing.

I approached the center of the celebration. My gaze met the large, glowing blue eyes of a boy hugging his father. He suddenly jumped at me and hugged me tightly as if we had known each other for a very long time. I felt amazed and honored by receiving such a pure, loving hug from a child, but I was also surprised. Why did it happen? I wondered. Children do not initiate and jump into a stranger's arms, especially when they are being held by their parents. We took a picture together. He put his hands on my neck and shoulder. I didn't give it any attention, still under the influence of the surprising hug. Later on when I looked at the photo, it was glowing with so much light around us, adding more to the magical moment I experienced. His joyful nature was the beginning of a spectacular journey.

The party felt like a real welcome for me. There was ultimate love and acceptance. In a town that is usually very quiet, now there was a big celebration. I enjoyed dancing with the people, even if they were total strangers to me. I felt at home. What a blissful start.

The next morning, we drove to a beautiful pastoral lavender field. It was the end of the season and there were no purple flowers growing, but something felt very unique about that place. I walked toward the tree that stood in the middle of the field and found a big brown-red rock in the shape of a heart. It was a gift of great love, both exciting and uplifting. It was only the second day there and I felt embraced by so much love already.

That is also when I learned for the first time about Master St.Germain. I lay under the tree to rest from the heat, set the stone on my heart, feeling deep relaxation but also strong currents from the earth throughout my body. This sensation was new to me. My friend took some pictures and we could clearly see purple all around us — the same color flame that represents St. Germain. I was enthralled. I was aware of energies, frequencies and the presence of our angelic guidance, but never had I experienced it in a physical form.

Our guide told us that some specific locations would be revealed to us only if it was meant to be. This felt odd to me, but soon I realized how it worked. We were taken to the area of a secret cave. Nobody knew exactly where it was except for the guide and the cave only revealed its location to a few of us. The entrance was huge. Inside, it was illuminated by a sunbeam that shone through a hole in the ceiling, creating magical light. I sat there on the cool damp of the rock and meditated, connecting to the earth.

Not everything was perfect and peaceful. I felt less than; I compared myself to the other woman I was traveling with. They were all seeing visions, talking with their guides and angels, and I witnessed nothing. It made me feel so disconnected and not deserving of being in such a high spiritual place. I wanted to know more, hear my guidance, be open to messages from beyond. But it felt as if those abilities were only for special people, definitely not me.

On the third day, at the base of the mountain, I felt a sense of pressure to find the right place to sit and meditate. I climbed a little way up before I reached a good spot. When I sat, a baby squirrel showed up next to me. I was a little surprised that he came so close. I started meditating, calling my light and soul guidance. I closed my eyes, feeling the warmth of the sun shining on my face and body. Enjoying this pleasant caress of the sun, I began to feel pulses all over my body. Tears began to fall uncontrollably, a sensation of strong energetic presence on my left side came like a gentle wave with a strong presence; my internal eye saw many vibrant colors.

When I opened my eyes from that deep meditation, I noticed the squirrel still sitting next to me. Wow! I thought to myself. All this time it was right beside me?! The squirrel started scurrying away, and I thought, "Wait, I didn't even thank you for your presence." Suddenly, the squirrel turned around, came back toward me, stood still, waiting. I said, "Thank you" and he left. That was a direct communication with an animal. I couldn't believe it. How can it be? I questioned. Am I going crazy? Is this what happens to people when they are on a spiritual journey? I was being so judgmental at that moment.

The Universe has many unique ways to talk to us and part of it is through nature. Society is accustomed to talking to dogs and cats. We humanized them and it becomes normal. But talking to other animals is very strange to many people. What if all animals represent something to us? And have a message for us? Ancient cultures and indigenous tribes have attributed and given significant respect to animals as part of their lives. I was aware of the connection certain cultures and people have with spirit animal guidance, but I never thought it would be part of *my* life. It took me a while to realize it actually happened. Since then, I've experienced more encounters with animals and my awareness is expanded to listen and pay attention to their presence and how their wonderful messages and guidance play in my everyday life.

On the fourth day, we hiked to the gorgeous alpine Panther Meadow. While we were walking on the stepping stones toward the location, I started feeling emotional, excitement in my heart and love enveloping me. Tears were falling down my cheeks. I couldn't control it, I didn't know why I felt that way, it just happened and it felt so GOOD, as something exciting is about to happen. When we arrived at the location, I couldn't believe my own eyes. My heart was almost exploding from overjoy and awe! What I saw was a meadow that I envision in my weekly meditation for almost a year. I thought it was an imaginary place where I'd take myself during my meditations, but now I saw it — real, physical, alive! How could it exist in this physical world? I was there standing in the middle of it as I always saw and felt it, down to the smallest details. I asked myself, "Is it possible that what I imagined *became* a reality? Or was it the reality projecting to my imagination? Is this the 'calling' that many who visit Mount Shasta are talking about?"

I thought that was the most significant experience of my visit to Mount Shasta. It was the most profound, but more was to come. Every day, my connection with nature became stronger and more meaningful.

Crossing the borders between our reality and our imagination… understanding how powerful our thoughts are… not taking them for granted because our subconscious mind gives us a glimpse of our reality, like opening a door to a magical world where everything is possible! When we repeat the same vision, over and over again, it is like we are engraving it into our mind. We are connecting new neuron pathways. If we repeat it enough it will become a permanent part of who we are.

Waking up early the following day, my friend and I decided to visit this location again before our day with the group started. The early morning was cold and we needed to wear many layers, but that didn't interfere with our plans. Excited, with a heart full of joy, I arrived. I had a strong urge to hug as many trees as I could. Actually, I felt I needed to hug at least 30 trees. Me?! Hugging trees??? Really??? And 30 of them? That's it, I must have lost it! What had I become?... Weirder than I have ever known.

The first tree, I approached carefully with a strange feeling and a sense of distance. I felt embarrassed for myself. I hugged it for few seconds and moved to the next tree, just to fulfill this urge as quickly as I could, feeling uncomfortable with myself. Until... I felt this click! I surrendered to that moment, not thinking, just being, hugging, loving, YES, the trees! Each tree was hugged longer. I hugged 30 trees that morning! THIRTY! With each tree I hugged, I felt the joy in my heart getting stronger. The last tree was the most profound experience I have had in my life. Thinking about it always brings tears to my eyes and opens my heart wider. I hugged the tree and it felt sooooo good! I couldn't leave. I felt as if we were glued together. The hug became longer until it became a feeling that my whole existence melted into the tree and became One. I couldn't feel my body; I *was* the tree, standing tall, strong, wide, with a sense of vastness, unfamiliar expansion accompanied by endless love. The tree was talking to me, assuring me this unconditional love and unity was our birthright. It was so beautiful; I felt like I was home for the first time in so long. It reminded me of a vision I had as a child where the world and nature could co-exist again. It is who we are and how we deserve to feel every day of our lives. We are all one with each other and nature. Since then, my philosophy and way of life is — happiness is the inner compass for a fulfilling life.

Just allow nature to be part of your life; connect with all living things, including the trees. Connect with mother earth and you will always find joy in your heart. My belief is that we are always in the right place at the right time. When we allow life to flow through us, it becomes more visible and we are freer to be who we really are, strengthening the trust within. When we experience nature from a different awareness, consciousness, perspective, curiosity, and wonder, we allow the Universe to speak to us more clearly. We have a habit of seeing it without really taking it in. Yet once we begin to notice it, we treat ourselves to an exquisite realm of subtle complex scents, miraculous forms, and ethereal light. The natural world enriches our entire being through the vehicles of our senses. When we are low, nature lifts our spirits. When we are tired, if we pause long enough to drink from its beauty, it rejuvenates us. If you have fallen out of the practice of taking time to observe the light as it filters through the leaves of a tree, or the concentric rings a raindrop makes as it plops into a puddle, retune yourself by dedicating time in your day to notice the magnificence in nature.

IGNITE ACTION STEPS

- **It's ok to rest** — nothing in nature blooms all year round. Allow yourself special time in nature daily, even if only 5 or 15 minutes at a time, to pause (of course it is wonderful if you can invest more time).

- **Be an observer** — Take the time today to really notice and appreciate the beauty that surrounds you. Use all your senses, touch the ground, the tree, smell the fresh-cut grass, the flower, listen to the birds singing, the sound of the breeze moving through the leaves. Look at the different colors of leaves, at the sky, the clouds. Pay attention to the gentle movement around you.

- **Box to God** — Write down what is worrying and bothering you and put in a special box to God. Trust it will be taken care of and allow the Creator to solve your challenges in mysterious and wondrous ways.

- **Pay attention to the signs** — The signs are feedback giving us clues if we are moving in the direction of the happiness compass or not.

Hanit Benbassat - United States
Integrative Holistic Coach
www.hanitbenbassat.com
⊙ hanit_benbassat
⨍ hanit.benbassat

MICAH NELSON

*"Travel opens the door for the Universe to speak to you
and sets you on the fast track for transformation."*

**My intention is to inspire anyone reading my story to know that it is okay
to set out on an adventure with a clear intention of where you are going,
to then discover a spark that Ignites a new path in a completely different
direction. Taking this path can feel like starting over but will lead you to
a more authentic life that reveals your true adventurous spirit.**

FROM INTERNATIONAL TO INNER DEVELOPMENT

In a world of infinite possibilities, choosing the right path as a new college graduate can be a challenge. I was ready to step into a career and felt
as if adulthood was finally settling in. Despite receiving amazing bursaries
and scholarships to pay for my education, I was still carrying a considerable
amount of student debt. I had a degree and postgraduate in International Development Studies and International Project Management and I was completing
a great internship at a law firm exploring potential development projects in
the Caribbean.

Of course, this was a low-paying internship and debts were calling. My next
step was clear: I had to make money. I decided to teach English in Korea while
completing my MBA online. I was feeling good about my choice, although
inside I felt like I was convincing myself that it was the right decision. Yes,
I was going to receive a much-needed bursary for my Masters; I had a great

job at a school outside of Seoul, Korea. I would be saving money on living expenses and making money, but it just didn't feel right.

It seemed like a logical step... until I saw a posting for an internship with the Canadian International Development Agency (CIDA) in Botswana. That internship involved working with a youth health organization promoting HIV awareness and helping with funding proposals. The second I saw that posting, I knew it was a dream internship for anyone in my program. It would be an amazing opportunity to finally visit the continent of Africa fully funded. I would be able to connect with my African roots, be immersed in the culture and gain professional experience. It was a win/win.

My family, however, was not supportive. They argued against it and I had almost talked myself out of applying since I felt discouraged. We sometimes lose ourselves in what other people want for us, and trust that those who love us have our best interests in mind. Needing to take a break from the family expectations, I took a spontaneous trip from Toronto to Montreal with a friend. I had such clarity being on my own and it was there that I decided I *had* to get that job in Botswana.

On the interview call for the internship, I was thrilled to discover the interviewer was a graduate of the very same program I had just completed. I instantly felt a connection. In that moment, I had never wanted a job more. I felt a huge pressure to find out if I had been accepted, as I was scheduled to leave for Korea within a couple of weeks.

When my acceptance call finally arrived, I was thrilled. I quickly gave up my job in Korea and dropped out of my MBA program, much to my friends' and family's surprise. In a matter of weeks, I headed off to Antigonish, Nova Scotia to attend the pre-departure training at the Coady International Institute with other amazing young Canadians preparing to embark on internships across the world.

As I stepped off the plane in Botswana, I could instantly feel the vastness of being on the continent of Africa and see the immense beauty of the majestic countryside. I was finally on the continent of my ancestors and I felt truly blessed to be chosen for this experience. I had a sense of freedom with endless possibilities. In many ways, Botswana was what I expected, a very beautiful country, rich in diamond wealth and economically stable.

My internship was not exactly what I had expected. For one thing, I had assumed that working with local youth out of portable trailers in a dirt field, the dress code would be casual. Everyone was dressed very professionally. At a staff meeting, a very direct comment about me being underdressed prompted me to step it up and rock some heels and nice skirts to fit in. It was a very awkward moment and the beginning of me feeling like I did not fit in. I did my best to 'assimilate' and was finally congratulated by an office mate for finally dressing like a 'Motswana' (a woman from Botswana).

I took that as a compliment. I may have looked the part, but I did not feel it. I also did not have time to learn Tswana, the second official language, which was the language of choice in the office. It was an odd experience, being a young black woman in an African country but feeling like an outsider in many ways. A word of advice: learn as much as you can about work culture from locals beforehand! Prior to leaving for Botswana, I asked a couple of Canadians who spent time there, but it turns out they were rather misinformed. I spent some time with a family from Botswana during pre-departure training, but I evidently missed asking some key questions. The real learning happens when you arrive.

Adding to my issue at work, my roommate and co-worker found me to be a bit odd. She was uncomfortable with me doing yoga in the living room and burning candles in my room. I was passionate about my new yoga practice; it helped me to stay grounded and manage some of the unexpected culture-shock I was experiencing. She wasn't into it. The stress grew in the household and her army general boyfriend added to it by making homophobic or Islamophobic comments as a joke. Tensions would rise as we had heated debates. He tried to defend his gay-bashing comments by reminding me that homosexuality was illegal in Botswana at the time or explain away his Islamophobia with how difficult it was to lose army friends to suicide bombers in Somalia due to Islamic extremists. I struggled to respect his point of view and personal trauma, but I just could not hold my tongue when these topics came up. It added to my disconnection.

One night, I felt very fortunate to finally be invited to a party by a local friend. I loved hanging out with my Canadian crew who I traveled with, but I really wanted local friends so I could immerse myself more deeply in the culture. Minutes after I arrived at the party, a very well-dressed man caught my eye. He was rather attractive, but he reminded me of someone I was trying to get over, so I decided to avoid him all night. I thought that was a great plan. It failed miserably.

It turned out that he too was born in Canada. Naturally, I was introduced to him. I was irritated that we were even being introduced, but once my guard fell, we had an instant connection. I thought I had found my perfect match in many ways. Even his family sounded amazing — his mother was a yogi and I was so excited to attend her yoga classes. It was such an unexpected relationship and I was so happy to have met Kavin. However, he came from a prominent Indian, Hindu family and they all held a certain image of the type of woman they intended for him. I thought it was insane that I had come all the way to the 'Motherland' only to be deemed unsuitable, essentially for being a black woman and not a 'suitable' partner. This was an incredibly challenging part of the culture for me and I shed more tears than I care to remember. Of all of the brilliant, beautiful and kind men in the country, I ended up with him, a man who did not want me to attend his mother's yoga classes and he certainly didn't want me to meet her.

At this point in my trip I was feeling overwhelmed with challenges. In my living situation, my roommate wanted me to move out. My relationship was very secretive, and I wasn't fitting in at work… it was all so difficult, and then, it felt as if the Universe heard my need for peace and space. I was invited to my first yoga retreat in South Africa by an amazing local friend. As I was loading my yoga mat and bags into my friend's car, I was stopped by my neighbor's children. One of the little girls asked me if I did yoga and if I'd teach her when I came back from my retreat. I didn't realize it then but the Universe was speaking to me through her. I was new on my yogic journey and this little girl wanted me to become her teacher. I was honored and it sparked something deep within me.

The retreat was held in a beautiful and peaceful border town in South Africa and the drive was amazing. The sunset sky was stunning. We spotted a baby hyena dash across the road in front of the car. The vegetarian meals were from local farms; our evening activities included a campfire under the stars with wine and chocolate. The days consisted of Ashtanga Vinyasa, Tai Chi and walking meditations. The experience was profound. I felt so incredibly inspired.

A couple of days after I returned, I held a yoga class in my backyard for the kids. Since I was not a trained yoga teacher, I was mindful of the postures we did and shared what I knew. Teaching the kids Ignited me. I had all the children on my block aged five to eleven years old knocking at my door for classes. They absolutely loved it! Yoga impacted me so deeply; I wished I had started it when I was a child.

The joy I felt from my newfound passion for teaching yoga was dimmed by the hurt of being unable to meet Kavin's mother or connect with her through yoga. For whatever reason, I had attached so much importance to meeting my boyfriend's mother. I had never experienced this with anyone I had dated before.

Finally, after asking many times and even crying about it, the three other Canadian interns and I were invited over to Kavin's house for dinner with his mom. Meeting his mother was not about seeking approval. I felt instinctively that there was a deeper reason. His mother was welcoming, warm, and even questioned why I had not come to her yoga class. I absolutely loved listening to her share her wisdom about yoga! She mentioned that she taught yoga to students at local schools. In that moment, hearing her say that, I just *knew* I wanted to do the same thing. I wanted to teach yoga to children to bring peace and harmony to their lives. Spending time with her truly Ignited something within me. I knew I had to study yoga and share it with children. My body was vibrating with the knowledge that this was the *right* path to take.

Only a few days after my enlightening dinner with her, I was scheduled to make my way back to Canada. My months in Botswana were drawing to a close. A few weeks before I left, my kids-yoga class came to an abrupt halt since my unsupportive roommate fertilized the lawn with manure, preventing us from doing our practice in the backyard. Nevertheless, my yoga students were all there to see me off. They begged me to one day come back to be their teacher again and to never forget them. They made me a birthday card as a going-away present since I was leaving shortly after my birthday. It said, *"You are a shining star, we love you. Happy Birthday. You are the best, I hope you enjoy your day. We all love you and we all care about you. Wish you all the best in life. With lots of love, your yoga class."* My amazing young neighbors were so inspirational and always brightened up my day.

It was a tearful goodbye leaving my yoga class, and leaving Kavin. I could see that there was a lot of pressure for him to maintain family traditions. I wanted to stay in Botswana, but I did not want to be in a situation where I was not fully accepted. He even told me, "You are the perfect partner for me, but I can't go against my parents." Looking back at this time in my life, I can't believe how I let this impact my self-esteem. I was really hurt. We made plans to see each other again, but family pressure prevented that from happening.

Despite everything, I kept in touch with his mother for several months after returning to Canada. She lovingly shared information and articles about Ayurveda and yoga. She was incredibly influential in my studies of yoga, Ayurveda and in becoming a holistic health practitioner. But as supportive as she was, I still was not a suitable match for her son. I believe everything happens for a reason and people come into my life as guides. I went to Botswana with a clear vision of the type of career I was building and how I was going to support people, but Botswana taught me the Universe had different plans for me. I'm glad I listened.

Before my departure, my older sister sent me information about a yoga teacher training happening near home. Although I had my heart set on studying yoga in India, upon my return to Toronto, instead, I attended Maureen Rae's yoga school in Canada. During the second year of yoga teacher training, I returned to university to become an elementary school teacher. I felt like I was starting to follow a more authentic path.

Two weeks before I began my education degree, Kavin called me out of the blue. He wanted me to come back to Botswana and try things again, assuring me that he was ready to go against his parents' wishes. We had not spoken in months after I ended things. It was too difficult being in love with someone that I could not be with. Had this conversation happened earlier I would have been on a plane the next day. Now, I was committed to my path and I had made peace with never seeing Kavin again. I was frustrated and oddly irritated that he had taken so long to reach out. Looking back, there was a lot of tension when I was in Botswana. I felt constantly judged and disapproved of. By the time he called, I had healed many of my emotional wounds and I had so much more love and respect for myself.

I continued to dive deeper into my new journey. I spent a month and a half in Costa Rica, living on the beautiful eco-resort Rancho Margot where I taught yoga and tutored kids after school. In the jungle, I connected with myself even more deeply. I realized I had so many more things to clear emotionally. In my heart, I knew that India was the next place I needed to go, but I wasn't sure how that was going to happen.

Back in Toronto, two weeks after leaving the jungle, I attended my first 10-day Vipassana Meditation course. It was challenging and so transformative, and led me to volunteer for the children's meditation course a couple of days later, which was a beautiful experience. There, the female meditation teacher invited me to go to India to visit the main Buddhist sites and attend another 10-day course in Bodh Gaya, India where the Buddha had his enlightenment. Four short days later, everything fell into place for me to spend a month in India traveling, meditating and immersing myself in another culture. Once again, the Universe sent me the right people at the right time to help me grow and evolve my soul.

My biggest takeaway from traveling is that when you step outside of your comfort zone and take a trip, sometimes life has magical plans for you. Traveling is like a fast track for transformational change and growth. The people you meet and the many situations you find yourself in can feel like carefully crafted steps along your soul's journey. This is what I want for you...

I invite you to travel, meet people, experience situations and take the steps in your own soul's journey. Travel opens the door for the Universe to speak to you and sets you on the fast track for transformation. When you feel that whisper and nudge to take that step, take it... the Universe will support you.

IGNITE ACTION STEPS

- **Expect the unexpected** when traveling. Although we try our best not to make assumptions about a place or a culture, it is important to be flexible with what comes up. Be open to learning and shifting your point of view.

- **Find ways to ground** especially during times of change. Yoga and meditation can help so much when trying to adjust to changes and cultural differences while traveling.

- **Be patient with yourself**. When exploring a new culture, sometimes challenging emotions or situations come up. Breathe in... and remember that when we enter a new culture, we are almost like children again learning rules and norms.

- **Connect with the local people**. The connections you make will be the highlight of all of your travel experiences. When we are curious about other cultures and points of view, it opens a world of new learning and new ideas.

Micah Nelson - Canada
Holistic Health Practitioner, Teacher and Yoga Instructor
www.Balancefirstworkshops.com
ⓘ micahjulia

DAMIAN CULHANE

*"Travel the world with the curiosity of an innocent child
to capture memories that will enrich your life."*

**My desire is for you to reach beyond your fear of the unknown, beyond your
threshold of resistance to embrace the enriching opportunity to experience
new cultures. Seeing the world through a new perspective advances your
understanding of yourself and develops your character. Travel is the fastest
way to grow as a person and connect from your core to people and places
that will progress your knowledge and arouse your curiosity. Travel can
be a healing therapy that soothes your emotional wounds.**

THE PARISIAN WEDDING FEAST

Imagine my delight as a five-year-old boy receiving my first fuzzy felt play
set. The farm scenery was made from brightly colored felt with shapes of pigs
and sheep; the carefully crafted trees, fences and farm workers were there to
create a scene and stick on to the cardboard landscape. The set was a present
from my Mum to keep me occupied during a particularly long journey — my
first trip on an airplane.

I don't recall packing or preparing much for this particular adventure. The
whole family was flying to a different country and I was so young that the only
thing I had to focus on was keeping the lid closed on my fuzzy felt set to ensure
I didn't lose any of the contents. The plane journey was uneventful for me,
largely because I was busy creating a far away scene in a distant make-believe

farm in my fuzzy felt world. The creative gift from Mum had suitably distracted me to not cause any disruption. I was 'very well behaved and a very good boy.' I still cherish that honor, however brief it may have been!

I can remember some details of that first adventure better than others. In particular, the Guesthouse where we were staying seemed quite large and breakfast was served in what seemed like a substantial dining room. My grandfather enjoyed his daily bowl of prunes and I was fascinated by the routine. With his enormous hands delicately wrapped around his spoon, he would carefully place a single prune into his mouth. Then, a few moments later, he would pop out the hidden stone onto the empty spoon, discarding the small almond shape on to his side plate. I was fascinated at the routine and rather than being indifferent to the alien ritual, I was quite eager to give it a go and eat some prunes for the first time. The squishy texture and syrupy dark sweet sauce didn't put me off. I learnt how to carefully chew around the stone in the centre, then politely pop the stone out of my mouth onto a spoon — leaving the discarded stone on the side plate. My grandfather and both parents bestowed considerable praise upon my fearless conquering of the small squishy fruit, glad that I had not choked on the stone. I felt very sophisticated and grown up to be eating such an adult-approved breakfast.

We were staying on the island of Guernsey, off the coast of France, full of charm with narrow country lanes, beautiful beaches and its colorful coastline — a key feature of all the channel isles. I remember exploring the sandy beaches with the hidden coves and at some point my parents arranged a day trip for the whole family. We were to leave our familiar holiday nest, embarking on a new adventure. I was entrusted with my own ticket to allow me safe passage and, filled with pride at having such a big responsibility, I clutched it firmly in my hand as I boarded the big boat. Our voyage began and we set sail for a faraway island. I kept looking over the railing for large sea creatures and pirates weaving in and out of the coves. Our epic voyage on board the Isle of Sark Shipping Company's boat came to a safe and monster-less end, terminating around 45 minutes after departure. It had seemed longer due to the absence of sea creatures, the lack of pirates and the fact that my beloved fuzzy felt play set had been left behind at the Guesthouse.

Disembarking from the uneventful crossing, I caught sight of what was waiting in the harbour. My whole body now filling with excitement; I jumped around with joy at what I could see. I hopped and skipped along the path with a flurry of enthusiasm, possessed with an eagerness to start our next adventure. For anyone who has visited the island of Sark, you will know that Sark is one of the few remaining places in the world where cars are banned from roads and only tractors and horse drawn vehicles are allowed.

My small palm, released of the burden of clutching my boat ticket, was now grasped by the gigantic outstretched hand of my grandfather. I was momentarily airborne as I was lifted up onto the enormous wooden carriage. The patient horse dutifully waited for the master's signal before setting off at a gentle trot. It was an open top carriage and I could feel the gentle breeze on my cheeks. The blue sky was endless, with just a wisp or two of faint white clouds — the beautiful green landscape opening up in front of us. The horse gathered speed and was now cantering along the cobbled pathway. My restless boyhood wiggles and fidgety spirit were now more settled — grounded by the tuneful rhythm of the hooves clicking. This was a delightful new experience and still one of the only ways to travel anywhere on the island of Sark.

Whenever I am traveling and see prunes at the breakfast buffet, I generally grab a bowl — savoring the memories of being a well-behaved and compliant five-year-old and the remembered adoration and adult approval gushing through me with each stone I successfully avoid choking on. Hearing the 'clippety-clop' of horses hooves on cobbles, I am taken straight back to those treasured memories on the island of Sark. I literally stop still in the street to admire the majestic sight of the horses trotting past, my body filling with happy hormones as I pause to savor the moment. Those early adventures are unforgettable due to the emotions and neural connections made. They're ingrained into my every cell, lying dormant awaiting the revival at any given moment. Traveling and the experiences on my journeys, have enriched me and helped me anchor the feelings and emblazon new neurological pathways into my memory forever.

Both my parents would enjoy taking trips around England and Scotland, but my Dad was always keen to take me on foreign trips. On one occasion, we flew to Paris to attend the wedding of my Dad's landlord. This was only my second trip on a plane. I remember we had to wake up before dawn to catch the early flight. I was an inexperienced traveler and anxious about the coming flight; I had not eaten much before we left. By then, I had outgrown the fuzzy felt set and was far more conscious of the motion of the plane. The bumpy approach to the airport provided evidence of my lack of resilience and fortitude, as the turbulence outside the plane caused turbulence inside my stomach — promptly ejecting the contents into my lap just as we touched down in France. The cabin crew were really kind in caring for my novice needs and I have since learned to always eat before I travel.

Upon arrival in Paris, Dad and I escaped the fracas of the French city streets and checked into our room. I loved unlocking the large double-height window and throwing the wooden shutters open onto the bustling street below. I was still at an age where I would be sharing a room with my Dad, which meant I was not going to get much sleep due to his snoring.

Spending time with Dad and exploring the world with the curiosity of an innocent child had a massive impact on me. The visit to the Louvre and the impressive Mona Lisa ignited a curiosity in me to explore art and artifacts from around the world. Visiting the Eiffel Tower left me in awe of the engineering magnificence of such structures. Walking to the Sacre-Coeur Basilica and visiting Notre Dame Cathedral has ignited a passion for visiting spiritual buildings and wandering the streets of the cities of the world. I still do this type of sightseeing even now as an adult, exploring new places with eyes wide open.

Dad and I ate croissants for breakfast and I remember dipping them in a large bowl filled with hot chocolate, the rich chocolatey liquid dripping on the white linen tablecloth as I refueled — the travel sickness a distant memory. I was curious to know what snails and frogs legs tasted like — a local delicacy. I was mildly disappointed that one tasted like chewy balls of garlic and the other was a garlicky chicken flavor. At least I had tried them and would have bragging rights with my friends! My adventurous spirit had been quietly awakened for what was coming — the Parisian wedding feast.

I'd never been to a French wedding before. I didn't understand much of the proceedings — mostly conducted in French — and the ceremony seemed to go on for ages. My schoolboy language skills made it difficult to follow the service; however, my schoolboy appetite for adventure and eyes bigger than my stomach meant I could understand the buffet fluently.

Festooned with an array of colorful food, beautifully created terrines, delightful plates decorated with delicious ingredients. There were enormous platters filled with cold meats and pâté, cheeses of all shapes and sizes, and bowls of fruit. It truly was a wedding feast. I traveled from one end of the buffet table to the next, making return journeys until I had tried almost everything. After navigating my way around the buffet several times, my excursions were interrupted by the ceremonial arrival of the wedding cake.

The four French waiters carrying the large silver platter were dressed in immaculate black outfits with crisp white shirts and black silk bow ties. Resting on top of the silver platter was the most incredible mountain of profiteroles dripping with chocolate sauce. My eyes opened wide as I gazed at my final destination on the exquisite banquet. After my hike around the buffet, I felt like I had reached base camp and now I just had to conquer the summit of the mountain of profiterole, a culinary challenge I felt worthy of embracing in my adventurous exploration of new flavors.

After two helpings of profiteroles, I was stuffed. The sightseeing had caught up with me and having not slept particularly well due to Dad's snoring, I was exhausted. Dad was still socializing and the wedding reception was in full swing. I quietly slipped away to the bathroom, relieved to be away from all the hustle and bustle. The stillness and tranquility of the bathroom was a peaceful haven. I locked the door of the cubicle and enjoyed the solitude. It occurred to me that due to my tiredness maybe I could rest for a few moments and return to the reception in due course. The floor was quite comfortable and I was so tired I probably could have slept anywhere. My eyes closed and I fell into a buffet coma. My Dad must have noticed my absence and he sent out a search party. I can remember groggily coming round from my slumber with my father banging on the door, sternly from not knowing where I was.

By the time I was 15 years old, I was barely mature enough to travel solo for the first time. I plucked up the courage and hopped on a coach with my newly acquired freedom, traveling the 100 kilometer trip into London. I changed coaches, dodging hectic travelers at a busy station and found my seat on the bus to North Wales. Several hours later, my newfound confidence was waning. I had left behind my familiar childhood surroundings and the beloved fuzzy felt set discarded in the loft storage of my childhood home. I was glad when we arrived safely into the port in Holyhead and slightly anxious to be reunited with my precious cargo — my suitcase containing my worldly possessions.

My mouth was dry as I walked to the awaiting boat, struggling to carry my bulging suitcase in one hand. My other hand was clutching my ferry ticket, a familiar feeling taking me back to my childhood; only this time, I would be making the solitary trip aboard the overnight boat. Having been traveling most of the day, the enormity of my adventure was dwelling on me. It was getting dark as we set sail for Ireland and I went outside to get some fresh air. As I peered out over the railings, there was not much to see; the Irish channel is not known for its sea creatures or pirates. I soon fell asleep on the deck, resting my head on my suitcase. I woke up barely able to move my neck — frozen by the cold sea breeze. Eventually, I found my way back inside to the warmth of the busy bar where an informal and impromptu celebration of life had already been in full swing for several hours. I soon learnt that my ancestors from Ireland were renowned for their singing and celebrations, all embraced with the Celtic enthusiasm I still admire and love so dearly.

I've spent over four decades learning through travel which is so enriching.

I recently moved to the island of Sardinia, part of Italy in one of the southern parts of Europe, where I am learning the language and experiencing the culture first hand. The island is well known for the amazing coastline, exquisite lace-making, ceremonial masks and basket weaving. Seeing this new experience through the wondrous eyes as if I was a child, I curiously observe the history and people, marveling in the extraordinary experience. The ancient traditions and customs have been handed down through generations, steeped in mystery. I have a vision… to bring small groups of people on educational retreats to discover and learn about the local culture, healing their emotional pain to liberate their souls. The experience of traveling to this mystical, curious and evergreen island igniting their adventurous spirit to take the journey inward to discover freedom from their emotional wounds.

My most recent 'big' adventure was the highlight of a six-week journey. Starting out on a road trip, traveling through France to stay for a few days in the Spanish resort of Barcelona. I glanced longingly out the window as I passed Paris, hoping to catch a glimpse of the Eiffel Tower and be reminded of my time spent there with Dad. That road trip was followed by a journey by air to Istanbul. It was my first time in the city and the first time I experienced an earthquake! Not something I am in a rush to repeat. I also survived the taxi journeys to and from the airport — the best way to describe them is 'hair-raising.' Having experienced a traumatic physical event, I was ready for something more relaxing.

My final destination was the main highlight of that trip. The beautiful landscape and mountains of Canada may not be a celebratory buffet or profiterole mountain, but they brought me back to my childhood travels to Paris and Canada with my Dad. I had not been in Canada since I was 10 years old, returning on this occasion to see Vancouver for the first time. It was amazing! Again, meeting great folks, learning about the culture and being in the moment as I enjoyed the wonderful and spectacular scenery — driving along the shores of Stanley Park, peering out to spot sea creatures. Visiting the Museum of Anthropology at the University of British Columbia, a place of world arts and cultures, was enthralling. The First Nations indigenous tribes living in what is now known as Canada were renowned for their storytelling, ceremonial mask rituals and basket weaving. This enriching and humbling experience brought to mind the similarities with the Sardinian culture. It was uncanny.

As a child, I traveled with effortless curiosity and unwavering wonder. As an adult, I strive to do the same. The experiences I shared with my Dad were some of the most memorable moments in my life. Just like my father persuaded me to travel and try new experiences, I urge my two sons to do the same whenever possible. When you travel, I encourage you to see the world through the eyes of an innocent child, explore with a beginner's mindset and be openly curious to what enriching experiences await you. Your growth as a person lies in readiness in the unknown — a parallel universe where the *real* you exists. Cast off your fears and be vulnerable to who you *truly* are — hidden beneath your mask. Be willing to explore how to heal your wounds from your experiences and awaken the Adventurous Spirit that lies within.

IGNITE ACTION STEPS

The lessons you can learn about yourself whilst traveling will be invaluable. Ask yourself: What adventures await you? What can you learn from the experiences you will encounter? Who will you meet on your next trip? What local cuisine can you try? What stories will you be able to share with your family and tribe?

Travel with an open mind. Try new foods. Try new adventures. Try to see things through the unbiased and inquisitive eyes of a child. What experiences can you emblazon and ingrain into your memory?

Damian Culhane
CMgr, FCMI, FISM, MIOD, MEMCC
www.damianculhane.co.uk

THANK YOU

Please know that every word written in this book and every letter on the pages has been meticulously crafted with fondness, encouragement and clarity to not just inspire you but to transform you. Many individuals in this book stepped up to share their stories for the very first time. They courageously revealed the many layers of themselves and exposed their weaknesses like few leaders do. Additionally, they spoke authentically from the heart and wrote what was true for them. We could have taken their stories and made them perfect, following every editing rule, but we chose instead to leave their unique and honest voices intact. We overlooked exactness to foster individual expression. These are their words, their sentiments and their explanations. We let their personalities shine in their writing so you would get the true sense of who each one of them is. That's what makes IGNITE so unique. Authors serving others. Stories igniting humanity. No filters.

A tremendous thank you goes to those who are working in the background, editing, supporting and encouraging the authors. They are some of the most genuine and heart-centered people I know. Their devotion to the vision of IGNITE, their integrity and the message they aspire to convey is of the highest possible caliber. They, too, want you to find your IGNITE moment and flourish. They each believe in you and that's what makes them so outstanding. Their dream is for your dreams to come true.

Editing Team: Alex Blake, Andrea Drajewicz, Carmelita McGrath, Jock Mackenzie & Wendy Albrecht
Production Team: Dania Zafar, Peter Giesin & JB Owen

A special thanks and gratitude to the project leaders: Yoram Baltinester and Faraaz Ãlì for their support behind the scenes and for going 'above and beyond' to make this a wonderful experience, ensuring everything ran smoothly and with elegance.

A deep appreciation goes to each and every author who made Ignite Your Adventurous Spirit possible — with all your exciting stories embracing this amazing idea of Igniting others while traveling the globe.

To all our readers, we thank you for reading and loving the stories, for opening your hearts and minds to the idea of Igniting your own lives. We welcome you to share your story and become a new author in one of our upcoming books. Sharing your message and Ignite moments may be exactly what someone needs to hear.

Join us on this magical Ignite journey!

BOOKS AND RESOURCES MEANINGFUL TO THE
IGNITE YOUR ADVENTUROUS SPIRIT AUTHORS

Charlene Ray
Anam Cara: A Book of Celtic Wisdom by John O'Donohue

Elena Rodríguez Blanco
www.elenarodriguezblanco.com
www.authenticitys.com

Janie Jurkovich
www.JanieJ.net

John D. Russell
www.johndrussell.com

Katarina Amadora
Temple of the Way of Light:
* youtu.be/PP647WCpBgc
* www.templeofthewayoflight.org

Micah Nelson
Trails Youth Initiatives
    www.trails.ca
The Coady International Institute
    www.coady.stfx.ca
Vipassana Meditation
    www.dhamma.org
Rancho Margot
    www.ranchomargot.com
Balance First Workshops
    www.balancefirstworkshops.com

Miguel Brighteyes
www.bebrighteyes.com/resources

Ravi Muti
Imiloa Institute
    www.imiloainstitute.com

Photo Credits

Upcoming Books in the
IGNITE SERIES

If you have story to share,
Please apply at www.igniteyou.life/apply

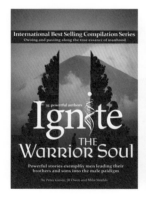

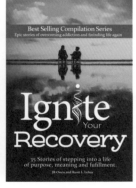